Kuwait's Foreign Policy

D0218317

Kuwait's Foreign Policy

City-State in World Politics

Abdul-Reda Assiri

Westview Press

BOULDER, SAN FRANCISCO, & LONDON

FEB 14 1991

DOUGLAS COLLEGE LIBRARY

Westview Special Studies on the Middle East

This Westview softcover edition is printed on acid-free paper and bound in library-quality, coated covers that carry the highest rating of the National Association of State Textbook Administrators, in consultation with the Association of American Publishers and the Book Manufacturers' Institute.

Map on p. xx prepared by Michelle Picard.

All rights reserved. No part of this publication may be reproduced or transmitted in any form or by any means, electronic or mechanical, including photocopy, recording, or any information storage and retrieval system, without permission in writing from the publisher.

Copyright © 1990 by Westview Press, Inc.

Published in 1990 in the United States of America by Westview Press, Inc., 5500 Central Avenue, Boulder, Colorado 80301, and in the United Kingdom by Westview Press, Inc., 13 Brunswick Centre, London WC1N 1AF, England

Library of Congress Cataloging-in-Publication Data
Assiri, Abdul-Reda.
  Kuwait's foreign policy : city-state in world politics / by Abdul-Reda Assiri.
     p. cm. — (Westview special studies on the Middle East)
  ISBN 0-8133-7636-X
  1. Kuwait—Foreign relations. 2. Kuwait—Foreign relations—Arab countries. 3. Arab countries—Foreign relations—Kuwait.
  4. Kuwait—Foreign economic relations. I. Title. II. Series.
DS247.K88A87 1990
327.53'67—dc19   88-19056
                                                                                    CIP

Printed and bound in the United States of America

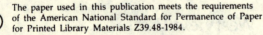

The paper used in this publication meets the requirements of the American National Standard for Permanence of Paper for Printed Library Materials Z39.48-1984.

10   9   8   7   6   5   4   3   2

Contents

Illustrations

Acronyms

AAM	Air-to-Air Missile
ACDA	U.S. Arms Control and Disarmament Agency, Washington, D.C.
AFV	Armored Fighting Vehicle
AIM	Air Intercept Missile
APC	Armored Personnel Carrier
AShM	Air-to-Ship Missile
ASM	Air-to-Surface Missile
ATGW	Antitank Guided Weapon
ATM	Antitank Missile
AWACS	Airborne Warning and Control System
BP	British Petroleum
CBK	Central Bank of Kuwait
CENTCOM	U.S. Central Command
CIA	Central Intelligence Agency
CRS	Congressional Research Service
FGA	Fighter/Ground Attack
FY	Fiscal Year
GCC	Cooperation Council for the Arab States of the Gulf, or the Gulf Cooperation Council
GDP	Gross Domestic Product
GNP	Gross National Product
IISS	The International Institute for Strategic Studies, London
ILO	International Labor Organization, Geneva

IMF	International Monetary Fund
KD	Kuwaiti Dinar
KFAED	Kuwait Fund for Arab Economic Development
KFTCIC	Kuwait Foreign Trade, Contracting, and Investment Company
KIA	Kuwait Investment Authority
KIC	Kuwait Investment Company
KIO	Kuwait Investment Office, London
KM	Kilometer
KOC	Kuwait Oil Company
KOTC	Kuwait Oil Tanker Company
KPC	Kuwait Petroleum Corporation
KPI	Kuwait Petroleum International
LCM	Landing Craft, Mechanized
LCU	Landing Craft, Utility
LPG	Liquefied Petroleum Gas
M b/d	Million barrels per day
MBT	Main Battle Tank
ME/GNP	Military Expenditure as Percentage of Gross National Product
MIDEASTFOR	Middle East Force
NATO	North Atlantic Treaty Organization
OAPEC	Organization of Arab Petroleum Exporting Countries
OECD	Organization for Economic Cooperation and Development
OPEC	Organization of Petroleum Exporting Countries
PFLP	Popular Front for the Liberation of Palestine
PLO	Palestine Liberation Organization
RDF	Rapid Deployment Force
ROPME	Regional Organization for the Protection of the Marine Environment, Kuwait

SAM	Surface-to-Air Missile
SIPRI	Stockholm International Peace Research Institute, Stockholm
SP	Self-Propelled
SSM	Surface-to-Surface Missile
UAE	United Arab Emirates
ULCC	Ultralarge Crude Carrier (Oil Tanker)
UN	United Nations
UNESCO	United Nations Educational, Scientific and Cultural Organization
UNIIMOG	United Nations Iran-Iraq Military Observer Group
UNRWA	United Nations Relief and Work Agency for Palestine Refugees
USGPO	United States Government Printing Office
VLPC	Very Large Petroleum Carrier

Preface

Kuwait, a welfare city-state in the Arabian (Persian) Gulf (henceforth "the Gulf"), has gained a preeminence in international politics in recent years. Throughout the 1960s and 1970s the country played a significant role in inter-Arab political and economic spheres. Since the outbreak of the Iran-Iraq war, Kuwait, being geostrategically located in a cumbersome triangle between the two combatants and Saudi Arabia, has undertaken a series of risky political maneuvers to maintain its security interests. The Gulf war has exposed the extent of Kuwait's fragility and its vulnerabilities, both internally and externally.

Despite worldwide attention from decision makers, the media, academia, and the wider public, there has been little if anything published on Kuwait's foreign policy per se. The following study attempts to fill this gap. The book is geared for students and specialists in political science and economics, governmental officials, the business community, media persons, and members of the general public with interests in Gulf politics, Middle Eastern affairs, and the role of small states in world politics.

The book assesses the dynamics of Kuwaiti foreign policy since 1961 (the year of independence) and explores the role of Kuwait as a small state in international politics. It seeks to analyze the impact of ideology, religion, and value systems on Kuwaiti foreign policy as well as the impact of domestic forces (elections, the constitution, the "free" press, associations, and ethnic groupings) on political actors in the small state and their concomitant ramifications for external behavior. It also examines how decision makers adopt different forces to achieve national goals and how and why a small state such as Kuwait can maintain a high profile in its foreign affairs.

Although the study covers almost three decades of Kuwait's foreign policy, it should not be construed as a holistic chronicle of each and every event in the state's external conduct. Rather, it emphasizes major developments, phenomena, and trends that have shaped Kuwait's foreign policy and left imprints in the course of Kuwait's external relations and the country's role in world politics. Certain case studies demonstrate this theme of political analysis and dynamism. The book by no means intends to rationalize Kuwait's external behavior; rather, it attempts to critically and systematically analyze and explain Kuwaiti foreign policy in a balanced and objective manner.

It is often assumed that small (geographically and/or in population) nations are insignificant in international relations and therefore play a marginal role in world politics. Their capabilities are too limited to make their presence, much less their influence, felt beyond their boundaries. However, this widely perceived notion of the smaller state is not necessarily valid. This study will show how some small states, because of a coalescence of factors or motives, can assume a role larger than their power matrixes would indicate. The sphere of influence for such smaller states is primarily regional and/ or within a bloc rather than on a global scale. Since small states can pursue only positive actions in world affairs,[1] among the hats such smaller countries can wear are those of bargainer, balancer, and mediator.

Clearly, Kuwait falls into the "small state" classification: It has 6,880 square miles of territory; a population of some 1,900,000, of whom only 42 percent are indigenous, constituting about one-fifth of the labor force; and its neighbors include the three regional "superpowers" Iran, Iraq, and Saudi Arabia.[2] Since Kuwait is a large, sprawling urban metropolis (over 90% is urbanized) around which revolve all political, social, economic, and other activities of the state, we use the concept "city-state" both territorially and demographically to imply both the basic elements of power of a small state and the actual conduct of its political activities. But despite its size, Kuwait has followed a unique path in its external orientation and its internal structure. Its foreign relations have been characterized by an activism disproportionate to the basic ingredients of state power. Simply put, Kuwaitis appear to be obsessed with something of a "siege mentality" and have historically calculated that outside powers would safeguard their survival. This attitude continued into the era of independence and nationhood, was aggravated by frustrations with neighboring Iraq immediately after independence, and developed into a grave crisis of confidence in the surrounding hostile environment.

Kuwait's post-independence foreign policy has been and is influenced by three major national goals: (1) political and military security; (2) Arabic ideology and Islamic values; and (3) the "mission" to invest and share the nation's wealth with less fortunate Arab and Moslem countries. With reference to political and military security, Kuwait's main objective is the survival, against great odds, of the state and the stability and integrity of the political system. The implications of these requirements have included the close identification with superpowers in the past (e.g., Great Britain), the ability to benefit from the contradictions between Arab and regional states in the 1960s and 1970s through mediator and/or donor roles, and the ability to enter into *entente* with like-minded nations (the Gulf Cooperation Council) in the 1980s. Having been vulnerable to Arab radical attacks during the heyday of Arab nationalism, Kuwait has continued to seek its objectives through quiet diplomacy.

The second foreign policy goal in Kuwaiti politics stems from its Arab and Moslem identities, which lend a pan-Arab ideology and Islamic overtones to its external outlook. Even though the Kuwaiti political regime is less dogmatic and ideologically bound than others in the region, the need to skirt the divisions within inter-Arab politics has forced Kuwait to follow a pattern that is acceptable both to Arab nationalist and to more traditional, fundamentalist, and conservative elements. The Kuwaiti goal has been to stay well toward the center in ideological cleavages within the Arab world, avoiding both the right (conservatives or traditionalists) and the left (nationalists or Arab radicals).

The emphasis on Arab and Islamic variables in Kuwait's foreign policy is evidence that it has sought to strike a balance in its policy, thereby attempting to moderate, deflect, even appease domestic opinion and external pressure. There has been a high degree of interaction between ideology and foreign policy. Domestic increases in Arab nationalistic attitudes and feeling led the government to accelerate economic aid and involvement in inter-Arab politics. Similarly, rising Islamic sentiment influenced the Kuwaiti government to expand involvement in and solidarity with Islamic causes and nations. Although Kuwait has urged a unified approach to the issue of mutual Arab security against Israel, its real concern was not Israel but its neighbors, aside from the influence of its own large Palestinian expatriate community, which could create mischief within Kuwait itself. In general, Kuwait is less a leader than a follower of Arab opinion and regimes.

The third foreign policy goal involves the moral sense of "duty" or "mission" felt by the policy makers toward less affluent Arab countries. Kuwait's economic well-being is based upon its plentiful oil resources (proved reserves of about 70 billion barrels, or three times those of the United States and about 10 percent of global reserves) and its enviable capital-surplus economy (a gross national product of some $20 billion by the mid-1980s, with a *per capita* income of $18,000). Aside from the wider attachment and identification with the Arab and Islamic worlds, there is the benefit of greater regional stability as the gap between "have's" and "have not's" is narrowed. The sense of mission, combined with the commercial mentality that pervades the private sector, has led Kuwait to foster public and private institutions for aid and investment in the Arab, Moslem, and Third World nations. One such example is the Kuwait Fund for Arab Economic Development, established in 1961 with an initial capital of $140 million that was raised to $6.7 billion by 1974. Nonetheless, lending by the various agencies in Kuwait exhibits political undercurrents in both orientation and execution. One might apply the term "dinar diplomacy" to Kuwait's financial role in regional politics.

Kuwait's foreign policy has undergone four phases to date in the 28 years since independence: state defense or survival; pragmatism and balanced approaches; ambivalence and tilting; and anxiety and uncertainty. The latter phase has been characterized by domestic ethnic and religious factionalism and fragmentation, influenced, in turn, by external polarization and threats.

This book analyzes the major crises that have beset Kuwaiti foreign policy—Iraq's encroachment on Kuwait in 1961; the Iraqi-Kuwaiti crisis of 1973; the Islamic revolution in Iran in 1979; the Iran-Iraq war of 1980–

1988; the creation of the Gulf Cooperation Council in 1981; Kuwait's campaign to charter and reflag its oil tankers in 1987; and Kuwait's ongoing role as economic aid donor and mediator—in light of Kuwaiti foreign policy goals and the fabric of the nation's politics. By examining Kuwait's behavior in its foreign relations on the regional and global levels, we may to some extent discern the course of the nation's policy in the future and, perhaps, a new framework for small states' role in world politics.

Abdul-Reda Assiri

Notes

1. A number of studies have looked at the role and power of small states in world affairs; see Annette Baker Fox, *The Power of Small States: Diplomacy in World War II* (Chicago: The University of Chicago Press, 1959), pp. 1–9 and 180–188; Gunnar Heckscher, *The Role of Small Nations—Today and Tomorrow* (London: University of London Athlone Press, 1966), pp. 1–34; David Vital, *The Survival of Small States: Studies in Small Power/Great Power Conflict* (London: Oxford University Press, 1971), pp. 1–131; Oscar J. Falnes, *The Future of the Small States* (Washington, D.C.: American Council on Public Affairs, 1942), pp. 1–21; Michael Handel, *Weak States in the International System* (London: Frank Cass, 1981), pp. 9–286; and Robert O. Keohane, "Lilliputians' Dilemmas: Small States in International Politics," *International Organization*, vol. 23, no. 2 (Spring 1969), pp. 291–310.

2. A United Nations study in 1971 classified Kuwait as a small state both in territory and population; see Jacques Rapaport, Ernest Muteba, and Joseph J. Therattil, *Small States and Territories: Status and Problems* (New York: Arno Press, 1971, for the United Nations Institute for Training and Research [UNITAR]), pp. 29–31 and 36.

Acknowledgments

This study was motivated by academic, intellectual, and patriotic curiosities to explore one of the basic facets of Kuwait's unique political system and to analyze systematically Kuwait's foreign policy. The temporal domain of the book is June 1961 to June 1989, a period of roughly 28 years, in which Kuwait emerged as a dominant actor in the political and financial fields in the Gulf region, the Arab world, and beyond.

The manuscript was completed during my tenure (1987–1989) as a visiting research scholar at the University of Colorado–Boulder Department of Political Science and International Research Center for Energy and Economic Development. My employer, the University of Kuwait, was generous in its grant of a two-year sabbatical. The combined assistance of these institutions helped me to complete this book.

During the course of this research, I had opportunities not only to discuss the basic issues with decision makers in Kuwait and elsewhere (see Bibliography) but also to review the literature in the various libraries of the University of Colorado–Boulder; UCLA Research Library; New York City Public Library; the United Nations Library; the Library of Congress; India Office Library and Records (London); Public Record Office (Kew, England); the University of Kuwait Commerce Library; the Gulf Archives Center at the University of Kuwait; and *Al-Watan* and *Al-Qabas* files and newsclippings.

A number of colleagues and friends have helped in the different stages of this research by giving advice, reviewing the manuscript or portions of it, and/or extending moral support. I cannot list them all here but must mention Mohammed Akacem, Shamlan Al-Essa, Faisal and Maria Al-Salem, Hassan El-Ebraheem, Dorothea El-Mallakh, and Mustafa Marafi. I am grateful to those interviewees (see Bibliography) who have given me their thoughts, expertise, and views. Richard Wilson did some initial research for this project. Nancy Mann performed fine editorial work. Wendy Klein-Reis of Phantom Court Laser Print provided good word processing services.

I would like to express my gratitude to the staff at Westview Press, including Fred Praeger, Barbara Ellington, Rebecca Ritke, and outside anonymous reviewers—their contribution was of immense value.

Special thanks are due to my family. My wife, Zahra, and my children, Adel, Basel, and Noor, provided the support and friendship that I needed to overcome long and at times frustrating research experiences. There is no way to express my love and admiration to all of them. My larger family—mother, brothers, sisters, and in-laws—has always been helpful and encouraging. Finally, I am grateful to the memory of my father, who instilled in me the lessons of hard and studious work. Any credit for the success of this book is due to them. The author alone bears responsibility for its contents and for any shortcomings.

The book follows the system of transliteration used by the Library of Congress, but some names which have been anglicized have not been transliterated. In order to simplify the transliteration, diacritical marks and signs have been omitted.

A.-R. A.

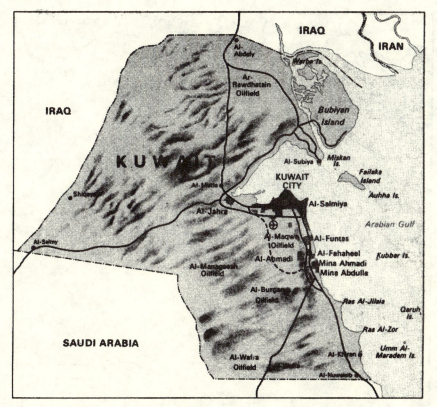

Map 1. Kuwait. Reproduced from Ministry of Information, *Maps of Kuwait* (Kuwait: Ministry of Information, January 1986).

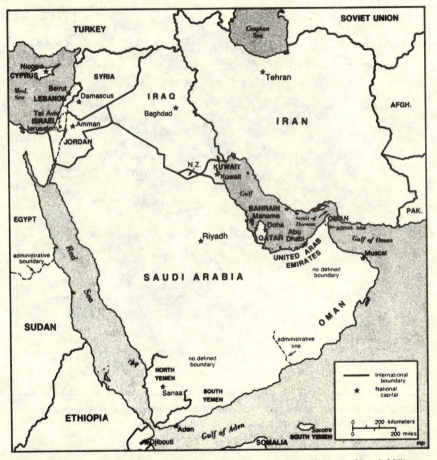

Map 2. Middle East. Reproduced from U.S. Department of Navy. Naval Military Personnel Command, *Arabian Peninsula: Saudi Arabia, Kuwait, Bahrain, Qatar, United Arab Emirates, Oman, North and South Yemen* (Washington, D.C.: U.S. Navy, March 1981).

1

Historical Overview
and Foreign Policy Goals

In comparison to its neighbors, Kuwait's ancient history is little known. It appears to be a country born out of a vacuum. In the early 1970s, European experts on the area (Winstone and Freeth) summarize this contradiction:

> In simple translation, Kuwait is the Little Fort. To Europeans who skimmed the surface of Arabia for five hundred years or so, it was a sandy littoral, a lip of the Gulf, south of Basra, which gave them no great need to pause in their tracks. They also called it Qurain, the Little Horn. Or Grane, or sometimes Grains.[1]

However, today Kuwait is considered one of the richest Third World nations. The country is engaged both in social transformation and political developments which have changed the basic tenets of its system yet still maintain the traditional Arabic and Islamic values.

Historical Overview

Some evidence has been discovered on the Kuwaiti island of Failaka that suggests that the Greeks had discovered it in ancient times. A stone found in 1937 bears a Greek inscription: "SOTEL (ES) An ATHENIAN AND SOLDIERS (?) TO ZEUS SAVIOUR POSEIDON ARTEMIS SAVIORS." According to the legends, a ship belonging to a Greek admiral, Nearchus, was wrecked in 325 B.C. while on an expedition for Alexander the Great, and Stoles and his men arrived on the shores of Kuwait, where they gave thanks for their rescue. Similarly, it had been claimed that Failaka was an important center for trade with India, and that the island was a port of call for Greek ships, and might have been used as a base for them as well.[2]

It has also been recorded that Moslem troops settled in northern Kuwait en route to proselytize the Persians. It is thought that Khalid Ibn Al-Walid faced the Persians in the battle of "that Al-Salasil" in Kadhima, north of Kuwait, about 633 A.D. Nothing specific was recorded about Kuwait, however, until the eighteenth century. The Danish traveller Carstein Neibuhr, who visited Arabia in the 1760s, referred to Kuwait as follows:

> Koueit or Graen, as it is called by the Persians and Europeans, is a sea port town, three days journey from Zobejeur, or old Basra. The inhabitants live by the fishery of pearls and of fishes. They are said to employ in this species of naval industry more than eight hundred boats. In the favourable season of the year, this town is left almost desolate, everybody going out either to the fishery, or upon some trading adventure. Graen is governed by a particular Schiech, of the tribe of Othema, who is vassal to the Schiech of Lachfa, but sometimes aspirs [sic] at independence. In such cases, when the Schiech of Lachfa advances with his army, the citizens of the Graen retreat, with their effects, into the little island of Feludsje. Near Graen are the remains of another Portuguese fortress.[3]

But the history and politics of modern Kuwait are synonymous with those of its ruling house, Al-Sabah, which migrated from the Arabian peninsula (Najd) to Kuwait with other tribes in 1716. The Al-Sabah family is a branch of the Utub tribe from Najd, which is in turn an offshoot of the Anaiza tribe. (The ruling families of Bahrain and Saudi Arabia trace their origin to the same tribe; thus social bonds reinforce the political links among the three ruling houses.) Within Kuwait a triumvirate ensued, with the house of Al-Sabah responsible for the affairs of the state; that of Al-Khalifa in charge of trade; and that of Al-Jalahma controlling maritime matters (i.e., pearl-diving and fishing). The pact continued up to 1756, when the Al-Sabah seized power, which they have virtually monopolized ever since. Thereupon, a primitive and uncomplicated system of government ensued. This is not to say that there is hereditary succession from father to son. In fact, hereditary succession has never been considered obligatory in Kuwait. The Al-Sabah choose a successor by the method traditional among tribes, that is, "by selecting a member of the ruling family who has already proved himself to have the requisite qualities of personality, leadership, and good luck."[4]

Despite its size, harsh climate, and bleak topography, its geographical location made Kuwait a bone of contention in the eighteenth and nineteenth centuries among the major powers of Germany, Great Britain, Russia, and Turkey. Regionally, Kuwait was engaged in the tribal struggle between Ibn Saud and Ibn Rashid.[5] As the Gulf became an arena for international competition and rivalry, Kuwait was marginally drawn into the power game.

The Persian occupation of Basra (1775–1779) opened up the first opportunity for an official Kuwaiti-British linkage, as British trade and desert overland mail from India, the Mediterranean, and Europe were diverted to Kuwait. The resulting economic prosperity, among other things, influenced the Kuwaitis to conquer Bahrain in 1783.[6] In addition, in 1793–1794, the British residence moved its office from Basra to Kuwait because of local sectarian fighting in southern Iraq. In 1821, the British office moved again to Failaka Island as a result of misunderstandings with the Ottoman governor in Basra.

On the regional level, Kuwait experienced a score of potential and real threats from its neighboring Arab tribes. In 1783, 1794, and 1796, both the Banu Kaab and the Ibn Saud attempted unsuccessfully to attack Kuwait. Ironically, the chief of the Ibn Saud and his family were later to seek asylum in Kuwait (1893–1901), until he was able with Kuwaiti help to regain his territory in Najd—a turnabout that illustrates the flexible posture Kuwait's leaders have adopted in dealing with their neighbors. During the rise of Wahhabi in the peninsula in the late eighteenth century, Kuwait could not fail to feel the effects of the general upheaval caused by the religious fervor of that movement.[7] The zealot Wahhabi order tried in 1792 and 1793 to attack Kuwait, but was repulsed by the combined forces of the British commercial office, the East India Company, and the ruler.

It has been argued that the Ottoman Empire maintained a quasi-sovereignty over Kuwait throughout the eighteenth century. Apparently, in 1756, the Kuwaiti ruler Sabah I negotiated with the Ottoman governor at Basra for the independence of his territory, under the suzerainty of the Ottomans. Later, Jaber I (1812–1859) helped the Ottoman governor of Basra to regain his territory after the latter was expelled by Iraqi tribes. Henceforth, and up to the reign of Mubarak the Great (1896–1915), Kuwaiti shaikhs "paid an annual tribute of 40 bags of rice and 400 Frasilah of dates" and received from their suzerain "every year a dress of honour."[8] In 1838–1839, the Ottomans placed an envoy in Kuwait in an attempt to lessen the impact of Wahhabism and strengthen the ties with the Empire.[9] In 1871, the Ottoman government bestowed on Sheikh Abdullah the title of Qaim-maqam, (governor of a sub-province) and abrogated the decree which had made Kuwait part of Al-Hasa province. This change also made Kuwait part of the more important Basra "Villiat" (province), and allowed it to run its own internal affairs. In return, foreign flags on Kuwaiti ships were replaced by Ottoman flags until World War I. There was a great deal of sympathy between Kuwait and Mohammed Ali (the Vali of Egypt); when in 1818 his troops occupied the coast of the Gulf in an effort to suppress the Wahhabis, Kuwait was left free since the Kuwaitis were sympathetic to the Ottomans and opposed to the Wahhabis. In sum, Kuwait's policy concerning Ottoman suzerainty over it was to "ignore the claim on most occasions, to deny it on others, and to tolerate it when danger threatened from another quarter."[10]

Despite the earlier connections with Britain, a real opportunity for Kuwaiti-British rapprochement arose only in the late 1800s, as a result of factors in and around Kuwait. Mubarak Al-Kabir (the Great) had assassinated his half-brothers Mohammed (ruler 1892–1896) and Jarrah in 1896. Mubarak, who was relegated by his ruling brothers to the undignified role of overseeing the bedouins outside Kuwait city, was in essence a warrior, a born conspirator, and a strong personality with a lust for power.[11] Mubarak accused his brother of incompetency and of being too closely aligned with the Ottoman empire. But Mubarak then needed a countervailing ally to buttress his claims, particularly after his slain brothers' sons and their supporters escaped to Basra and sought aid from the Ottomans and from other tribes to regain their father's throne. Thus, to resist Ottoman pressures, Mubarak sought and received British protection in a bid to escape absorption by the larger neighboring countries.[12] On January 23, 1899, Mubarak signed an agreement with Britain stating that he

> does hereby pledge and bind himself, his heirs and successors not to receive the Agent or Representative of any Power of Government at Kuwait territory, without the previous sanction of the British government; and he further binds himself, his heirs and successors not to cede, sell, lease, mortgage, or give for occupation, or for any purpose any portion of his territory to the Government or subjects of any other Power without the previous consent of Her Majesty's Government for these purposes.[13]

The forces that compelled both parties to reach this agreement were numerous. The Russians had attempted in December 1898 to gain Ottoman approval to build a railroad from Tripoli (Lebanon) to Kuwait. Similarly, in 1899, Germany tried to build a railroad from Berlin through Istanbul and Baghdad, with a terminus in Kuwait. In 1897 the Ottomans sent a health inspector to Kuwait, and in January of that year, the Ottoman government issued a decree appointing Mubarak Qaim-maqam of Kuwait. In 1899 Mubarak rejected a request by the Ottomans that he leave Kuwait for Constantinople, with the promise that he would be appointed to the consultative council and that he would be granted a monthly stipend. In 1901 the Ottoman government tried to expel him from Kuwait but was prevented from doing so by the presence of a British naval ship. These developments, taken together, gave Britain the incentive to sign a treaty of protection with Mubarak. The treaty was meant to protect Kuwaiti rulers from external threats and internal opposition; it also tended to reduce the role of the tribes in politics,[14] since the Shaikh would rely more on British support for his rule and perhaps adventures. Explicitly, the treaty stated that Mubarak and his successors were linked to Britain, and were not allowed to lease or sell any part of their territory without British consent. Implicitly, it meant that externally Kuwait had entered into the British sphere of influence, while remaining a free emirate (principality) in its internal affairs; and that the succession was limited to Mubarak's lineage of Al-Sabah.[15] Despite the limitations in the treaty, Mubarak was widely held to be the only independent Shaikh in the Gulf region.[16]

Mubarak thus managed in one stroke to eliminate the possibility that his brothers' heirs might reclaim the sheikhdom, to reduce local opposition to his rule, and to shield Kuwait against external threats. The alignment with Britain proved to be a far-sighted policy, both for the ruler and his country. After the treaty was signed, Mubarak did not "care the least about foreign affairs," merely appointing "an agent in Bombay . . . to look after the needs of Kuwaitis who travelled over there."[17]

In 1903, Lord Curzon, Viceroy of India, visited Kuwait, and as a result a British Residence was established in Kuwait, despite Ottoman protests. The visit marked the consolidation of British influence in Kuwait.[18] Between

1900 and 1906, when the Gulf became a market for contraband arms trade to India, Persia and Afghanistan, the British, who feared that arming the tribes there might lead to insurrection against British rule, were able to convince the ruler to impose a ban on arms trade to Kuwait. Britain and the Ottoman Empire resolved their disagreements about Kuwait in a 1913 treaty, but the outbreak of World War I prevented its ratification.

The new arrangement made Britain responsible for the defense and external relations of Kuwait. Despite the 1899 treaty, the Russians attempted, through visits by Russian emissaries (for example, there was a Russian consul in Bushire [Iran] in 1901) and through visits by their naval ships *Askold, Varyag,* and *Boyarin,* to lure Mubarak away from the British, but to no avail.[19] During World War I, Britain stationed troops in Kuwait to blockade the Ottoman Empire and as a link in the broader context of special British security interests.[20]

Although the Kuwait authorities were free to conduct their own affairs, British advice and influence proved important to the Al-Sabah, as the merchants and nationalists demanded a share in the ruler's power. When a group of Kuwaitis tried in the 1920s and the 1930s to ask for the establishment of an elected council, ostensibly to create a "representative" system of government, but actually to loosen the ties between the ruler and Britain, the British, fearful of any external influence on the movement, decided to find a solution satisfactory to both parties, before Kuwait's neighbors exploited the issue. The British, it was reported, pushed for one of two approaches: either to change the protective relationship to indirect rule as in the case of Bahrain, or to move to direct British rule as in the case of Aden. Neither course was adopted; instead, a council was elected in 1938 but failed to achieve its goals and soon faded away.[21]

Kuwait became a center for regional politics in November 1923, when Britain arranged a conference among representatives from the Ibn Saud and the sharifs (notables) of Hijaz, Iraq, and the Trans-Jordan to find a stable solution for the situation in Arabia by the delimitation of permanent boundaries, mainly because Ibn Saud was constantly attacking Hijaz and Iraq.[22]

Kuwait's relations with its three neighbors have fluctuated among indifference, friendship, and hostility. The tribes of Najd (the Wahhabis or Ikhwan [brotherhood]) had attempted to influence and on several occasions to invade Kuwait. Ibn Saud, the ruler of Najd, once sought asylum in Kuwait; and in his grand design to unify the peninsula under his dominion, Kuwait was not out of his mind. In fact, from 1928 to 1937, he imposed trade sanctions against Kuwait because it had refused to collect customs and transit duties, on behalf of Ibn Saud, on merchandise destined for Najd. In the 1920s, tribes loyal to Ibn Saud might have taken over Kuwait if it had not been for the British airplanes and ships in Kuwait Bay, which not unlikely influenced the invaders (Al-Duwish) to withdraw.

In December 1922, the Al-Uqair boundary agreement was reached between Ibn Saud and Kuwait, which was represented by a British agent. The agreement deprived Kuwait of almost two-thirds of its territory and gave the land to Najd. Kuwait's boundary was pushed back a hundred and fifty miles. The British justified their relinquishment of Kuwait's territory by saying that otherwise "the sword had been mightier than the pen" and that "had . . . Kuwait not conceded the territory, Ibn Saud would certainly have soon picked a quarrel and taken as much, if not more, by force of arms."[23] This border agreement symbolized the foundation of the nation-state in the Arabian peninsula, and drew a new boundary between nations linked with a new concept of sovereignty.[24]

Although during Ottoman rule and up to Mubarak's era Kuwait's relations with Iraq had been pragmatic and close, Mubarak's pro-British attitude caused rapid deterioration. After World War I, the Iraqis supported the nationalist elements inside Kuwait in order to reduce the British role in Kuwait. The nationalist demands for a share in the ruling family's power and for a union with Iraq found support from King Ghazi of Iraq, Qasr Al-Zuhoor radio station, and the Iraqi press, which broadcast nationalist messages and propaganda inside Kuwait.[25] This agitation from Iraq continued up to the 1950s. Furthermore, Iraq charged that Kuwait was the source of arms and other smuggling to Iraq. In the 1930s and 1940s the Iraqi government expressed a willingness to appoint a consulate in Kuwait, but as Kuwait estimated that there were only about 30 Iraqi subjects in Kuwait by the 1930s, Britain turned down the Iraq request.[26]

In Iran, Kuwait's interests were primarily directed toward the southern provinces, which were either under British rule or under the control of shaikh Khazal of Muhammerah (Khuzistan). Kuwaiti rulers and Khazal had maintained cordial relations, but Kuwaiti officials were reluctant to get involved in Iranian politics. When, in the 1920s, Khazal was arrested and was taken to Teheran, they refused to provide him with weapons or even to collect his debts from Kuwaiti merchants. This policy is explained in part by Kuwaiti unwillingness to offend the central Iranian government, and in part by British wishes.[27] In the 1920s, Iran proposed to appoint an honorary agent, "to issue passports to fellow Persian subjects in Kuwait." However, Britain refused on the grounds that "it was contrary to the agreement of 1899, and might set a precedent for other powers."[28]

With the discovery of oil in the early twentieth century, the United States acquired more than a negligible influence in Kuwait. The initial approaches took place through humanitarian channels. In 1914 American missionaries opened up a hospital that played an appreciable role in the social development of Kuwait until the late 1960s. In the 1930s, American interests extended to oil as well. Earlier, in 1914, shaikh Mubarak had agreed not to give any concession to any party without British approval, "if in their [British] view there seems hope of obtaining oil therefore we shall never give a concession in this matter to any one except a person appointed from the British government."[29] Under a compromise between American and British oil interests, a joint company, Kuwait Oil Company (KOC), was set up to explore oil in Kuwait. In the 1940s, with a growing American presence in

KOC and other interests, the U.S. government requested that an American consulate in Kuwait be opened. The British responded once more that they did not desire to set a precedent, and that the "shaikh would endeavor to 'play off' the British and USA representatives against each other and that this might weaken our influence with him."[30]

As to the importance of Kuwait to the Western economies, in the 1950s a secret British memorandum warned that "Kuwait's importance to us and the Western world outweigh absolutely any temporary advantage we reap from the Iraqis or Persians by weakening or surrendering our special position here."[31] The fact is that, by then, Kuwait's proven oil reserves and production had become important for Western economies.

As political trends in the Third World took a turn toward self-reliance and independence in the aftermath of World War II, and since Kuwait was allowed a margin of "leeway" in the conduct of its foreign politics, it was imperative that independence be granted soon. A number of actions proves that Kuwait was in fact "independent" before the official announcement. Kuwait and Saudi Arabia had signed a mutual defense pact in July 1947, albeit with British consent. Kuwait had participated in economic and social meetings of the Arab League since early 1952.[32] Kuwait became a member of several specialized international agencies such as the International Labor Organization (ILO) and UNESCO and in 1960 became a founding member of the Organization of Petroleum Exporting Countries (OPEC). A confidential British letter advocated in 1957 that Kuwait deal with its neighbors concerning boundaries and other related issues; the British wanted "to let Kuwait do more of its own dirty work in dealing with its neighbors."[33] And according to the 1914 British promise, the British government did "recognize and admit that the Shaikhdom of Kuwait is an independent Government under British protection."[34]

On June 19, 1961, Kuwait and Britain signed an agreement terminating the protection agreement of 1899. However, in order for Kuwait to be prepared for any unforeseeable events, both parties signed a new understanding, a friendship treaty, according to which "(c) When appropriate the two Governments shall consult on matters which concern them both. (d) Nothing in these conclusions shall affect the readiness of Her Majesty's Government to assist the Government of Kuwait if the latter request such assistance."[35]

As Kuwait was celebrating its first week of independence, Iraq declared, to the surprise of everyone, its intention to annex Kuwait on historical grounds, i.e., that Kuwait had once been part of Iraq under the rule of the Ottoman Empire. British and later Arab League troops thwarted such a threat (see Chapter 2).

Meanwhile, Kuwait's internal structure followed a new model that added legitimacy and support to its besieged political regime. For a number of reasons, most urgently the Iraqi threat, the ruler, Abdullah Al-Salem, agreed to surrender some of the ruling family's power and prerogatives to the people by permitting the citizens to participate with the ruling house in decision making. In general, "the dominant families of the Arabian Peninsula were prepared to acknowledge that their stability and future were intertwined with their capacities to adapt to changing conditions as well as to respond to the pleas of a youthful, politically conscious public." And the Al-Sabah were "judged by observers to be among the most enlightened of the ruling families in the Arabian peninsula."[36]

A constituent assembly (Majlis Al-Tasisi) was elected in late 1961, and a constitution was promulgated in November 1962. Accordingly, a national assembly (Majlis Al-Ummah) made up of 50 members was elected in 1963 for a four-year term. This assembly lent support, and occasionally opposition, to the government's domestic and, to a lesser extent, foreign policies. Kuwait stands as the only regional state with an established modern legal system.[37]

Foreign Policy Goals

As the scope of Kuwait's external interests and involvements has widened and become multifaceted, so have the goals that serve as a driving force for its foreign policy. First of all, state security and the ruling family's stability have been in the forefront of Kuwaiti concerns since the country's inception in the 1700s. This concern culminated in 1899, when Mubarak requested and received British protection in order to safeguard his own rule against his brothers' heirs and also to maintain the state's integrity against external threats. In fact, "alliance" with Britain was seen as a reasonable way out, since Britain was a credible and recognized force in the Gulf. During the independence era, security implied staying clear of regional and inter-Arab rivalries, and establishing friendly relations with as many countries of the world as possible, regardless of their political inclinations. The obvious assumption is that more friends equal more leverage, and more leverage is a better deterrent.

Second, the ideological tendencies of Kuwait as an Arab state and a Moslem religious community did bear some fruit after independence; however, the Islamic tendencies remained marginal until the late 1960s. Before independence the strong tide of Arab nationalism in Kuwait alarmed the British, who warned in a secret letter that there was "noticeably greater anti-British and pro-Egyptian feeling in Kuwait than in Iraq and Lebanon."[38] Furthermore, a 1956 British confidential report stated that the Kuwaitis were still solid in condemning London's Suez action. The British authorities speculated in 1957 whether the increased number of Palestinians in government positions might influence the policies of the Kuwaiti government.[39] In the late 1950s, after a meeting in Damascus among Nasser, the ruler of Kuwait, and the new regime of Iraq, it was rumored that Kuwait might join the United Arab Republic of Egypt and Syria. Such reports had an upsetting effect on the oil market and on shares in London. Likewise, Nuri Al-Said of Iraq tried unsuccessfully to convince the Kuwaiti ruler to join the Hashemite Union of Jordan and Iraq. Nonetheless, after visits to Baghdad, Ankara, and Teheran, the ruler reasserted his decision in 1958 not to join either the Baghdad Pact or the Hashemite Union.[40]

Arab nationalism is a deep-seated phenomenon in Kuwait. In the 1920s and 1930s, a group of elitist nationalists had called for setting up elected councils, but its ultimate goal was to undermine the ruling house, to unite with Iraq, and to loosen the ties between Kuwait and Britain.[41]

The influence of Arab nationalism is epitomized in the Kuwaiti constitution. Article 1 states that "Kuwait is an Arab State. . . . The people of Kuwait are a part of the Arab Nation." Moreover, Article 2 states that "the religion of the State is Islam, and the Islamic Sharia shall be a main source of legislation." The influence of Arab nationalism is embodied in Kuwait not only in the indigenous population, but also in non-Kuwaiti Arabs of various backgrounds. The combined Arab influence on the press, education, professional associations, and the national assembly is clearly identifiable. The demography of the population plays a role which the government cannot ignore, and clearly affects its behavior. The dominant group—by their longevity in Kuwait, sheer numbers, and penetration into almost all areas of Kuwaiti political, social, and economic life—consists of the Palestinians.

One must realize that native Kuwaitis make up only 39.1 percent (some 700,000 out of an estimated 1,958,477) of the 1988 population, down from 40.1 percent in 1985 and 47.5 percent in 1975, whereas non-Kuwaitis form 69.0 percent of the 1988 population (over one million), up from 59.9 in 1985 and 42.2 percent in 1975.[42] Out of the Arab population, the Palestinians made up about half (300,000) by 1978, up from 204,178 in 1975. Their number reached 350,000 by 1985 and was estimated at around 400,000 by the end of 1988.[43] Thus, Palestine has become a major domestic as well as a foreign policy issue. Palestinians "have a ready-made card of entry into local politics and local public opinion."[44]

Kuwait's concern about the Palestinian issue as the core of Arab politics was evident in the first formal Kuwaiti address to the General Assembly of the United Nations, right after the country was admitted to the UN in 1963. Kuwait's foreign affairs minister, Sabah Al-Ahmad, stated categorically:

> Kuwait raises its voice . . . to the sad plight and the immeasurable injustice under which . . . the people of Palestine have been living. . . . The mere lapse of time does not deprive the people of Palestine of their legitimate rights to an honourable return to a country which is their own. . . . A fait accompli can never be a stable foundation for peace. . . . Justice and a humane attitude towards the catastrophe of Palestine is the only remedy.[45]

Kuwait's emphasis on Arab solidarity against external threats was reflected in the foreign minister's statement that solidarity was "the only way to force . . . others to respect the Arabs."[46]

At first, despite the fact that the state official religion is Islam, Kuwaiti decision makers tended to follow a secular orientation in their foreign policy. In fact, Kuwaiti legislation is based not solely on Islam, but on a mixture of religious and secular laws and traditions. In other words, Kuwaiti officials tried not to mingle politics and religion in foreign policy. Yet the Arab cold war of the 1960s and King Faisal's emphasis on Pan-Islamism were not irrelevant to the Kuwaitis. By the late 1960s, because of the 1967 war with Israel and the failure of Pan-Arabism, the burning of Al-Aksa Mosque in Jerusalem, the first Islamic summit in Morocco in 1969, and the increased power and influence of Islamic fundamentalism at home, Islam began to significantly affect the formulation of foreign policy. Such changes were evident in Kuwait's foreign aid scheme, which was initially limited to Arab states. In fact, "Islamic countries are the favored borrowers reflecting Kuwait's Islamic identity and cultural interests. This serves to neutralize criticism from within the Kuwaiti community or the National Assembly."[47] In part, foreign aid to Islamic nations is a manifestation of religious "zakat" (an almsgiving charity duty based on around 10 percent of one's annual profits) to impoverished Moslems.[48]

In the 1970s and 1980s, Kuwait's devotion to Islamic causes and purposes equaled, if not outweighed, its other purposes in allocating aid. It established a private Islamic bank (Kuwait Finance House), set up the Al-Zakat House, called for setting up an Islamic International Court of Justice, and spent over $400 million on a 99-acre conference center to host the heads of the 46 members of the Islamic Conference in January 1987. In addition, in 1984 Kuwait established the International Islamic Charity Foundation, and by 1987 it had financed 59 projects in 13 Moslem countries at a cost exceeding $8 million.[49]

Finally, the state's sudden change from "rags to riches" enticed the Kuwaitis to assume a new missionary role: to spread and share their wealth with less fortunate people. As early as the 1950s, Kuwaiti decision makers felt a humane responsibility to distribute the oil wealth to their brethren in the lower Gulf and southern peninsula in the forms of social, educational, medical, and other essential services. Kuwaiti's foreign minister phrased this sense of moral duty as "brothers sharing a loaf."[50] The director-general of Kuwait's Fund for Arab Economic Development (KFAED), established in 1961, has said, "if you look at our record you will find we put greater emphasis on poorer, smaller countries . . . countries that don't really matter politically."[51]

One Arab aid official, comparing the lots and living conditions of many Third World states with the Arabs' own before oil, stated that countries like Kuwait win a measure of respect in the world because of their generosity. Kuwait's aid schemes were widely perceived as a monument to its foresight and generosity.[52]

The sense of mission continued, but was later politicized, and on occasion humanitarian and political purposes paralleled each other or overlapped. In effect, Kuwait successfully used "dinar diplomacy," the power to capitalize on the financial might of the state for political and security purposes, i.e., to win friends and thwart enemies. Kuwaiti support in the area of human developments served as a means of assisting regional growth and security.[53] In other words, Kuwaiti foreign aid "essentially has been used either to ward off a particular, clearly identifiable danger, or to improve the donors' broader security environments."[54] Although until the 1980s Kuwaiti officials were reluctant to admit the political dimension of foreign aid, after Nicaragua and Zimbabwe abstained on the Security Council resolution condemning Iran's attack on oil tankers, Kuwaiti officials publicly demanded that Kuwaiti aid should be reviewed in light of these developments and linked to other states' behavior towards Kuwait. One high-ranking Kuwaiti official said, "all countries of the world, in giving loans or aid or taking political positions in any particular issue, make their own national interests the goal."[55] A government committee to review all cases of foreign aid was formulated. In order to grasp the humane dimension of Kuwait's foreign aid policy, one must realize that Kuwait's aid exceeds 3 percent of its GNP, far above the industrial nations' average of 0.39 percent annually, and way ahead of the minimum 0.70 percent recommended by the United Nations. Kuwait's development aid between 1983 and 1985 reached 3.8 percent of its GNP.[56]

Kuwait's investment attitudes and actual policies have also been influenced in part by the trading and entrepreneurial mentalities that have permeated the minds of both rulers and ruled since the seafaring era. Public, private, and joint public and private investment have sprung from this city-state into the four corners of the globe. In fact, because of the increasing volume of Kuwait's investment and the government's share in private corporations, it eventually became difficult to draw a line between public and private investment. In addition, humanitarian, economic, and political purposes became blurred. Although Kuwait's investment behavior has been conditioned by political and economic criteria, economic factors often outweigh the political.[57]

What has historically forced the Kuwaitis into an external orientation and involvement, sometimes under great duress and even beyond their own capabilities, is a need to escape the hostile environment that have found themselves locked into. Indeed, long before the oil, trade and commerce with faraway places such as East and South Asia and East Africa had become a means of survival as well as interaction with other societies. Thus, the Kuwaiti mentality and outlook over the years has been characterized as "open, renewable and flexible," so that, in general, Kuwaiti society tends to "influence, and be influenced by other societies' conditions, . . . norms . . . and . . . rules."[58] Since seafaring demands cooperative work and a collective spirit, the Kuwaitis became willing "to accept everything new but useful. . . . They also became pragmatic in dealing with . . . life."[59] The new environment in Kuwait and the interaction with other societies, it has been assumed, created "a new man . . . unrelated to his original roots . . . of a new breed and character."[60]

In all fairness, however, it should be emphasized that in general, whatever its motives or goals, Kuwait's foreign policy is not active or initiatory, but rather reactive, triggered by events and stimuli outside its boundaries. Since it is small, exposed, and vulnerable, events in its immediate environment may have a farther-reaching impact on Kuwait's policies than the forces discussed above. Thus, the range of actions for decision makers is limited and the interdependence between external development and foreign goals is relative, since Kuwait needs first of all to satisfy the aspirations and goals of its immediate neighbors and adjust its motives accordingly. Kuwait is basically a migrant society, and native Kuwaitis trace their background and roots to three main neighbors: Iran, Iraq, and Saudi Arabia. Since the phenomenon of national loyalty and patriotism is a recent one in Arabia, events in the vicinity of Kuwait affect the emotions of its citizens, and sympathy with one state or another has the potential to polarize Kuwait. In particular, by the early 1930s, out of a Kuwaiti population of 65,000, some 18,000 persons were Shiite Moslems, while the rest were Sunni. In the mid-1980s, the Shiites constituted some 25 percent of the population.[61] Regardless of where the Shiites come from, they have historically looked to Iran as their guardian. The Sunnis—except for those of Persian origin, who are simply riding along in the Sunni bandwagon—have identified with Saudi Arabia, Iraq, or Arab nationalism. By mere logic, then, about one-fourth to one-third of the Kuwaiti population might identify with each of the neighboring states, a loyalty that could create security problems if the Kuwaiti government could not manage to create a national consciousness unbounded by primordial and sectarian loyalties (see Chapter 4). It is not in the interest of Kuwait, therefore, to tilt the political pendulum to any one of its neighbors against another. Such a policy could set in motion a backlash or a chain reaction among a certain section of the population, perhaps one beyond the capability of the political system to control, and might lose some of the domestic support needed for a fully successful foreign policy.

Conclusion

In two centuries and a half, Kuwait has been transformed from a minor principality buried in oblivion into an important, active, prosperous city-state. The most remarkable period has been the last forty years or so, during which Kuwait began to assume an active role, sometimes beyond its actual power, and perhaps unrelated to its "passive" ancient history.

Two major developments shaped Kuwait's foreign policy from its origins up to 1961: the 1899 Kuwaiti-British protective treaty, and the 1950s oil bonanza, which transformed Kuwait from a mini-state "principality" into a city-state. The motive behind Mubarak's treaty with Britain can be summarized as the maintenance of the status quo, both in ensuring the succession of Mubarak's descendants and in preserving the state's security against external odds. British pressures and forces helped to achieve that end, Saudi usurpation of about two-thirds of Kuwaiti's territory notwithstanding. Generally speaking, throughout Kuwait's history, peaceful transition of power has characterized its political processes, except for the palace coup of 1896.

The discovery of oil in the 1930s and the commercial export of oil in the 1940s not only brought an influx of expatriate labor to Kuwait, but also made conditions in Kuwait more complicated and Kuwaiti people more sophisticated, albeit still fatalistic on occasion.

The goals of Kuwait's foreign policy became multiple and interdependent. Although state security and the ruling family's stability were still paramount, Arab nationalism, Islamic tendencies, humanitarian mission, and a trading mentality pervaded decision making and characterized Kuwait's behavior. Britain lived up to its 1914 promise, and its protective status became "benign," indeed. Whether because it was losing its grip on its overseas territories after World War II, or because it wanted to gain favor with Kuwait, where the Americans were pressing for a foothold, or simply because it was preparing Kuwait for self-rule, Britain allowed Kuwait a large margin of leeway and flexibility in conducting its own affairs. At any rate, Kuwait began to assume a role in world affairs much larger than its size would warrant. In contrast to the Mubarak era, when the protection treaty made the ruler lose interest in foreign relations, the oil boom made external affairs a way to guarantee the state's survival, and gave those involved in conducting them psychological satisfaction and publicity. Therefore, in contrast to Mubarak's reign, which was characterized by a bond with one superpower, the oil era marked the beginning of the end of such formal, "unrestrained" relationships.

The common denominator between the two eras is the importance of regional forces, whether tribes, mini-states, or regional powers, in the minds and the realpolitik of foreign policy formulators. In fact, dealing with the neighboring powers has been complicated and heartbreaking in both periods (see Chapters 2, 3, 4, and 5). Kuwait tends to react with anguish to pressures and demands put on it from its immediate vicinity. Kuwait's alternative choice is to take advantage of its neighbors' contradictions to reduce their pressure on Kuwait itself, realizing that each state might not allow the others to have a larger influence.

In short, just as the interests, scope, and intensity of Kuwait's foreign policy were limited before the 1950s, so were its goals. As those interests, scope, and intensity have broadened, so have the goals.

Not only have the scope and orientation of Kuwait's foreign policy changed since its foundation, but in the last generation the whole character of Kuwait, both internally and externally, has changed. Socially, economically, culturally, and politically, Kuwait has witnessed a "face-lift." An observer wrote in the 1960s, "In less than two decades the whole face of Kuwait has changed beyond recognition."[62] Such changes, in turn, have broadened Kuwait's interests and its activities and have spilled over into Kuwait's external behavior.

The gush of oil forced the government to deal with a mixed, cosmopolitan population, in which natives gradually became a minority. This mixture began to change people's value system and general expectations. The political actors were not limited to natives, but included a growing majority of expatriates, whose degree of influence is not fully documented yet must not be underestimated. The tension between the two groups was based on social background and economic competition. At the same time, oil revenues became an impetus for as well as a sedative against outside demands and pressures. As its immediate environment looked to Kuwait for assistance, Kuwait successfully took the initiative to redistribute its wealth to neighboring states. Its financial capabilities became both a goal and a means. The need to distribute oil surplus and invest globally simultaneously served as an indirect instrument of foreign policy. Kuwait, as a small state, had few means at its disposal to reach its political ends; financial channels became an effective means to achieve those state's goals.

Notes

1. H.C.D. Winstone and Zahra Freeth, *Kuwait: Prospect and Reality* (London: George Allen and Unwin Ltd., 1972), p. 11.

2. C.A.P. Southwell, "Kuwait," *Journal of the Royal Society of Arts*, vol. 102 (December 11, 1953), p. 27; Husayn Khalaf Al-Shaykh Khazal, *Tarikh Al-Kuwayt Al-Siyassi* (Political History of Kuwait), vol. 1 (Beirut: Dar Al-Kutub, 1962), p. 11; and Qadri Qalaji, *Al-Khalij Al-Araby* (The Arabian Gulf) (Beirut: Dar Al-Kitab Al-Araby, 1965), pp. 115–120.

3. Carstein Neibuhr, "Travel in Arabia," in John Pinkerton, ed., *A General Collection of the Best and Most Interesting Voyages and Travels in All Parts of the World*, vol. X (London: Longman, Hurst, Rees, and Brown, Paternoster-Row; and Cadell and Davies, in the Strand, 1811), p. 121.

4. Husayn Khalaf Al-Shaykh Khazal, *Tarikh Al-Kuwayt Al-Siyassi*, vol. 2, p. 294; Winstone and Freeth, *Kuwait: Prospect and Reality*, p. 65; for the Sabah's history and politics see Rosemarie Said Zahlan, *The Making of the Modern Gulf States: Kuwait, Bahrain, Qatar, the United Arab Emirates and Oman* (London: Unwin Hyman, 1989), pp. 79–82.

5. Laurence Lockhart, "Outline of the History of Kuwait," *Journal of the Royal Central Asian Society*, vol. 34 (1947), p. 268.

6. Ahmad Hasan Joudah, *Al-Massaleh Al-Britania Fil Kuwayt Hata 1939* (British Interests in Kuwait Up to 1939) (Basra: Centre for Arab Gulf Studies, 1979), p. 37; Robin Bidwell, *The Affairs of Kuwait 1896–1905*, vol. 1, 1896–1901 (London: Frank Cass and Co., 1971), xi; and Winstone and Freeth, *Kuwait: Prospect and Reality*, pp. 62–63.

7. Winstone and Freeth, *Kuwait: Prospect and Reality*, p. 59.

8. Winstone and Freeth, *Kuwait: Prospect and Reality*, p. 12; and J. C. Lorimer, *Gazetter of the Persian Gulf, Oman, and Central Arabia*, vol. 1, Pt. 1 (Calcutta: Superintendent Government Printing, 1915), p. 1008.

9. Winstone and Freeth, *Kuwait: Prospect and Reality*, p. 64.

10. Husayn Khalaf Al-Shaykh Khazal, *Tarikh Al-Kuwayt Al-Siyassi*, vol. 1, p. 138; and J. B. Kelly, *Britain and the Persian Gulf, 1795–1880* (Oxford: Clarendon Press, 1968), p. 33.

11. Salah al-Akad, *Al-Tiyarat Al-Siyasiah Fil Al-Khalij Al-Araby* (Political Trends in the Arabian Gulf) (Cairo: Anglo-Egyptian Printing, 1983), pp. 191–192; and Abd Al-Aziz Al-Rushaid, *Tarikh Al-Kuwayt* (The History of Kuwait) (Beirut: Dar Maktabat Al-Hayat, 1971), p. 189.

12. Richard Coke, *The Arab's Place in the Sun* (London: Thornton Butterworth Ltd., 1929), p. 184.

13. Jacob C. Hurewitz, *The Middle East and North Africa in World Politics: A Documentary Record*, vol. 1 (New Haven & London: Yale University Press, 1975), p. 476.

14. Khaldoun H. Al-Naqeeb, *Al-Mujtama Wa Al-Dawlat Fil Al-Khalij Wa Al-Jazirah Al-Arabiya* (Society and State in the Gulf and the Arabian Peninsula) (Beirut: Center for Arab Unity Studies, 1987), p. 96.

15. Abd Al-Aziz Husayn, *Al-Mujtama Al-Araby Bil Kuwayt* (Arab Society in Kuwait) (Cairo: Institute for Higher Arab Studies, 1960), pp. 29–30.

16. Richard Coke, *The Arab's Place in the Sun*, p. 184.

17. Husayn Khalaf Al-Shaykh Khazal, *Tarikh Al-Kuwayt Al-Siyassi*, vol. 2, p. 297.

18. Rasim Rushdi, *Kuwayt Wa Kuwaytion: Dirasat Fil Madhi al-Kuwayt Wa Hadireha* (Kuwait and Kuwaitis: Studies in Kuwait's Past and Present) (Beirut: Al-Rahbania Al-Lubaniah Press, 1955), p. 58; and Harold R. P. Dickson, *Kuwait and Her Neighbours* (London: George Allen and Unwin Ltd., 1956), p. 140.

19. For the arms ban see Najat Abdul-Kadir Al-Qinaei, "Hadher Tinarat Al-Isleha Fil Al-Kuwayt Wa Al-Khalij Al-Araby" (Arms Trade Sanctions in Kuwait and the Arabian Gulf, 1900–1906), *Al-Biyan*, no. 198 (September 1983), pp. 34–59; and for the Russian attempts see Badr Al-Din Al-Khususi, "Al-Nishat Al-Russi Fil Al-Khalij Al-Araby, 1887–1907" (Russian Activities in the Arabian Gulf), *Journal of Gulf and Arabian Peninsula Studies*, vol. 5, no. 18 (April 1979), pp. 113–130.

20. Richard H. Sanger, *The Arabian Peninsula* (Ithaca, N.Y.: Cornell University Press, 1954), p. 151.

21. Khalid Sulaymin Al-Adsani, *Nisf Aam Lil-Hukum Al-Niyabi Fil Al-Kuwayt* (Half a Year of Parliamentary Rule in Kuwait) (Beirut: Al-Qashaf Press, 1947), p. 6; Richard H. Sanger, *The Arabian Peninsula*, pp. 168–169. For the Majlis developments, see Jacqueline S. Ismael, *Kuwait: Social Change in Historical Perspective* (Syracuse: Syracuse University Press, 1982), pp. 71–77 and 83–86.

22. Richard Coke, *The Arab's Place in the Sun*, pp. 254–255.

23. For discussion on Kuwait's relations with its neighbors see Harold R. P. Dickson, *Kuwait and Her Neighbours*, pp. 256 and 274–279; also Rosemarie Said Zahlan, *The Making of Modern Gulf States*, pp. 118–120. For Kuwait's influence on Ibn Saud during his asylum in Kuwait see Jacob Goldberg, *The Foreign Policy of Saudi Arabia: The Formative Years, 1902–1918* (Cambridge and London: Harvard University Press, 1986), pp. 3–4, 31, and 35.

24. Khaldoun H. Al-Naqeeb, *Al-Mujtama Wa Al-Dawlat Fil Al-Khalij Wa Al-Jazirah Al-Arabiya*, p. 112.

25. Khalid Sulayman Al-Adsani, *Nisf Aam Lil-Hukum Al-Niyabi Fil Al-Kuwayt*, p. 7; Majid Khadduri, *Independent Iraq 1932–1958: A Study in Iraqi Politics*, 2nd ed. (London: Oxford University Press, 1960), p. 141; and India Office and Library Records (IOR), London File R/15/5/226, a confidential letter No. D.O.C.-250, from the Political Agent in Kuwait to the Political Resident in Bushire, on August 8, 1935, and a confidential report no. c/104, March 13, 1939.

26. See India Office and Library Records, London, File R/15/5/226, on August 8, 1935; File 15/5/228, a restricted letter from the Gulf Residency in Bahrain (#149/39/49), and a confidential letter from the British Embassy in Baghdad (#852/2/49), on July 18, 1949, May 16, 1949 and March 26, 1930; and File 15/5/226, a telegram from the Political Resident in Bushire to the government of India.

27. Husayn Khalaf Al-Shaykh Khazal, *Tarikh Al-Kuwayt Al-Siyassi* (Political History of Kuwait), vol. 5, pt. 1 (Beirut: Dar Al-Kutub, 1970), pp. 224–260; for Iran's relation with shaikh Khazal see Rouhollah K. Ramazani, *The Foreign Policy of Iran: A Developing Nation in World Affairs, 1500–1941* (Charlottesville: University Press of Virginia, 1966), pp. 197–203.

28. India Office Library and Records, File R/15/5/126, telegram from the Political Resident in Bushire to the Government of India, New Delhi, no. 155, on February 14, 1930.

29. Mohammad Khalil, *The Arab States and the Arab League: A Documentary Record*, vol. 2, International Affairs (Beirut: Khayats, 1962), pp. 668–669; for the role of the American missionaries see K. S. Twitchell, *Saudi Arabia*, 3rd ed. (Princeton: Princeton University Press, 1958), p. 161; Cordell Hull, *The Memoirs of Cordell Hull*, vol. 2 (N.Y.: The Macmillan Co., 1948), p. 1499; and for the missionaries' accomplishments and hardships, see Eleanor Taylor Calverly, *My Arabian Days and Nights* (N.Y.: Thomas W. Crowell Co., 1958), and Joseph J. Malone, "America and the Arabian Peninsula: The First Two Hundred Years," *The Middle East Journal*, vol. 30, no. 3 (Summer 1976), pp. 406-424.

30. For KOC see Archibald H. T. Chisholm, *The First Kuwait Oil Concession Agreement: A Record of the Negotiations, 1911–1934* (London: Frank Cass, 1975), pp. 130-131; and Richard H. Sanger, *The Arabian Peninsula*, pp. 164–166. For American requests see India Office Library and Records, File 15/5/317, telegram from London to Political Agent in Kuwait on March 27, 1948 (the American community was estimated at 2000 persons); and File 15/15/317, telegram No. 258, from the Political Agent in Kuwait on March 30, 1948 (which estimates the American community in Kuwait at only 200).

31. Public Record Office (Kew, England), File 3/18/88, F.O. 371/126905, a confidential letter from the Political Agency in Kuwait to the British Residency in Bahrain, on November 14, 1957 (#EA 1022/2).

32. Sayed Nuwfal, *Al-Awdah Al-Siyassiah Li Amarat Al-Khalij Al-Araby Wa Janoub Al-Jazirah* (Political Situations for Arabian Gulf Emirates and the Southern Peninsula) (Cairo: Dar Al-Marifat, 1960), pp. 215–220.

33. Public Record Office, File 3/18/88, F.O. 371/126905, a confidential letter from the British Residency in Bahrain to the Foreign Office on December 3, 1957 (EA# 1022/2).

34. Jacob C. Hurewitz, *The Middle East and North Africa in World Politics: A Documentary Record*, vol. 2, British-French Supremacy, 1914–1945 (New Haven and London: Yale University Press, 1979), pp. 6–7.

35. Husain M. Al-Baharna, *The Legal Status of the Arabian Gulf States: A Study of Their Treaty Relations and Their International Problems* (Manchester: Manchester University Press, 1968), p. 322.

36. Lawrence Zirig, *The Middle East Political Dictionary* (Santa Barbara, CA and Oxford: ABC-CLIO Information Services, 1984), pp. 125, 94; and Alan Rush, *Al-Sabah: History and Genealogy of Kuwait's Ruling Family 1752–1987* (London and Atlantic Highlands: Ithaca Press, 1987), pp. 1–10.

37. Lawrence Zirig, *The Middle East Political Dictionary*, pp. 93–94.

38. Public Record Office, File 3/18/88, F.O. 371/126899, a strictly confidential report from the Political Agency in Kuwait on January 9, 1957 (EA #1018/1); for a review of Nasser's influence and support in Kuwait see Michael Adams, "Is Kuwait Next on Nasser's Timetable?" *The Reporter: The Magazine of Facts and Ideas*, vol. 19, no. 2 (September 4, 1958), pp. 27–28.

39. Public Record Office, File 3/18/88, F.O. 371/126899, a strictly confidential report on January 25, 1957 (EA# 1081/5) and a confidential Political Agency Report on May 2, 1957 (EA# 1018/9).

40. *Coventry Evening Telegraph* (July 23, 1958), p. 2; *Western Mail (Cardiff)* (July 23, 1958), p. 2; and *Al-Ahram*, (July 7, 1958), p. 5. For Nuri's pressures on Kuwait see Michael Ionides, "Iraq: The End of an Era," *The Reporter: The Magazine of Facts and Ideas*, vol. 19, no. 1 (August 7, 1958), pp. 14–15.

41. India Office and Library Records, File R 15/51/226. A confidential report (C.104) on March 13, 1939 from the Political Agent at Kuwait to the Political Resident

in Bushire. For the impact of Arab nationalism on contemporary Kuwaiti politics, see *Al-Taliat Fil Marakat Al-Dimikratiah* (The Vanguard in the Battle for Democracy) (Kuwait: Kadhima, 1984), pp. 1–50; and Riad E. EL-Rayyes, "Arab Nationalism and the Gulf," in B. R. Pridham, ed., *The Arab Gulf and the Arab World*, (London: Croom Helm, 1988), pp. 67–94.

42. Ministry of Planning, *Annual Statistical Abstract, 1986*, (Kuwait: Al-Mughwi Press, 1986), p. 27. The new 1988 data are based on the census of the civil card registration in Kuwait, provided to the author (December 27, 1988), and on Ministry of Planning, *Annual Statistical Abstract 1988* (Kuwait: Central Statistical Office, 1988), p. 27.

43. Moslem Students of Khomeini's Line, *Dikalathai Amerika Der Kishwarhay Islamy Kuwait, II* (American Interventions in Islamic Countries) (Teheran: University of Teheran and Islamic Guidance Ministry, N.D.), a confidential report from U.S. Embassy in Kuwait to State Department, #A-25, July 28, 1979; and Shafeeq N. Ghabra, *Palestinians in Kuwait: The Family and the Politics of Survival* (Boulder and London: Westview Press, 1987), p. 9. For the noncitizens' numerical and other challenges in Kuwait see J. S. Birks, "The Demographic Challenge in the Arab Gulf," in B. R. Pridham, ed., *The Arab Gulf and the Arab World*, pp. 131–152.

44. Sir Anthony Parson, "The Gulf States in the Eighties," *The Arab Gulf Journal*, vol. 6, no. 1 (April 1986), p. 12.

45. United Nations, *Official Records General Assembly*, N.Y. 18th Session, (September 17–October 14, 1963), p. 11.

46. *Al-Watan* (January 13, 1988), p. 1.

47. Walid E. Moubarak, "The Kuwait Fund in the Context of Arab and Third World Politics," *The Middle East Journal*, vol. 41, no. 4 (Autumn 1987), p. 542.

48. *Aramco World Magazine*, vol. 30, no. 6 (November-December 1979), p. 3.

49. *Al-Watan* (January 10, 1988), p. 13; for the role of Beit Al-Zakat (Al-Zakat Houe), see Kuwait Oil Company, *The Kuwaiti Digest*, vol. 16, no. 4 (October/December, 1988), pp. 11–13; Kuwait Finance House was listed as the leading Arab Islamic banking institution in 1988 in terms of assets; *The Banker*, (December 1988), p. 87. By the end of 1988 its assets were estimated at K.D. 1200 million (some $4.13 billion); see *Asharq Al-Awsat* (May 3, 1989), p. 7.

50. Ministry of Guidance and Information, *Kuwait Today: A Welfare State* (Nairobi: Quality Publications Ltd., n.d.), p. 9.

51. *Aramco World Magazine* (November-December 1979), p. 3.

52. Ibid., p. 3; and Fakhri Shehab, "Kuwait: A Super-Affluent Society," *Foreign Affairs*, vol. 42, no. 3 (April 1964), p. 474.

53. Saud N. Al-Sabah, *A Kuwaiti View of Middle Eastern and International Affairs*, addresses and remarks by the Ambassador of the State of Kuwait to the United States of America (Washington, D.C., N.P.: 1983), p. 17.

54. Shireen Hunter, *OPEC and the Third World: The Politics of Aid* (Bloomington: Indiana University Press, 1984), p. 55.

55. *Al-Anba* (June 5, 1984), pp. 15, 22; see also "Do Our Loan Policies Serve Our Political Goals?" *Al-Mjtama* (November 8, 1988), pp. 12–13.

56. *Aramco World Magazine*, (November-December 1979), p. 2; see also *Al-Rai Al-Aam* (February 2, 1989), p. 16. For Kuwait's aid between 1983 and 1985 see a statement of Kuwait's minister of foreign affairs, *Al-Watan* (September 16, 1987), p. 2. Kuwait's aid as a percentage of its GNP has fluctuated over the last few years; 1988 (0.4%); 1987 (1.23%); 1986 (2.91%); 1985 (3.17%); and 1984 (3.85%); see *The Middle East Economic Survey* (June 26, 1989), p. B3.

57. Richard P. Mattione, *OPEC: Investments and the International Financial System* (Washington, D.C.: The Brookings Institution, 1985), p. 120.

58. Abd Al-Aziz Abdallah Al-Sarawi, *Dirasat Fil Al-Shuoun Al-Ijtimaiah Wa Al-Omaliah* (Studies in Social and Labor Affairs) (Kuwait: Government Printing Office, 1965), p. 35.

59. Abd Al-Aziz Husayn, *Al-Mujtame Al-Araby Bil Kuwait*, pp. 80–81.

60. Personal Interview, Kuwait (March 31, 1988).

61. The Shiite population of Kuwait is not accurately known, and estimates vary from one source to another, since there is no category of Shiite in the general census. Khalid Sulayman Al-Adsani, *Nisf Aam Lil-Hukum Al-Niyabi Fil Al-Kuwayt*, put their number at 50,000 or about half of Kuwait's population by the mid-1930s, pp. 32–33. Alan Rush, *Al-Sabah*, estimates their number at 18,000 out of a total of 65,000 in the mid-1930s, p. 57. Harold R. P. Dickson, *Kuwait and Her Neighbours*, estimates their number to be 30,000 out of a total population of 160,000 by the early 1950s, p. 40. By the mid-1980s, the Shiites' number was estimated at 137,000, or about 24 percent of the native population; see James A. Bill, "Resurgent Islam in the Persian Gulf," *Foreign Affairs* (Fall 1984), p. 120.

62. Fakhri Shehab, "Kuwait: A Super-Affluent Society," p. 464.

2

Self-Defense and Survival (1961–1963)

The single most important event in Kuwait's contemporary politics and history is the Iraqi encroachment of the early 1960s. This event still imbues the memories of the Kuwaitis, and, given the lukewarm attitudes of the successive Iraqi regimes toward Kuwait, it will not be easily or soon forgotten. Indeed, it has shaped the future of the Kuwaiti-Iraqi relationship, and the national attitude, mood, and trust of each party towards the other.

The Kuwaiti-Iraqi Crisis (1961–1963)

As Kuwait was celebrating its political independence, which took effect June 19, 1961, and building its foundation as a sovereign state, a dramatic challenge to the new state was in the making. The expected Iraqi congratulation turned into a confrontation when the Iraqi premier, Abdul-Karim Qasim, laid irredentist claims on the whole territory of Kuwait. Qasim's allegations were based on the shaky historical grounds that Kuwait had once been under the control of the Ottoman Empire, and that Iraq, as the successor of that empire, was legitimately and rightfully the proprietor of its territories. This episode penetrated the national consciousness of the Kuwaitis and has complicated any future rapprochement between the two states.

During a press conference in Baghdad, on June 25, 1961, Qasim announced that he did not recognize any "forged treaty" imposed on Kuwait by "imperialist" Britain. He further claimed that Mubarak's signature on the 1899 agreement had been given in exchange for 15,000 rupees, i.e., that the shaikh had been bribed to sign the treaty. He stated that a decree would be issued appointing Kuwait's ruler, Abdullah Al-Salem, as Qaim-maqam of the Kuwait district of Iraq: "The era of sheikhdom is over. . . . We shall extend Iraq's borders to the south of Kuwait." In words that were to become famous, he claimed that Iraq's border extended from "north of Zago to south of Kuwait." The Kuwaiti representatives who had signed the 1961 treaty were "irresponsible people who are under the sway of imperialism." His warnings to the ruler were clear-cut: "if he . . . were to misbehave he would receive . . . a severe punishment and be considered a rebel."[1]

However, Qasim chose to emphasize that his tactics to achieve his goals were peaceful ones and in something of a brotherly reunification. Yet the Iraqi premier reiterated a veiled threat that "peaceful means are of no avail with the imperialists." Moreover, Qasim extended his threats to Britain as well: "I remind Britain to keep out of Kuwait, or . . . we shall kindle an internecine war in the Middle East and force Britain to get out."[2]

An Iraqi Foreign Ministry statement justified the Iraqi case this way:

> Foreign powers, including the British government itself, recognized the sovereignty of the Ottoman State over Kuwait. The Ottoman Sultan used to appoint the Shaikh of Kuwait by a decree conferring on him the title of Qaim-maqam and making him a representative of the Governor of Basra in Kuwait. Thus until 1914 the Shaikhs of Kuwait continued to derive their administrative powers from the Ottoman authorities in Basra and to affirm their allegiance to the Ottoman Sultan.[3]

In short, the Iraqi regime viewed Kuwait's new status as only nominal independence and still under British protection.[4]

Kuwaiti officials and the public were caught off guard by this unpredictable pronouncement, and found themselves ill prepared and powerless to cope with the Iraqi potential and real threats. In fact, Kuwait possessed an army of only 2,000 to 3,000 men, plus twelve planes, four of which were helicopters, whereas Iraq had an army of 60,000, with modern Soviet equipment and MIG aircraft.[5] The basic Kuwaiti goal was self-defense and the survival of the Kuwaiti political system and its ruling dynasty, Al-Sabah. Not surprisingly, the Kuwaiti ruler responded to Qasim's threats, "The Government of Kuwait and the Kuwaiti people have decided to defend their independence. The Government of Kuwait, in declaring this, has full confidence that all friendly and peace-loving countries—especially Arab countries—will support Kuwait in safeguarding her independence."[6] Thus the ruler invoked the friendship agreement with Britain of June 19, 1961, amid popular demonstrations supporting government policies.

The British government announced on June 30, 1961, that it was taking some precautionary measures in response to Kuwait's request and in compliance with its own obligations toward Kuwait.[7] British frigates, commando carriers, and air carriers moved towards Kuwait, and on July 1, 600 British soldiers landed in Kuwait and were deployed on the border with Iraq. Eventually the number of British troops reached 5,000. In what was called a "vantage operation," the contingents "had penetrated to within 5 miles of the border, covering all 100 miles of it."[8] Kuwait's limited military capabilities were boosted, in addition to the British forces, by some 2,000 Saudi troops and some 5,000–6,000 Kuwaiti volunteers.[9]

The British authorities admitted that they had put a military force into Kuwait and at the Kuwaiti government's disposal.[10] In part, Britain rationalized its assistance to Kuwait in terms of its commitment to the ruler rather than as a response to an actual threat. But it should be pointed out that in such a weak, powerless, and "easy-going" state, even the perception of a potential threat would most likely have endangered the existence of the state altogether.

Besides Britain's legal obligations towards Kuwait, the two maintained a political and economic relationship whose dimensions and importance should not be underestimated. Kuwait supplied nearly 40 percent of Britain's oil.[11] The shaikh of Kuwait had invested hundreds of millions of pounds on the London stock market, becoming the market's largest individual investor, and by the late 1950s he had over $90 million invested in London.[12] The British government, it was assumed, had encouraged the ruler to invest one-third of his annual revenue in Britain. The British government owned one-fourth of KOC shares, and the ruler awarded most of the major projects in Kuwait to British firms. In 1961, the ruler's treasure made up about 16 percent of the total liquidity in sterling; and Kuwait's new currency, the dinar, was tied to sterling.[13]

The significance of Kuwait to the potential well-being of Western economies was equally important. Kuwait's oil reserves, estimated at about 62 billion barrels in 1961, are the largest in the Middle East and represent about one-third of the total reserves of the region. Kuwait was then the world's fourth largest producer of oil. Its production ran about 1.7 million barrels per day (b/d), and Kuwait received estimated revenues of $450 million a year.[14]

Thus it is not surprising that Kuwait's wealth "provoked envy in Arab lands and attracted the jealous eyes of Arab leaders who sought to achieve pan-Arab goals through territorial aggrandizement."[15] It was reported that if Britain lost Kuwait, other British assets in the Gulf might follow. If Qasim occupied Kuwait, what would the Soviet Union do? A new world conflict could be on its way.[16]

The Iraqi government, in responding to the British landing with claims of imperialistic intervention, massed its troops along the border with Kuwait. Iraq asserted that this foreign military presence was a direct threat to Iraqi security and it urged Arab support for its goals that included so-called liberation of the Arabian peninsula.[17] The Iraqi representative in the United Nations termed the British troop landing "gunboat diplomacy."[18] An "unholy alliance of a feudal sheikhdom and a colonial power" he claimed, was "trying to rob an Arab nation . . . of its rightful wealth."[19]

In the meantime, the Kuwaitis, realizing the impotence and division within the Arab world, took their complaint to the international community for recognition and a blanket of security. Kuwait's state secretary asked the Security Council of the United Nations to consider "threats by Iraq to the territorial independence of Kuwait which are likely to endanger the main-tenance of international peace and security." Moreover, Kuwait's Amir informed the council of the Iraqi declarations that had been "followed by movements and concentration of Iraqi troops on the Kuwait frontiers." Britain and Iraq also requested a meeting of the council, the Iraqis protesting threats to their state "arising out of the armed threat by the United Kingdom." On the inconvenient date of Sunday, July 2, 1961, the Security Council met for four consecutive sessions.[20]

The British representative at the UN stated during the council debates that among the Arab states Kuwait's welcome "to the family of nations was very widely approved." Therefore, it was "with surprise and shock that the news was received that Iraq had reacted not with approval, but with a threat."[21]

The Iraqi representative insisted that "Kuwait is not and has never been an independent State. It has always been considered, historically and legally, a part of the Basra province of Iraq. There can be no question of an international dispute arising between Iraq and Kuwait since the latter is an integral part of the Iraqi Republic."[22]

The Egyptian position, on the other hand, was characterized by ambiguity and vacillation. Egypt's representative at the Security Council emphasized the inter-Arab nature of the conflict, and that it should be resolved within Arab principles and tradition. "To our way of thinking, all of Arab territory belongs to the Arab nation, in accordance with the logic of history." In other words, the Egyptian delegate's position echoed Nasser nationalism and Pan-Arabism and his distaste for foreign forces in the region. In order to mitigate the Arabs' and others' fear of a foreign army on its territory, Kuwait's ruler informed the council that "as soon as the crisis is over these British forces will be withdrawn immediately."[23]

The Iraqi team at the UN reacted by saying that "the Sheikh [sic] of Kuwait has been brought into the picture in order to give this whole sordid operation some pretence of legality and legitimacy, however spurious and unfounded it may be." Moreover, the ruler of Kuwait was "involved to the extent that he allows himself to be a tool of UK policy."[24] In return, Kuwait's delegation at the council meetings summarized Qasim's assertions as "a distortion of history that reveals. . . . Kassim's [sic] illegitimate ambitions of territorial expansion."[25]

Despite a number of proposals submitted by its members, the council was unable to pass any resolution, primarily because the Soviet Union has used its veto power to block Kuwait's application for UN membership, as well as its complaint against Iraq. The Soviet pretext was that Kuwait was an "overgrown village," not qualified to be an independent state, and that the new 1961 agreement subjected Kuwait to British domination, so that it remained in essence a "British colony."[26] But the real Soviet motive was support for its client in Baghdad. Still, the presence of a Kuwaiti delegation, albeit with no voting rights, at the council proceedings was a victory for Kuwait and its supporters, since this represented a real recognition at the highest international levels.

The international community having failed to deter Iraq, Kuwait was pushed by its Arab identification to take its case before the regional Arab League, i.e., to find an Arab solution to an inter-Arab conflict, and to avoid the possibility of East-West confrontations at the height of the Cold War era. In order to nullify Arab protests against British troops in Kuwait and minimize the uneasiness of the Soviet Union about British interference in the Arab world, Kuwait proposed that a contingent from the Arab states—

excluding Iraq—should replace British troops. In a letter to Nasser, delivered by Jaber Al-Ahmad, the then chief of the Finance Department, on July 12, 1961, the Amir of Kuwait requested recognition by Arab states and Kuwait's admission to the Arab League.[27]

Despite Iraqi protests and withdrawal, the league was able to admit Kuwait to its membership on July 20, 1961. The league's resolution stipulated, however, that

(a) . . . Kuwait undertakes to request the withdrawal of British troops from (its) territory.

(b) . . . Iraq undertakes not to use force. . . .

(c) The Council undertakes to support every wish Kuwait may express for a union or a federation with other countries of the Arab League.[28]

It seems in retrospect that Nasser used his prestige and influence with other Arab states to obtain recognition and admission of Kuwait to the league. Seeking to replace his enemy the British in Kuwait, he was able to extract two major concessions from Kuwait: the withdrawal of British troops, and a commitment to share Kuwait's wealth with other Arab nations. Thenceforward oil revenues and politics became increasingly intertwined in inter-Arab relationships, and Kuwait's aid and investment became a major instrument of Kuwait's foreign policy. "Dinar diplomacy" thus emerged and took a real shape at this period.[29]

It was assumed that Kuwait's offer to invest oil revenues in development projects in the Arab world was thought in Cairo to be Egypt's price for supporting Kuwait against Iraq.[30] Yet these concessions were not totally incongruent with Kuwait's existing beliefs and practices. Kuwait had already extended social and economic aid to poorer Arab states in the lower Gulf and Peninsula; and it was natural that in due course Kuwait would let the other Arab nations share its wealth. Such aid would in part minimize criticism and resentment of a prodigal nation in a poverty-stricken neighborhood. Likewise, opposition to the concentration of British troops in Kuwait was widespread, although muted locally. Replacing them with Arab troops was a wise and highly calculated choice.

On August 14, 1961, Kuwait signed the Arab League agreements for joint defense and economic cooperation, thus forming the legal basis for the presence of an Arab League force in Kuwait. The league contingents began to arrive in Kuwait on September 10, and by October 3 all contingents had arrived. On October 10 the British troops completed their withdrawal, except for a few advisers.[31] The league deployed a total force of about 3,300 men, of whom 1,200 were provided by the United Arab Republic (Egypt and Syria), 1,200 by Saudi Arabia, 400 by Sudan, 300 by Jordan, and 200 by Tunisia.[32] The Egyptian troops left Kuwait in December 1961, after a coup in September in Syria. Jordanian and Saudi troops were withdrawn in January 1963, and the last of the league's forces departed Kuwait on February 19, 1963.

A unique combination of opposing forces and ideologies came to Kuwait's rescue. Britain, Egypt, Iran, Saudi Arabia, and the United States all helped Kuwait in different ways and to different degrees. The main Arab states, except Saudi Arabia, hesitated to support Kuwait because they feared to antagonize Iraq and to create frictions within the Arab world,[33] and wished not to support a system whose survival was presumably built on foreign troops. After a period of uncertainty and indecision, however, Nasser announced his opposition to any Iraqi attempts at annexation—once he was assured of Kuwait's financial assistance. King Saud, on the other hand, dispatched his troops to Kuwait in July, before the Arab League decision, and declared that "any mishap that befalls Kuwait affects Saudi Arabia and vice versa."[34]

Iran supported Kuwait on two fronts, political and economic. The shah dispatched a goodwill mission to Kuwait, with a message to the ruler and a declaration that he intended to establish diplomatic relations and promote economic and cultural linkages. Moreover, Iran effectively used commerce to achieve its foreign policy goals towards Kuwait.[35] After merchants in Basra refused to send supplies to Kuwait, motor launches loaded with vegetables and foodstuffs left Abadan for Kuwait, even though Iraqi gunboats opened fire on them.[36] Iran's exports to Kuwait amounted to only $7 million in 1962–1963, but reached $24.4 million in 1965–1966. In fact, Qasim's policies served to draw Iran's attention to Kuwait.[37]

The United States supported Kuwait's case before the United Nations, and established diplomatic relations with it.

Meanwhile, Kuwait undertook a campaign to enhance its international legitimacy and reputation by increasing the number of its friends and supporters. In August 1961, it sent four goodwill missions to different countries of the world to explain Kuwait's viewpoint vis-à-vis Iraq and to seek political recognition. By September 1961, 34 states had recognized Kuwait, and by the end of 1961, an additional 28 states had extended political recognition.[38]

Between June 1961 and October 1963, the Kuwaiti-Iraqi crisis went through various phases, from the immediate military threat to a political confrontation, and then to occasional heated propaganda warfare. However, by February 8, 1963, when a military coup overthrew and assassinated Qasim, the crisis had subsided. But it took the new Iraqi regime a few months to "put its house in order," in the process extracting financial and political gains in return for political recognition and dropping the state's claim on Kuwait.

In the interim, in order to assuage Arab nationalists at home and abroad and conciliate the new regime in Baghdad, Kuwait's government announced in parliament on April 9, 1963, that it would review its friendship agreement of 1961 with Britain and "adopt a Kuwaiti position" in keeping with the political realities in the region. The government statement referred to Arab unity as an "historical eventuality," but gave no promise to work towards such a goal with any Arab state.[39]

On October 4, 1963, during a visit to Baghdad by a Kuwaiti official delegation, Iraq officially recognized the independence of Kuwait, and announced that it would adhere to the borders established in the exchange of letters in 1932. On October 19, 1963, Kuwait gave Iraq an $80 million interest-free loan, to be paid in 19 installments over 25 years.[40] A joint commission to delimit the border was set up, but during the course of those negotiations the terms of discussion shifted significantly. Iraq made it known that its 1963 recognition of Kuwait "should not be construed as a blanket acceptance on Iraq's part of the territorial status quo."[41]

Meanwhile, Kuwait renewed its application for membership in the United Nations. On April 20, 1963, the Security Council unanimously recommended the admission of Kuwait, despite Iraqi objections. The Iraqi delegate reconfirmed his country's opposition to accept Kuwait as a sovereign state, and viewed the Kuwaiti question as an Iraqi national issue. Furthermore, "the Government of Iraq, therefore, has no alternative but to declare solemnly and unequivocally its reservations regarding any decision that may be taken today, and to state categorically that it affirms its legitimate rights and will never allow anything to affect the historical ties with Kuwait and its people."[42] In May 1963, the General Assembly admitted Kuwait as the one hundred and eleventh member of the United Nations. Since the UN was facing financial difficulties, Kuwait donated $200,000 to UNRWA, and bought $1 million worth of UN bonds. Earlier, in July 1962, Kuwait had joined the IMF and the World Bank, and Kuwait's initial contributions to these and other agencies were estimated at $120 million.[43] In the spring of 1963, Kuwait established diplomatic relations with the Soviet Union and the Eastern bloc nations. The new Kuwaiti-socialist linkage manifested, among other things, Kuwait's willingness to neutralize the Iraq threats, to reduce its own reliance on the Western powers, and to seek more political options. Moreover, this policy may have reflected recommendations from Arab advisers in Kuwait that Kuwait should detach itself from the West and meet the demands of Kuwaiti nationalists and the Arabs at large.

It seems unambiguously clear that Turkish sovereignty was never established over Kuwait. However, suzerainty was established up to 1896, when shaikh Mubarak refused the title of Qaim-maqam, repudiated a Turkish health inspector, and imposed a 5-percent duty on all Turkish goods. Nevertheless, as a successor to former Ottoman territories, Iraq was legally bound by the limitations imposed upon Turkey by the Treaty of Lausanne (1923).[44] Moreover, in summer 1932, in exchanges of letters between the ruler of Kuwait, Ahmad Al-Jaber, and Iraqi Prime Minister Nuri Al-Said, both parties reaffirmed "existing frontiers between Iraq and Kuwait," including the islands of Warba and Bubiyan. In fact, Kuwait indicated that it had never been subjected to Ottoman sovereignty and that the title of Qaim-maqam "was never used in Kuwait and never influenced the course of life or the independence of Kuwait from the Turkish empire."[45]

In retrospect, Qasim's irredentist claims were a surprise to everyone, perhaps to himself as well. The relationship between Kuwait and Iraq early in Qasim's rise to power had been neighborly and warm.[46] A number of plausible motives, however, might explain his move. First, Qasim wanted

Kuwait and its resources in a regional union espousing pan-Arabism and neutralizing Nasser. Qasim desired to increase his bargaining power in other inter-Arab spheres. He wanted to counteract Nasser's influence in Kuwait, contain Saudi leverage in Kuwait, and perhaps extort money from Kuwait.[47] It has been claimed that both Nasser and Saud had "covetous eyes on Kuwait."[48]

In addition, Qasim was engaged in negotiations with Western oil companies in Iraq to increase Iraq's oil revenues. He may have thought that should those negotiations fail to produce sufficient monies, the combined financial and political resources of the two countries were to provide the funds necessary for Iraq's various schemes.[49] Moreover, in spring 1961 rumors were circulating that Kuwait might join the British Commonwealth,[50] and he may have wanted to preempt British designs. The Kuwaiti-Iraqi crisis had influenced the British authorities to maintain a symbolic rapid deployment force in the Gulf on a ship loaded with half a squadron of Centurion tanks kept permanently in the Gulf.[51] Kuwait's case fit perfectly with Qasim's use of foreign adventures and misadventures to divert the attention of divisive domestic factions from the internal problems.[52] In retrospect, the incident made Iraq place greater emphasis on its interests in the Gulf states as well as reinforcing Baghdad's image as both an expansionist and a radical state.[53]

With the failure of Qasim's policy vis-à-vis Kuwait, the Iraqi leader's prestige was seriously damaged.[54] Kuwait emerged stronger and more powerful as a result of individual and collective actions.[55]

Dinar Diplomacy

In the meanwhile, Kuwait began to realize the value of money politics. It became clear that Arab support to the besieged regime warranted a serious redistribution of Kuwait's oil wealth. Therefore, the era of Kuwait's dinar diplomacy began with the Kuwaiti-Iraqi crisis of 1961. After a visit by a Kuwaiti financial team to Egypt, Saudi Arabia, Sudan, Libya, Tunisia, Morocco, Lebanon, and Jordan in summer of 1961, on December 31, 1961, Kuwait set up the Kuwait Fund for Arab Economic Development, with an initial capital of K.D. 50 million ($140 million), in part as a price for Arab protection of Kuwait. In the 1970s, the fund's capital was augmented to K.D. 2 billion ($6.7 billion), and it began to extend loans not only to Arab states but also to other Moslem and Third World countries. Although the creation of the fund was motivated by political as well as human factors, its general policy has been determined more by economic considerations. From 1962, when the fund began its activities, until June 30, 1989, KFAED distributed 361 loans totalling K.D. 1, 592 million ($5.73 billion) among 65 countries. Up to the end of 1963, the fund extended loans of $21 million each to Jordan, Sudan, and Tunisia. Loans to Egypt totalled some K.D. 17.5 million up to 1973.[56] During 1962–1973, Egypt was the largest recipient of the fund's aid (20 percent), followed by Sudan (17 percent) and Tunisia (14 percent).[57]

On the other hand, aid to the Arab countries of the Gulf and the Peninsula was basically channeled through the General Board for the South and Arabian Gulf, which was set up in 1953 to direct projects aimed at social and economic infrastructure, such as schools, hospitals, housing projects, mosques, etc. Between 1966 and 1969, the board disbursed some $14.6 million.[58]

Despite the economic nature of Kuwait's fund, a few cases of political interference in its activities have been reported. In 1973, a fund loan to Iraq was dropped after an Iraqi occupation of a Kuwaiti police post. Likewise, in 1978, new loans to Egypt were stopped after it signed the Camp David Treaty.[59]

The government undertook a parallel scheme of loans that were strictly politically oriented, a sort of quid pro quo, and were taken from the state reserve fund. This type of aid was directed either toward Arab countries or toward Arab causes and political movements, including Arab frontline states and liberation movements such as the Algerians and the Palestinians. Between 1961 and 1966 such State Reserve loans amounted to K.D. 125 million, compared to K.D. 64 million disbursed by KFAED over the same period.[60]

By the 1970s, with tenfold gains in oil revenues, Kuwait embarked on an aggressive worldwide investment policy in order to diversify its economic structure and efficiently utilize its surplus oil revenue. In the 1950s Kuwait had established the Kuwait Investment Office (KIO) in London to manage the royal family's investment, mainly in England. KIO became in due time the official state agency to channel the majority of public investment abroad.[61]

In the first few years of independence, Kuwait set up a host of companies to carry out the investment policies and schemes of the government. In November 1961 the government established the Kuwait Investment Company (KIC), a semipublic venture (50 percent public and 50 percent private) with a capital of K.D. 10.4 million (later raised to $76 million). In 1964, the state formed the Kuwait Foreign Trade, Contracting and Investment Company (KFTCIC), with 80 percent official participation and an initial capital of K.D. 20 million, which was raised to $100 million by the mid-1970s.

In order to work with other Arab states and show its progressive and caring credentials, Kuwait joined Egypt in 1964 to form the Arab African Bank (each held 42.4 percent). By 1970, the bank had a portfolio of 14 direct investment projects in Africa and the Arab countries (37 percent and 49 percent, respectively).[62]

The international banking and investment fervor of the Kuwaitis extended beyond their own boundary when private banks combined with KIC and KFTCIC to create the London-based United Bank of Kuwait (UBK) in 1966.

These schemes and enterprises were less politically motivated than the State Reserve loans, being based rather (supposedly) on sound financial returns and a safe investment environment. However, as the investment volumes became larger and the cycles longer, the chances for political influence and external ramifications became greater (see Chapter 3).

Conclusion

Irrespective of one's own perception of the Kuwaiti-Iraqi crisis of 1961, Qasim's politics and personality left their imprint on future relations between the two countries, and brought to the surface the hidden Iraqi resentment and hostility toward Iraq's southern neighbor. Yet, on the positive side, Qasim should be credited with accelerating Kuwait's move toward political modernization and an active world role. Kuwait's government, as a result, followed a dual scheme of domestic reforms and external deterrence.

For the first two years of its independence, Kuwait's preoccupation was dealing with the Iraqi threat, in a variety of ways. Fortunately, the Kuwaiti government was able to spend simultaneously on guns and butter. In order to build up its meager army, it ordered a substantial number of Britain's latest antitank missiles, the "Vigilant," and airplanes worth more than half a million dinars.[63] On the domestic level, a new constitution, a relatively liberal press, and an elective form of government were set in motion in a society that had until then been, at least in a political sense, traditional and evolutionary. Socially and economically, Kuwait was viewed as a model for development, because it provided free education, health care, and housing. According to a Kuwaiti official, "Kuwait is a welfare state which is today the pride of the Middle East."[64] Thus, the Iraqi crisis catalyzed radical change in a traditional society. The political reforms presumably were meant to contribute, either directly or indirectly, to the socioeconomic prosperity, political stability, and international status of Kuwait. The new patterns of political reform and social development involved mutual benefits for the citizens and the government alike. Indeed, the new schemes reflected in part the regime's "benign," paternalistic attitude.

Externally, Kuwait followed a middle-of-the-road approach in mainstream Arab, regional, and world politics. It avoided both ideological and political clashes and close identification with any particular political system within the Arab world. As a reflection of its "missionary" responsibilities, in appreciation for the Arab states' help in protecting Kuwait, as a means of distributing its wealth, to safeguard itself against potential future threats, and to satisfy domestic Arab nationalist aspirations and commercial tendencies, it initiated a three-pronged set of assistance programs: "economic" development aid, "political" financial subsidies, and foreign investment. In general, Kuwait was "the first Arab country to use economic assistance systematically to advance its national security and political goals."[65]

Iraq's failure was conversely a success story for Kuwait and those who supported it. Yet Qasim taught the Kuwaitis a lesson about the interdependence between the security of Kuwait and that of its three main neighbors. Stability and security in Iraq and the other neighboring states have become an important factor for Kuwait and vice versa. Indeed, regional politics became entrenched in Kuwait's polity and society. On the other hand, the era of politicization of Kuwaiti economic and social assistance took place.

Although Iraq dropped its irredentist claims on the whole Kuwaiti territory, the crisis shifted after October 1963 into a question of border adjustments, which have remained a matter for negotiation ever since. In recent years, for example, Iraq had demanded that it be allowed to lease the Kuwaiti islands of Warba and Bubiyan. It should be realized that Iraq is an almost landlocked state which, given its quest for leadership in the area and its continuous competition and hostilities with neighboring Iran, needs a deep-water outlet. It is then merely a matter of time and right circumstances before Iraq presses its demands on Kuwait. The only consolation for Kuwait is that its other two neighbors might not tolerate such an infringement of Kuwait's sovereignty, for the sake of their own national and regional interests. In essence, the 1961 crisis and the constant Iraqi pressures on Kuwait generated an "Iraqi complex" on the part of Kuwaitis.

Notes

1. United Nations, *Security Council Official Records* (New York: 957th meeting, July 2, 1961), p. 5.

2. *The New York Times* (June 26, 1961), pp. 1, 4; Hussein A. Hassouna, *The League of Arab States and Regional Disputes: A Study of Middle East Conflicts* (Dobbs Ferry, New York: Oceana Publications, Inc., 1975), p. 93; and *The New York Times* (December 4, 1961), p. 9.

3. Ministry of Foreign Affairs, *The Facts about Kuwait, II* (Baghdad: Ministry of Foreign Affairs, August 1961), p. 24.

4. Ibid., p. 20.

5. *The New York Times* (June 27, 1961), p. 1.

6. *The New York Times* (June 27, 1961), p. 1; for a Kuwaiti interpretation of the Iraq claim, see Kuwait Government, *The Kuwaiti-Iraqi Crisis* (Kuwait: Government Printing Press, 1961), pp. 1–35.

7. *Keesing's Contemporary Archives* (July 8–15, 1961), p. 18187.

8. *The New York Times* (July 4, 1961), p. 1.

9. Martha Dukas, *Azmat Al-Kuwayt: Al-Ilakat Al-Kuwaytiah Al-Irakiah, 1961–1963* (Kuwait Crisis: Kuwaiti-Iraqi Relations) (Beirut: Dar Al-Nahar, 1973), p. 40.

10. United Nations, *Security Council Official Records* (New York: 957th meeting, July 2, 1961), p. 4.

11. *The New York Times* (June 27, 1961), p. 1.

12. Don Peretz, *The Middle East Today*. 3rd ed. (New York: Holt, Rinehart and Winston, 1978), p. 453; and Michael Adams, "Is Kuwait Next on Nasser's Timetable?", p. 27.

13. Martha Dukas, *Azmat Al-Kuwayt*, p. 14.

14. *The New York Times* (June 30, 1961), p. 35.

15. Majid Khadduri, *Republican Iraq: A Study in Iraqi Politics since the Revolution of 1958* (London: Oxford University Press, 1969), p. 169.

16. *The New York Times* (July 2, 1961), p. 2.

17. *The New York Times* (July 4, 1961), p. 1.

18. United Nations, *Security Council Official Records* (New York: 958th meeting, July 5, 1961), p. 8.

19. United Nations, *Security Council Official Records* (New York: 957th meeting, July 2, 1961), p. 13.

20. Ibid., p. 3.

21. Ibid., p. 4.

22. *United Nations Security Council Records*, S/4844 (New York: 16th Year, Supplement for July, August and September, 1961), p. 3.

23. For the Egyptian position and Kuwait's response see United Nations, *Security Council Official Records* (New York: 957th meeting, July 2, 1961), pp. 8 and 7.

24. Ibid., p. 9.

25. United Nations, *Security Council Official Records* (New York: 958th meeting, July 5, 1961), p. 12.

26. *The New York Times* (December 1, 1961), p. 1.

27. *The New York Times* (July 12, 1961), p. 3.

28. Hussein A. Hassouna, *The League of Arab States and Regional Disputes*, p. 101.

29. Martha Dukas, *Azmat Al-Kuwayt*, p. 69.

30. *The New York Times* (July 25, 1961), p. 5.

31. Hussein A. Hassouna, *The League of Arab States and Regional Disputes*, pp. 102–103 and 105.

32. *Keesing's Contemporary Archives* (October 7–14, 1961), p. 18355.

33. Martha Dukas, *Azmat Al-Kuwayt*, p. 27.

34. *The New York Times* (June 28, 1961), p. 1.

35. Rouhollah K. Ramazani, *Iran's Foreign Policy 1941–1973: A Study of Foreign Policy in Modernizing Nations* (Charlottesville: University Press of Virginia, 1975), p. 406.

36. *The New York Times* (June 28, 1961), pp. 1, 6; and (June 30, 1961), p. 1.

37. R. K. Ramazani, *Iran's Foreign Policy 1941–1973*, pp. 406 and 420.

38. Martha Dukas, *Azmat Al-Kuwayt*, p. 64.

39. Martha Dukas, *Azmat Al-Kuwayt*, p. 67; and *Sout Al-Khalij* (April 14, 1963), p. 1.

40. Martha Dukas, *Azmat Al-Kuwayt*, p. 69; and *New York Times* (October 29, 1963), p. 34.

41. Robert Litwak, *Security in the Persian Gulf II: Source of Interstate Conflict* (Allenheld, PA: Osmun for International Institute for Strategic Studies, 1981), p. 28.

42. United Nations, *Security Council Official Records* (New York: 1034th meeting, May 7, 1963), pp. 2–4.

43. Martha Dukas, *Azmat Al-Kuwayt*, pp. 69 and 65.

44. Husain Al-Baharna, *The Arabian Gulf States: Their Legal and Political Status and Their International Problems*. 2nd ed. (Beirut: Libraire du Liban, 1975), pp. 252–255 and 256.

45. Ibid., p. 250.

46. Uriel Dann, *Iraq under Qassem: A Political History, 1958–1963* (Pall Mall, New York: Praeger, 1969), p. 350; and for further analysis of the crisis see Avraham G. Mezerik, "The Kuwait-Iraq Dispute, 1961," *International Review Service* (New York), vol. 7, no. 66 (1961), pp. 1–35; Lorenzo K. Kimball, *The Changing Pattern of Political Power in Iraq, 1958 to 1971* (New York: Robert Speller and Sons, Publishers, Inc., 1972), pp. 106–107; Phebe Marr, *The Modern History of Iraq* (Boulder, CO: Westview Press, 1985), pp. 180–181; Erskine B. Childers, "Kassem and Kuwait," *The Spectator* (July 7, 1961), p. 7; "Kuwait: Time to Depart," *The Spectator* (July 14, 1961), p. 49; Edith and E. F. Penrose, *Iraq: International Relations and National Development* (London: Ernest Benn and Boulder, CO: Westview Press, 1978), pp. 274–276; Humphrey Trevelyan, *The Middle East in Revolution* (Boston: Gambit Incorporated, 1970), pp. 182–198; and Marion Farouk-Sluglett and Peter Sluglett, *Iraq since 1958; From Revolution to Dictatorship* (London and New York: KPI, 1987), p. 82.

47. Uriel Dann, *Iraq under Qassem*, p. 352.

48. Majid Khadduri, *Republican Iraq*, p. 169.

49. Ibid., p. 168.

50. Robert Litwak, *Security in the Persian Gulf, II*, p. 27.

51. Alvin Cottrell, ed., *The Persian Gulf States: A General Survey* (Baltimore: Johns Hopkins University Press, 1980), p. 97.

52. Majid Khadduri, *Republican Iraq*, p. 187.

53. Edmund Ghareeb, "Iraq in the Gulf," in Frederick W. Axelgard, ed., *Iraq in Transition: A Political, Economic and Strategic Perspective* (Boulder, CO: Westview Press, 1986), p. 63.

54. Uriel Dann, *Iraq under Qaseem*, p. 352.

55. Majid Khadduri, *Republican Iraq*, p. 172.

56. Kuwait Fund for Arab Economic Development, Nashat Al-Sandouq Fil Al-Duwal Al-Nameyat Hata April 30, 1988, *The Fund's Activities in the Developing Nations up to April 30, 1988* (Kuwait: The Fund, International Cooperation Department, May 1988), pp. 1, 3, 4, and 6; and information provided to the author by the fund, (February 6, 1989), and (June 30, 1989).

57. Naim A. Sherbiny, *Arab Financial Institutions and Developing Countries* (Washington: The World Bank Staff Working Papers, No. 794, 1986), pp. 14–15.

58. Shireen Hunter, *OPEC and the Third World*, p. 77.

59. Walid Moubarak, "The Kuwait Fund in the Context of Arab and Third World Politics," pp. 541, 542, and 549.

60. *The Middle East and North Africa 1967*, 18th ed. (London: Europa Publications Ltd., 1967), p. 421.

61. *The Financial Times* (February 22, 1988), p. 18; and "Inside the KIO," *Euromoney*, (March 1988), pp. 52–60. The original Kuwait Investment Board was set up in London in 1952; for the board's roles see M. W. Khouja and P. G. Sadler, *The Economy of Kuwait: Development and Role in International Finance* (London: Macmillan, 1979), pp. 195–201.

62. Naim A. Sherbiny, *Arab Financial Institutions and Developing Countries*, p. 17; for a review of the impact of oil surpluses on the producing nations, including Kuwait, see Johangir Amuzegar, "Oil Wealth: A Very Mixed Blessing," *Foreign Affairs*, vol. 6, no. 4 (Spring 1982), pp. 814–835.

63. *The New York Times* (April 16, 1962), p. 11.

64. United Nations, *Security Council Official Records* (New York: 958th meeting, July 5, 1961), p. 12.

65. Shireen Hunter, *OPEC and the Third World*, p. 246.

3

Pragmatism
and Balance (1963–1979)

The subsiding of the immediate Iraqi threat by the end of 1963 altered in turn the dimensions and dynamism of Kuwaiti foreign policy. After that time, Kuwait began to play an active, expansive, and multifarious role in inter-Arab and regional politics, employing a variety of strategies and tactics, both political and financial, to achieve its foreign policy goals. In inter-Arab politics, Kuwait played the roles of donor, investor, mediator and, indeed, honest broker. While its hereditary, tribal system classified it as a traditional and conservative state, its strong pan-Arabist orientation, its new political structure, and regional political exigencies attuned it to the so-called liberal and progressive camp. Thus, for ideological, historical, and practical reasons, Kuwait opted to play a "centrist" role, a role that made it a reliable source of support for both ends of the political spectrum in the Arab world. Kuwait's quick response to an array of human and political causes in the region, and its reasonable experience in mediating among competing Arab political interests and forces, made it credible and respectable as a centrist. In other words, Kuwait's surplus money was the lubricant for its political action.

Kuwait's Foreign Aid and Financial Schemes

Kuwait employed different mechanisms, both private and public, to achieve its national goals. Aid, investment, and loans, stemming from humanitarian, financial, and political compulsion, proved to be the most effective means of influence. Traditionally, Kuwaiti funds for economic and human development were channeled through the Kuwait Fund for Arab Economic Development. In spite of the fund's original political motivations, its conduct and commitments reflected a human dimension and economic considerations that made Kuwait and, indeed, the Kuwaitis respected throughout the Third World. One report remarked that the fund "rapidly became a vital force for progress in the Third World."[1]

From its inception in late 1961 up to June 30, 1989, the fund extended a total of 361 loans to 65 countries, reaching over K.D. 1,592 million (about

TABLE 3.1 Geographical Distribution of Kuwait's Loans (K.D. million)

	No. of Countries	No. of Loans	Amount	%
Arab countries	16	172	809.653	50.8
African countries	30	98	297.587	18.6
Asian countries	15	79	457.852	28.7
Others	4	12	27.490	1.7
Total	65	361	1,592.582	*100.0

*The total is less than 100% because of rounding.

Source: KFAED, *The Fund's Activities in the Developing Nations Up to April 30, 1988* (Kuwait: KFAED, International Cooperation Department, May 1988), section 3, p. 5, and information provided to the author by the fund, February 6, 1989, and June 30, 1989.

$5.73 billion). Of these loans, the Arab states received 50.8 percent, African states 18.6 percent, Asian countries 28.7 percent, and other countries 1.7 percent (see Table 3.1).[2] The fund also gave 90 packages of technical aid to 38 states, surpassing K.D. 20,015 million ($71.9 million). Thus the combined fund loans and aid reached some K.D. 1,612 million (about $6.00 billion).

Clearly, Kuwait's priority has been the Arab world. Indeed, up to 1974, the fund extended loans to the Arab states only, and over the whole period the sixteen Arab states received more than half of the total amount (50.8 percent). Within this group, Kuwait's concern for stability and security was reflected in its disproportionate allocation of loans to the status quo regimes of Jordan, Tunisia, Sudan, Morocco, Egypt, and North Yemen, which received a total of more than K.D. 529 million, or over 65.3 percent of the loans to Arab countries (see Table 3.2). Jordan tops the list with K.D. 118 million, or 14. 5 percent of the Arab loans and 7.4 percent of the total loans followed by Tunisia with K.D. 117 million, or 14.4 percent and 7.3 percent, respectively. Lebanon is at the bottom of the list with less than K.D. 2.5 million, or 0.30 percent of the Arab loans and 0.12 percent of the total.

Kuwait's identification with and concern for Islamic states was on the rise as well. The nineteen Islamic (non-Arabic) nations (29.2 percent of all recipient countries) received 22.3 percent of the total loans (see Table 3.3). Pakistan tops the Islamic nations with K.D. 53 million, or 15.0 percent of the total Islamic loans; 3.3 percent of the total loans, and 11.7 percent of all loans to Asian states.

The Asian Islamic nations of Pakistan, Bangladesh, Indonesia, Turkey, Malaysia, Afghanistan, and the Maldives received loans of over K.D. 211 million, or 46.1 percent of all loans to Asian states (see Table 3.4). India

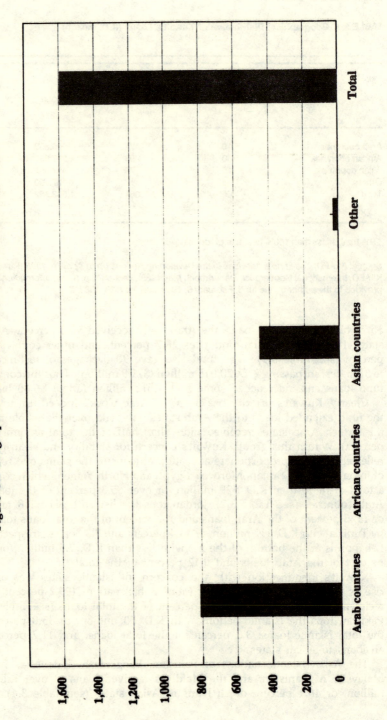

Figure 3.1 Geographical Distribution of Kuwait's Loans (K.D. million)

TABLE 3.2 Loans to Arab States (K.D.)

	No. of Loans	Amount	% Share
Jordan	21	118,619,090	14.6
Tunisia	26	117,407,329	14.5
Sudan	18	91,514,432	11.3
Morocco	13	77,544,514	9.5
Egypt	12	76,700,191	9.4
N. Yemen	17	48,503,769	5.9
Syria	9	46,070,482	5.5
Mauritania	10	45,819,550	5.6
Oman	9	44,772,820	5.6
S. Yemen	13	38,808,276	4.7
Bahrain	7	30,959,541	3.8
Somalia	4	30,044,385	3.7
Algeria	3	18,998,372	2.3
Djibouti	6	15,039,563	1.8
Iraq	2	6,385,523	0.7
Lebanon	2	2,465,448	0.3
Total	172	809,653,285	

Source: KFAED, *The Fund's Activities in the Developing Nations up to April 30, 1988*, (Kuwait: KFAED, International Cooperation Department, May 1988), section 4, p. 1, and information provided to the author by the fund, February 6, 1989, and June 30, 1989.

led the Asian countries in terms of total loans allocated. It received loans of over K.D. 88.8 million, or 19.3 percent of Asian loans, and 5.5 percent of the total fund's loans.

The Islamic countries of Africa (Senegal, Mali, Niger, Cameroon, Guinea, Gambia, Guinea Bissau, Comoros Islands, Uganda, Benin, Burkina Faso, and Sierra Leone) received over K.D. 140 million or over 47.1 percent of all loans to African states (see Table 3.5). Senegal tops the African states with K.D. 35.7 million, or 2.2 percent of the total loans and 11.7 percent of the African loans.

Kuwait's concern for human development in the Third World and its sense of moral mission were reflected in the sectoral appropriation of the fund's aid. Over 80 percent was consigned to the basic fields of agriculture, water, electricity, and transportation (see Table 3.6). Transportation accounted for 35.7 percent, electricity 18.2 percent, agriculture 19.1 percent, and industry 16.3 percent.

A complementary minor, albeit older, channel of aid is the General Board for the South and Arabian Gulf. Established in 1953, primarily out of a sense of "missionary" and "fraternal" responsibility, the agency played a valued role in the human development of the then poorer lower Gulf states,

TABLE 3.3 Loans to Islamic Countries (K.D. million)

	No. of Countries	No. of Loans	Amount	% of Total Amount
Arab & Islamic	35	258	1,165.583	73.1
Arab countries	16	172	809.653	50.8
Islamic countries (non-Arabic)	19	86	355.929	22.3
Non-Arabic & Non-Islamic	30	103	427.002	26.8
Asian countries	8	39	246.140	15.4
African countries	18	52	153.372	9.6
Other countries	4	12	27.489	1.7
Total	65	361	1,592.585	100.0

*The total is less than 100% because of rounding.

Source: KFAED, *The Fund's Activities in the Developing Nations up to April 30, 1988* (Kuwait: International Cooperation Department, May 1988), section 6, p. 1, and information provided to the author by the fund, February 6, 1989, and June 30, 1989.

the Trucial States (now the United Arab Emirates). In 1966, the then Kuwaiti prime minister and crown prince, Jaber Al-Ahmad, indicated Kuwait's humane obligations toward its southern brethren: "we have not liked for ourselves to benefit exclusively from the bounty which God has bestowed upon our country. We see in the strengthening of the economies of these states . . . a backing for the entire Arab nation of which we are an indivisible part."[3] In the late 1960s and 1970s, the board extended its services to Bahrain, Oman, North Yemen, South Yemen, and Southern Sudan, where it built more than 250 schools, hospitals, housing projects, mosques, etc. Between 1975 and 1988, the board's budget reached K.D. 182.3 million ($620 million).

It has been argued that a large portion of these funds and projects were targeted for Bahrain (presently a member of the GCC), whereas the funds earmarked for South Yemen were drastically cut during the 1980s because of Kuwait's displeasure with Aden's position vis-à-vis the Iran-Iraq war. It should be noted, however, that since detailed appropriations of the board's funds are not revealed, this allegation cannot be independently verified.

TABLE 3.4 Loans to Asian Countries (K.D.)

	No. of Loans	Amount	% Share
India	8	88,853,189	19.4
China	11	74,357,169	16.2
Pakistan	10	53,738,936	11.7
Indonesia	6	45,142,361	9.8
Bangladesh	7	44,482,771	9.7
Turkey	7	34,314,511	7.4
Thailand	5	22,413,642	4.8
Sri Lanka	3	20,930,000	4.5
Malaysia	4	16,613,072	3.6
Nepal	3	13,000,000	2.8
Vietnam	3	13,000,000	2.8
Afghanistan	1	8,845,000	1.9
Maldives	5	8,576,008	1.8
Bhutan	4	7,850,000	1.7
Philippines	2	5,736,132	1.2
Total	79	457,852,132	

Source: KFAED, *The Fund's Activities in the Developing Nations up to April 30, 1988* (Kuwait: KFAED, International Cooperation Department, May 1988), section 4, p. 2, and information provided to the author by the fund, February 6, 1989, and June 30, 1989.

As noted in Chapter 2, in addition to these conventional means of aid, Kuwait, by December 1966, had extended loans exceeding K.D. 125 million to Arab states from the State General Reserves.[4]

A more politicized means of financial and political influence in the Arab world has been the government's direct cash contributions to many causes in the region, contributions made either out of a true belief in these causes or in the hope of immediate or long-term political gains. Although Kuwait was genuinely and perhaps nonpolitically committed to Arab causes such as the Algerian war of independence, its later cash contributions to the confrontation states, to the Palestinian struggle, and to Iraq were determined both by national and emotional allegiances and by political motives, including internal influence and security considerations, among other factors. Kuwaiti policy makers assumed that these cash grants might serve as a "protective shield" against both internal instability and external threats.

As the richest state in the region, Kuwait was expected to respond most quickly to the needs and causes of its neighbors. Thus Kuwait was to play the role, whether by choice or by force, of benefactor or, better, "milch cow" of the Arab world, a role that took no small toll on Kuwait's budget. In fact, the Gulf states have not only "become the financial cornucopia of the Arab world but also a moderating and indeed mediating influence."[5]

TABLE 3.5 Loans to African States (K.D.)

	No. of Loans	Amount	% Share
Senegal	10	35,719,349	12.0
Tanzania	5	28,950,000	9.7
Mali	4	22,239,741	7.4
Zimbabwe	4	16,849,248	5.6
Ghana	3	16,470,000	5.5
Niger	5	14,372,273	4.8
Mozambique	4	11,750,000	3.9
Burundi	7	11,187,040	3.7
Rwanda	4	10,700,000	3.5
Congo	3	10,700,000	3.5
Burkina Faso	3	10,500,000	3.5
Cameroon	3	10,295,888	3.4
Comoros Islands	5	9,235,653	3.1
Botswana	4	8,751,100	2.9
Guinea	2	8,570,946	2.8
Gambia	3	8,238,760	2.7
Togo	2	8,000,000	2.6
Guinea Bissau	4	7,855,000	2.6
Benin	3	7,689,640	2.5
Uganda	3	6,500,000	2.1
Mauritius	2	5,500,000	1.8
Central African Republic	4	5,120,000	1.7
Losotho	3	4,997,180	1.6
Madagascar	2	4,807,500	1.6
Angola	1	3,700,000	1.2
Sierra Leone	1	3,000,000	1.0
Liberia	1	2,200,000	0.7
Seychelles	1	1,620,000	0.5
Equatorial Guinea	1	1,100,000	0.3
Cape Verde	1	970,000	0.3
Total	98	297,587,315	

Source: KFAED, *The Fund's Activities in the Developing Nations up to April 30, 1988* (Kuwait: KFAED, International Cooperation Department, May 1988), section 4, p. 3, and information provided to the author by the fund, February 6, 1989, and June 30, 1989.

In summarizing Kuwait's political cash contributions or grants, one must recognize that many of these are secret—not reported—and out of public scrutiny. Furthermore, some of these and some of the early economic aid, given through the state reserves or in the form of grants for food or medicine, may not be quantifiable. On the other hand, some amounts were merely committed rather than actually delivered, and since the oil slump of the early 1980s there has been a slow and inconsistent pattern of payment. The

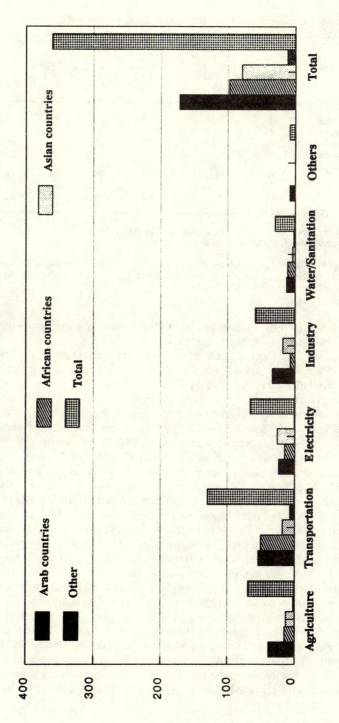

Figure 3.2 Sectoral Allocation of Loans (by number of loans)

TABLE 3.6 Allocation of Loans by Sector (No. of Loans and Percentage)

	Agri-culture	Trans-portation	Elec-tricity	In-dustry	Water & Sani-tation	Others	Total
Arab states	39	54	24	34	13	8	172
African states	15	50	15	7	11	–	98
Asian states	13	18	26	18	4	–	79
Other states*	2	7	1 .	–	2	–	12
Total	69	129	66	59	30	8	361
%	19.1	35.7	18.2	16.3	8.3	2.2	100%**

*Includes Malta, Cyprus, Papua, New Guinea, and Solomon Islands.
**The total is less than 100% because of rounding.

Source: KFAED, *The Fund's Activities in the Developing Nations up to April 30, 1988* (Kuwait: KFAED International Cooperation Department, May 1988), section 5, p. 1, and information provided to the author by the fund, February 6, 1989, and June 30, 1989.

following figures may therefore be conservative and are certainly inconclusive, and should be read with caution.

The total Kuwaiti cash contribution to Arab causes since 1961 may exceed $29,960 million—some $16,650 million or 55.5 percent to the frontline states and the Palestinian cause, and $13,310 million (44.4 percent) to Iraq, with more than $6 billion in cash and the remainder ($7.3 billion) from the sale of oil for the benefit of Iraq (see Appendix B). Egypt's share, all given before 1979, was $7,129.5 million or 23.7 percent of the total. Syria received $2,813.5 million or 9.39 percent; Jordan received $2,154 million or 7.18 percent; and the PLO received $891.9 million or 2.97 percent. In addition, $3,594.1 million or 11.99 percent went to those and other states and organizations without verification of which parties received how much. The political contributions to the Palestinian cause do not include an average of $5 million per year deducted from Palestinian workers' salaries in Kuwait, in a collection scheme that began in 1965. In the period 1965–1989, this amount reached around $122.5 million. The Kuwaiti government also charged a nominal stamp fee for "Palestinian liberation" (i.e., the PLO) from moviegoers, but this practice was discontinued by the end of the 1970s. We estimate that in the period 1965–1980, these fees totaled $2.0 million. Although the government decreed in 1964 that 5 fils (1.4 cents) for each gallon of oil locally consumed should be given to the PLO, this provision has never been implemented.[6] Since the uprising in the occupied Palestinian territories in 1988, the salary monies are given to and distributed by the private Kuwaiti "people's committee." Contributions to Iraq increased greatly after the beginning of its war with Iran in 1980, although they go back a long way; the first reported Kuwaiti "political" cash grant was $80 million in "aid" to Iraq in 1963 in return for Iraqi recognition of Kuwait. These "grants" were allocated in exchange for Iraqi protection of the Gulf. As the Iraqis stated, "They [the Gulf countries] know that had it not been for Iraq, they would have been taken as prisoners to the lands of the Persians. . . ."[7] The crux of Kuwait's grants to Arab states and to the Palestinians has been Kuwait's obligations under the terms of the Arab summit conferences of 1964, 1967, 1973, 1978, 1988, and 1989. These grants and financial assistance could be viewed as something of an insurance policy for a small and vulnerable Kuwait.[8]

Besides the role of donor, Kuwait assumed the role of savvy investor in the free markets of the Western economies. Investment was viewed within Kuwaiti official circles as part of the country's sociopolitical responsibilities. A Kuwaiti oil minister explained that investment "should be considered not purely from the commercial point of view, but from that of the economic and social profitability for the nation, especially in the long-run—and also as part of the social costs as a means of filling the technological gap and widening the industrial base."[9] The new activity of Kuwaiti investment and petroleum agencies has made Kuwait the eighth sibling-sister of the world's great multinational oil companies,[10] and may indeed place it in an equally exploitative role. Through acquiring a number of energy and other industrial firms, Kuwait intends, according to the *Wall Street Journal*, "to establish itself as a potential competitor to . . . other international companies for the burgeoning exploration and production business in both the U.S. and Third World countries."[11] However, limited market opportunities and political instability have restricted Kuwaiti investments in Third World countries.

In its efforts to diversify its economy and utilize its surplus oil revenues, and to invest the ruler's private treasure, Kuwait has traditionally turned to Britain. The Kuwait Investment Office (KIO) in London and its predecessor, the Kuwait Investment Board (established in 1952), have joined the major players in international finance and real estate investment.[12] In order to streamline the investment posture already established, in January 1966 Kuwait set up the International Investment Advisory Committee, which functioned as a consultative body to the ministry of finance. The committee was headed by the minister of finance, and included four Kuwaiti and four international experts.

Up to mid-1989, the state's surplus and investment abroad has varied from as little as $50 billion to as high as $200 billion. Since very little is known about it, it is perhaps speculative to conclude that the total Kuwaiti investment locally and internationally exceeds $120 billion, about one-third in the State Reserves and two-thirds in the Fund for Future Generations. Kuwaiti's investment portfolio is classified into two categories, external investment (Istithmarat Kharijiya) and foreign investment (Istithmarat Ajnabiya). "External assets" refers to local and international holdings, whereas "foreign investment" is exclusively foreign ventures. Some $20–$30 billion fall within the realm of external investment, and $90 to $100 billion within that of foreign investment.

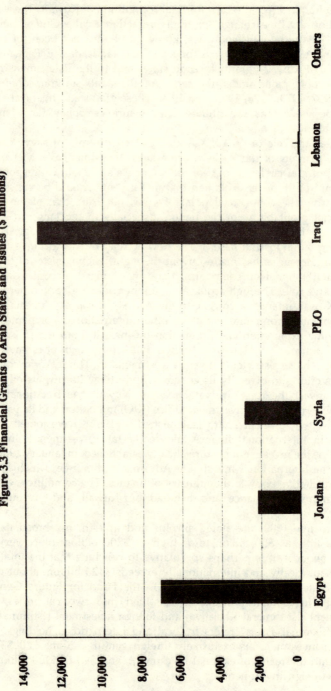

Figure 3.3 Financial Grants to Arab States and Issues ($ millions)

Although Kuwait Investment Authority (KIA) is the state's instrument for carrying out Kuwait's foreign investment policy, and Kuwait Investment Office (KIO) is technically an arm of KIA, in reality KIO operates independently, and perhaps very few people are aware of its multifarious activities. Both agencies use a number of cover companies to conduct business for them, and KIO has lately become very aggressive in the business field. KIA holds shares in a number of joint (private-public) companies in Kuwait; moreover, Kuwaiti private sector asset portfolio is estimated at around $30–40 billion.[13] In 1967–1968, the interest on Kuwaiti investment was K.D. 25 million; in 1972–1973, it reached K.D. 60 million; in 1986–1987, K.D. 2.5 billion ($8.9 billion), about one-fourth of the 1986 GDP. By 1987, the foreign investment return was estimated at $6.3 billion and had, for the first time, overtaken the oil revenue yield of $5.4 billion.

By the early 1980s, Kuwait's surplus accounted for about 23 percent of the OPEC surplus. Two-thirds of Kuwait's surplus was invested globally, most by KIO. Kuwait's investments are for the most part divided among Western Europe, the United States, the Far East, and some Third World states. More than 90 percent are in Europe and the United States, of which $60 billion are in dollar holdings.

The massive network of Kuwait's investment transcends economic and ideological boundaries, however. According to Kuwait's crown prince and prime minister, Saad Al-Abdullah, this pattern of assistance and investment has played a "positive role in the economy of many countries." In England, Kuwait owns St. Martin's Property Group and is an 11.9 percent sharehold in the Royal Bank of Scotland and a 10.3 percent shareholder of Midland Bank. Kuwait owns some $4 billion in British government bonds. In 1989, Kuwait Petroleum Corporation bought Carless Lubricants for $51.5 million. Kuwait's concern for the well-being of the Western economies was exemplified in 1974, when Kuwait gave Britain a £750 million interest-free loan for two months, to help its balance of payments.[14]

By late 1987, KIO moved to buy interests in British Petroleum (BP), the third largest oil company in the world, initially purchasing 19 percent of the stock, and eventually reaching a 22 percent stake at over $5.7 billion.[15] The purchase represented about 10 percent of Kuwait's total international funds, and brought KIO's sterling holdings to over £30 billion.[16] Kuwait's purchase might be viewed as having rescued the British government when a BP stock offering was poorly received by the public.[17] In response to appeals by the British authorities, Kuwait stepped in to purchase the shares. Since the deal created a public uproar in England, however, the Kuwaiti minister of finance declared that the purchase was "strictly commercial . . . and no political decision or goal was behind it." By June 1988, KIO had agreed not to augment its shares until the appropriate British authorities completed their investigations of BP's deal.[18]

Meanwhile, Kuwait Petroleum International, a London-based arm of the state's Kuwait Petroleum Corporation, "indulged" in purchasing oil facilities in Europe, in order to run downstream operations there. By early 1989 it

TABLE 3.7 State Reserve and Investment Income (K.D. million)

Fiscal Year Ended	June 1984	June 1985	June 1986	Projected June 1987	Projected June 1988
State General Reserve	11,760	11,433	10,680	9,769	8,950
Net Income Accrued during FY	463	452	276	258	236
Implied Effective Drawdown		(780)	(1,029)	(1,169)	(1,055)
Apparent Drawdown		(328)	(753)	(911)	(820)
Implied Rate of Return (%)		3.85	2.42	2.42	2.42

Reserve Fund for Future Generation	10,822	11,843	14,323	15,345	16,476
Income Accrued during FY	818	702	2,217	859	921
Statutory Increment	315	274	235	163	210
Total Increment (Official)		1,021	2,479	1,022	1,131
Total Increment (Implied)		976	2,452	1,022	1,131
Implied Rate of Return (%)		6.48	18.72	6.00	6.00
Total State Reserve	22,582	23,276	25,003	25,114	25,425
Total Income Accrued during FY	1,280	1,154	2,493	1,118	1,157
Total Increment		694	1,727	112	311
Implied Rate of Return (%)		5.11	10.71	4.47	4.61

Source: The National Bank of Kuwait, *Kuwait and Gulf Cooperation Council: Economic and Financial Bulletin* (Kuwait: NBK, Fall 1987), p. 10.

operated around 5,000 gas stations under the logo "Q8" in seven European countries, as well as two refineries in Denmark and Holland. Its share of the retail gasoline market was more than 23 percent in Denmark, 15 percent in Sweden, and around 5 percent in England. It is assumed that Kuwait's European installations consume about one-fourth of its oil production.[19]

Kuwait's investment in West Germany reached about $3 billion by 1982. It owns 18 percent of Daimler-Benz, 10 percent of Volkswagen do Brasil, and 24 percent of Hoechst Chemicals.[20] In 1987, Kuwait bought a 37 percent share in Union Explosives Rio Tinta, Spain's second largest company. Kuwait's plan to restructure the company evoked an unresolved controversy in Spain. Moreover, Kuwait owns over 12.5 percent of Banco Central. In early 1989, KIO decided to resell its Spanish banking interests for more than $400 million. Even after this sale, Kuwait's investment in Spain is estimated to reach $2 billion.[21]

In Japan, Kuwait has stakes in Nissan, plus 23 percent of New Tokyo Trust and 7.1 percent of Crescent in Japan. By mid-1988 Kuwait's holdings in Japanese equities reached some $7 billion, even though Kuwait's entry into the Japanese market was limited by Japan's regulations. In early 1988, a financial team headed by the Kuwaiti finance minister visited Japan in order to convince the Japanese to allow greater Kuwaiti investment.[22]

Kuwait made its first major investment inroads into the American market in 1974 by purchasing Kiawah Island, a resort facility in South Carolina, for $17.4 million. However, this operation was sold in 1988 for $105 million. Before this, Kuwait had bought some bonds and shares which reached some K.D. 536 million ($1.8 billion) by 1976. In 1976, it purchased Columbia Plaza, an office block in Washington, D.C., for $22 million. But its biggest and boldest act was the purchase of Santa Fe International Corporation, a California-based oil exploration and drilling-rig company, for $2.5 billion in October 1981. Later, in November 1984, Santa Fe acquired Occidental Geothermal, Inc. for $350 million. These deals raised some political and public eyebrows.[23] The *Wall Street Journal* stated that "the transaction would far outstrip any other Mideast investment of petroleum revenue in a publicly traded U.S. corporation."[24]

The Kuwaitis had to calm public fear and outrage and convince the Congress of their strictly financial intentions. An official from the Kuwait Petroleum Corporation testified that "we expect that Santa Fe will continue to be run as a business enterprise, subject, as an American company, to the political and economic policies of the U.S. government."[25] Kuwait's ambassador to Washington, Saud Al-Sabah, explained that Kuwait had made this deal "in order to benefit from [Santa Fe's] technical know-how, especially in downstream technology, and not . . . to strangle the U.S. economy and energy industry."[26] These public and private fears led Santa Fe to announce in December 1981 that it would discontinue its defense-related nuclear work at U.S. government facilities because of the ongoing negative and unwarranted public and media criticism.[27]

The purchase created a political storm in Kuwait as well. Members of the National Assembly questioned the decision of the minister of oil to buy the corporation on the grounds "that the purchase was both economically unjustified and makes Kuwait vulnerable to U.S. pressure."[28] In February 1985, however, the U.S. Interior Department reversed a 1983 ruling and allowed Santa Fe to acquire oil, natural gas, and other mineral leases on federal lands. Kuwait's investment in the United States makes up some 30 to 35 percent of its total global funds, and was estimated by early 1988 to have approximated $30 billion.[29] By the mid-1980s Kuwait was listed as the only non-OECD large investor in the United States.[30]

On the other hand, only 5 percent of Kuwait's funds are invested in developing countries, including Arab states. And it is not unlikely that investment outside the industrial world is affected by foreign policy considerations.[31] Kuwait's concern for domestic and regional security and promotion of Third World solidarity, and its preference for certain political regimes, are but a few reasons for such investments. Kuwait has joined in ventures in Mauritania, Brazil, Yugoslavia, Morocco, India, Pakistan, Tunisia, Jordan, and Senegal in livestock, hotel and tourist facilities, housing projects, ship repair yards, construction, cement plants, etc.

Kuwait owns the largest skyscraper outside the United States, the Overseas Union Bank in Singapore, which costs about $247 million. Kuwait owns 8.2 percent of Sime Darby, the largest industrial holdings group and biggest plantation owner in Malaysia, and part of the second largest plantation group, Harrison Malaysian Plantations. Moreover, it has a 20 percent holding in the Hong Leong Company, a financial group linked to the Hong Kong financial market. By early 1989, Kuwait was viewing the investment opportunities in China and the Soviet Union. By late 1987, Kuwaiti investment in Egypt was estimated to have reached some $3.5 billion.[32]

Likewise, Kuwait has cemented its relationship with the Eastern bloc not only through diplomatic means, but also through finance. In the 1980s Kuwait extended numerous loans to the socialist states. In 1980, China received a $300 million loan for five years—reportedly the first foreign loan China received after its open-door policy of the 1970s. By 1982, Yugoslavia had received aid and loans reaching $1 billion. In mid-1988, Kuwait agreed with other countries to reschedule $946 million worth of Yugoslavian debt for 10 years. And in early 1987 the Soviet Foreign Trade Bank received a loan of $150 million. In 1989, the Soviet Union was awarded a $60 million contract for desalting and dehydration facilities at Kuwait Oil Company's facilities.[33] One may therefore assume that Kuwaiti's extensive economic and financial roles are not inseparable from the political tenets of the regime.

However, these aggressive and venturesome tendencies in investment abroad have created some problems for Kuwait. It would seem that the managers of these funds are professionals within the field of finance, and rarely review the political implications of investment in Western economies. In addition, decisions are made by a closed circle involving few people. Since the closure of the Majlis Al-Ummah in 1986, investment agencies have not been accountable to popular pressure, and bureaucratic feuding and complications generate intra-agency rivalry between the two main bodies, the KIO and KIA.

In fact, the private financial sector complements the role of the state's foreign policy. Certain Kuwaiti private banks were listed among the top 500 banks in the world in terms of assets in both 1987 and 1988. Moreover, 12 Kuwaiti or Kuwait-based banks led the top 50 banks in the Arab world in 1987 and in 1988 in terms of equity. The financial credibility of the state was augmented by its ranking in terms of credit rating or worthiness for 1989 (twenty-ninth among 112 countries).[34] This banking and financial reputation has doubtless given Kuwait the wherewithal to act "aggressively" in world affairs.

Kuwait's Mediating Role

The systematic pattern of Kuwait's financial powers gave it the leverage and credibility to assume the role of a mediator in regional disputes, thus lessening tensions within the Arab world and the Middle East region, and increasing its own credentials as a "centrist" state in Arab politics. In fact, mediation has become a main feature of Kuwait's foreign policy. Whether Kuwait is invited to mediate, or whether it takes the initiative itself, in the words of the former foreign ministry undersecretary, Rashed al-Rashed, "many expect Kuwait to play a mediation role in regional problems and conflicts." The undersecretary explained Kuwait's motives as follows: "Kuwait recognizes that peace and cooperation among countries and peoples of the world are not only an ideal of goodwill rooted in the Kuwaiti . . . people's [mind and behavior], but [rather] an immediate pragmatic need, and certainly for definite geopolitical reasons."[35]

The first test of Kuwait's mediation took place in the mid-1960s, when it arranged a meeting between the rival factions of republicans and royalists in Yemen, and the two states of Egypt and Saudi Arabia. The outcome of this meeting, however, was inconclusive. Kuwait's then crown prince and prime minister Sabah Al-Salem visited Riyadh in June 1965 and held talks with King Faisal to find a means for the settlement of the crisis in Yemen. In August 1966, a meeting took place in Kuwait between representatives of Egypt and Saudi Arabia and the two Yemeni factions. Kuwait presented a proposal, agreed upon by the parties but never implemented, to form a transitional government made up of republicans and royalists, with a republican majority and with Egyptian troops being withdrawn and replaced by a joint Arab force.[36]

In the late 1960s, Kuwait set the conditions to settle the Iranian claim on Bahrain. Kuwait arranged a number of meetings between representatives of both governments in its mission in Geneva, before their agreement to take the case to the UN for a good-office mediation effort. It also tried unsuccessfully to mediate the Shatt Al-Arab dispute between Iran and Iraq in 1969. Kuwait's prime minister stated that the Amir would "exert his . . . efforts to settle the crisis," and Kuwait's representatives visited Baghdad and Teheran with messages from the Amir to heads of both states.[37]

In the early 1970s, Kuwait attempted to settle the dispute between East and West Pakistan. Kuwait's foreign minister, Sabah Al-Ahmad, led a good-office delegation from the Islamic Conference to Dhaka and Islamabad, a delegation that eventually succeeded in lessening the tension between Bangladesh and Pakistan and normalizing relations between the two states.

Kuwait attempted to mediate between North and South Yemen in September 1972, after border clashes between the two states. Kuwait's single efforts did not bear fruit, but a UN committee with representatives from several countries including Kuwait visited the two states in October 1972 and was eventually able to settle the differences.[38]

Kuwait participated in the concerted Arab effort to settle the September 1970 civil war between the Palestinians and Jordan. Kuwait's then minister of defense and interior, Saad Al-Abdullah, played an important role in the Arab League committee's efforts to find a satisfactory compromise.[39] Such conduct undoubtedly enhanced Kuwait's prestige with the Palestinians and pan-Arabist elements, both in Kuwait and outside.

But the most successful Kuwaiti effort at settling regional crises was ending the Omani-South Yemeni disputes in the 1980s, in collaboration with the Gulf Cooperation Council. After many lower-level meetings, in an October 1984 meeting in Kuwait between the foreign ministers of Oman and South Yemen in the presence of the foreign ministers of Kuwait and the United Arab Emirates, both parties agreed basically on noninterference in the domestic affairs of each state, respect for the sovereignty and territorial integrity of both states, cessation of propaganda warfare, and establishment of diplomatic relations. The agreement, in the words of ex-undersecretary Al-Rashed, "builds a relation of greater trust . . . and prevents superpower intervention."[40]

One of the frustrating issues that Kuwait had tried in vain to mediate —either individually or collectively—was the Lebanese civil war. Since the 1970s, Kuwait's foreign minister, Sabah Al-Ahmad, had tried, albeit to no avail, to utilize Kuwait's moral, political and financial leverage to reach some understanding. In the 1980s, Kuwait revived its mission by leading an Arab League delegation. The various Lebanese political and religious leaders met in Tunis and Kuwait in early 1989, in order to work towards a satisfactory solution to the thorny Lebanese crisis.[41]

Kuwait's success in mediation, in the words of foreign ministry undersecretary Sulaiman Majid Al-Shaheen, emanated from the "credibility of Kuwait's behavior, the uncompromising tendencies of Kuwaiti foreign policy, the unchanging pattern of Kuwaiti policies, and the financial power of Kuwait."[42] Kuwait's financial capabilities, whether exercised in loans, aid, or investment through public institutions or private channels, added leverage and impetus to Kuwait's foreign policy and made its mediating role more possible, and often welcome.

It has also been stated that credit for the success of Kuwait's diplomacy should go to its astute foreign minister, Sabah Al-Ahmad, who has been managing the ministry or, better, the conduct of Kuwait's foreign policy, single-handedly for over a generation. His role as the architect of Kuwait's foreign diplomacy has been termed "the other phase of Kuwait's foreign policy."[43] It is generally assumed that the personalization of a nation's foreign policy may have contributed to some of its successes, but such personalization also tends to make the conduct of the state's foreign relations depend on personal tastes, mood, and preferences, and may lead to complications with other states, confusion and, often, bureaucratic inertia.

Kuwait's Support of the Palestinian Cause

Kuwait's Arabism has been strikingly exemplified in its championship, in a variety of ways, of the Palestinian issue as the core of Arab identity. The Palestinian community in Kuwait is the largest minority and the second largest group after the native Kuwaitis, making up some twenty-one percent of the total population. The presence and penetration of Palestinian advisers and influences throughout Kuwaiti society made the government simultaneously conscious of the Palestinians' human suffering and their political clout, and built mutual relationships between the Kuwaiti political and financial establishments and the Palestinian elite. But the Kuwaiti understanding of and sympathy toward the Palestine problem is not a recent phenomenon.

The beginning of Kuwaiti-Palestinian relations dates back to the 1920s. In 1922 the Mufti of Jerusalem visited Kuwait to collect donations to rebuild the Aksa Mosque. In the 1930s, the Kuwaiti Youth Association formed a committee to study the Palestine issue, and in 1936 it collected about 7500 rupees to aid the Palestinian struggle. The initial Palestinian influence on Kuwait's future social and educational life began to take shape in 1936, when the first Palestinian education mission, which included four schoolteachers, came to Kuwait. Many of the original founders of the Palestine Liberation Organization began their careers and formed their revolutionary strategy in Kuwait in the late 1950s. In fact, Al-Fatah made Kuwait its headquarters until it moved to Syria in 1966. In 1964 Kuwait permitted the Palestine Liberation Organization (PLO) to open up an office.[44] The private People's Committee has been active since the 1940s in collecting donations for the Palestinians, and until 1962 for the Algerians.

Kuwait's financial assistance to the PLO has already been described. Beginning in the mid-1960s, Kuwait allowed the opening of camps to train the Palestinians in Kuwait, and in the aftermath of the 1967 war, with the influx of Palestinian refugees to Kuwait, the government acquiesced in the PLO's request to use Kuwaiti public schools to teach the Palestinian children.[45] In addition, Kuwait agreed to permit Palestinian students to use any scholarships given by Arab states and universities and not filled by Kuwaitis.[46]

The Palestinian youths spend their spring vacation in Kuwait at camps geared to military training and political indoctrination. An officer in charge of such camps in Kuwait stated: "these youth camps are the leading experiment of the Palestine revolution. . . . They give the youth the ability to live in the battlefield, and learn how to regain their lost homeland."[47] In the early 1980s, Al-Fatah's representative in Kuwait, Abul Adib, graduated 500 Palestinian youth and reiterated, "we feel as if we are in our own land."[48]

In solidarity and sympathy with the Arab states' 1967 war preparations, Kuwait formed a symbolic military unit, the Al-Yarmouk Brigade. On May 30, 1967, the unit was dispatched to Egyptian territory to work along with other Arab troops against Israel. In the meanwhile, Kuwait declared a defensive war against Israel, and the National Assembly demanded the nationalization of oil companies, called for the organization of volunteers, and initiated a campaign of blood and money donations. On June 6, the council of ministers decided to suspend oil shipments to Britain and the United States because of their support for Israel, and requested that Iran cease supplying Israel with oil.[49] The ruler, Jaber Al-Ahmad, then prime minister and crown prince, summarized Kuwait's support for the Arab struggle this way: "Kuwait utilized all its resources, military, political and economic, for the battle. . . . This is what Kuwait did and cared about. There is no need or reason to list the details of our role. . . . Words must be brief and useful . . . we need say only as much as the situation demands . . . that the Arab nations may be confident and trust that . . . Arab governments mobilized all their resources in the battlefield to win the ultimate victory against all their enemies."[50] In keeping with Palestinian objections, Kuwait refused to accept resolution 242 of the Security Council, which considered the Palestinians as mere refugees.

In essence, the 1967 war and the Arab defeat, and Arab reliance on the financial subsidies and political support of the Gulf states, not only increased the credentials of oil states such as Kuwait, but also showed the vested interest of all Arabs in the operation of oil facilities and the survival of the Gulf regimes. Moreover, it made the radical Arabs more amenable to the demands of the so-called moderate and traditional systems.[51]

Kuwait has supported the Palestinian cause even against Arab brethren. Kuwait suspended all aid to Jordan in the aftermath of the 1970 civil war, reinstating it only during the October war of 1973. Furthermore, the Amir of Kuwait appealed to King Hussain to reconsider the sentence passed on Abu Dawoud and his colleagues in 1971.[52]

Kuwait has supported the Arab economic boycott of Israel since the 1950s. In the late 1950s and early 1960, the United States protested Kuwait's alleged "unwarranted interference in the commercial relationships of business firms," following a Kuwaiti request for American companies to verify their relations with Israel and Israeli companies.[53] In the October war of 1973, in addition to paying "political" subsidies, Kuwait sent two symbolic military units to the Egyptian and Syrian fronts.[54] In addition, in 1973, it led the movement for an Arab oil boycott of the United States and the Netherlands and for cuts in oil production. A Organization of Arab Petroleum Exporting Countries (OAPEC) conference in Kuwait in October 1973 made the decision on price increases and oil reductions, and Kuwait was instrumental in these decisions. It cut back its national oil output from 3.7 m b/d to 3.0 m b/d in late 1973, and to 2.5 m b/d in 1974.[55]

In defense of the Palestinian cause, Kuwait has repeatedly spoken out in international bodies. Kuwaiti foreign minister Sabah Al-Ahmad, in a 1974 address to the General Assembly of the United Nations, demanded that it invite "the Palestinian people to participate in the discussions through its legitimate representative [PLO] . . . which alone can authoritatively explain its viewpoints, voice its aspirations, and define its objectives."[56]

Reinforcing Kuwait's role as a member of the Security Council, and reflecting its concern for Palestinian/American dialogue, on July 26, 1979, Kuwait arranged a meeting between Andrew Young, U.S. ambassador to the U.N., and Zehdi Tarzi, the PLO's U.N. observer, at the residence of Abdullah Bishara, Kuwait's delegate to the United Nations. The meeting led to public and newspaper protests and outcry, both in Israel and in the United States. Eventually, on August 15, 1979, Andrew Young resigned.[57]

In the 1980s, Kuwait and Saudi Arabia froze a multimillion-dollar loan to the World bank to protest a decision to deny the PLO observer status at the bank. Kuwait's share of the loan was $86 million. In September 1980 President Jimmy Carter, appealing to the bank not to politicize the international monetary agencies, said, "any political pressure or unwarranted influence from any international forum which might undermine your integrity would be neither necessary, nor desirable."[58]

In the summer of 1983, Kuwait's zealous concern over the Palestine case caused a minor diplomatic row between Kuwait and the United States. Kuwait refused the nomination of Brandon W. Grove, Jr., as American ambassador to Kuwait, on the grounds that he had previously served as American consul in Jerusalem. "Shocked" State Department officials said that Kuwait's decision might "set an ominous precedent for U.S.-Arab relations," and that Israel might serve as a "diplomatic ghetto" for American personnel. A Kuwaiti official justified Kuwait's decision as expressing Kuwait's "national stand toward the Palestinian cause in general and the status of occupied Jerusalem in particular."[59] Palestinians of various political ranks and ideologies applauded Kuwait's decision. Yasser Arafat, the head of the PLO, termed it "the first genuine Arab position taken by Arab states against the official unfriendly policies of the United States . . . and its disregard for the rights of other nations."[60]

Kuwait has in the past identified principally with the mainstream of the PLO, Al-Fatah, with which most of the Palestinians in Kuwait and elsewhere are affiliated, especially those rich members of the Palestinian elite close to centers of power in Kuwait. In the 1980s, however, Kuwait has attempted to increase its credentials and leverage with other Palestinian factions, and to extend its mediation into intra-Palestinian rivalries. Kuwait invited George Habash, of the Popular Front for the Liberation of Palestine, to visit and meet officials of the Kuwaiti government, to resolve the differences between the various factions that might lead to a meeting of the Palestine National Council. An official of the PFLP called the Kuwaiti position toward the Palestinian conflict "unique," and by 1988 Kuwait permitted the PFLP to open an official office in Kuwait.[61]

Kuwait broke off diplomatic relations with West Germany in 1965, when the latter recognized Israel. Likewise, it severed its relationship with Costa

Rica and Zaire in 1982, when the former moved its embassy to Jerusalem and the latter reestablished diplomatic relations with Israel. In January 1986, after Spain recognized Israel, Kuwait recalled its ambassador in Madrid.[62]

In December 1985, the National Assembly asked the Egyptian government to free an Egyptian border policeman, Sulaiman Khatir, who on October 5 had shot to death seven Israeli tourists at a Sinai beach resort. The Assembly's justification was that Khatir had "restored to the Arab people some of its dignity."[63]

During the 1987–1988 Intifadah (uprising), the Kuwaiti cabinet called for a general strike in sympathy with the uprising and as a mark of respect for its martyrs. Moreover, the cabinet decided to deduct one day's salary from the pay of all employees to subsidize the popular uprising.[64] The ongoing Kuwaiti assistance and backing led Abul Adib to emphasize that Kuwait's security was inextricably interwoven with the Palestinian struggle.[65]

The Palestinians are the only non-Kuwaiti community who are allowed political and cultural activities and organizations inside Kuwait, but the Kuwaiti government remains anything but permissive toward extralegal actions. It will not tolerate Palestinian demonstrations or public gatherings, except those sanctioned by the authorities in advance. Frankly, they are chary of such approval. For example, in early 1988, Palestinian youngsters were permitted to organize a demonstration in front of the embassies of the five permanent members of the Security Council, and to present a letter expressing their sympathy with the uprising and demanding that these countries interfere to stop the killings by Israel.[66] But in March 1982, the security special forces used clubs, tear gas, and water cannons to prevent a student demonstration in support of the Palestinians in Lebanon. It was reported that dozens of demonstrators were injured and dozens were arrested. A student demonstration in February 1988 encountered the same harsh treatment.[67]

Kuwait's continuous support to the Palestinians has caused uneasiness in Israeli diplomatic circles. In 1969, Israel complained to the United Nations about Kuwait's "open support of Arab commandos and collecting funds for them." The Israeli complaint created fear of Israeli attacks against Kuwait's vital desalination plants.[68]

In a nutshell, it seems that because of historical ties between Palestinians and Kuwaitis, particularly between the elites, Kuwait's political, financial, organizational, media, and other public and private support has by far exceeded the commitment of many other Arab states to the Palestinian struggle. This support is important for the Palestine revolution, despite some fluctuations in the financial commitment of the Kuwaiti government. As a result, an unwritten pact has emerged between the Kuwaiti and Palestinian elites, whereby the Palestinians are free to conduct their political activities as long as they do not meddle in the domestic policies and security of the state, and the Palestinian elites mediate between the Kuwaiti government and the Palestinian masses in the country.

The Kuwaiti-Iraqi Dispute of 1973

Despite Kuwait's generous and great achievements in foreign policy, Iraqi politics of intimidation towards Kuwait have continued unabated. As Chapter 2 explained, since the 1950s, Iraq has been attempting, despite the 1932 exchange of letters, to gain greater maritime access to the Gulf waterways by incorporating within its territories the island of Warba and a portion of the coastline of the island of Bubiyan. Since it built the Umm Qasr seaport at the mouth of the Gulf in the 1950s, Iraq has harped on its need for a deep seaport and access to the waterways, on both maritime and naval grounds. In return for this access, Iraq promised to provide Kuwait with fresh water, which Kuwait lacks, from Shatt Al-Arab. Despite British pressures, the Kuwaitis turned down this demand, fearing that Iraq would eventually occupy the two islands[69] and perhaps hold Kuwait hostage by manipulating its water supply. In 1961, Iraq announced its intention to annex all of Kuwait, and despite the 1963 agreement and a joint boundary commission, the border was never demarcated because of Iraqi procrastination.

In the late 1960s, with the British departure from the Gulf region imminent, and Iran-Iraq relations worsening over the issue of Shatt Al-Arab, the Iraqis employed a combination of persuasion and pressures on Kuwait to station an army on Kuwaiti territory as part of a military force to protect the Iraqi port of Umm Qasr from an impending Iranian attack.[70] During an April 1969 visit by the Iraqi defense and interior ministers to Kuwait, the Kuwaitis seem to have tacitly acquiesced that Iraqi troops should be stationed on Kuwaiti territories. Thus it was claimed that an "unwritten agreement"[71] was reached which was in essence a "form of modus operandi."[72] The "temporary" stationing of Iraqi troops continued after the Iranian threats subsided, and it appears that the Iraqis wanted to convert the de facto presence into a de jure one. By the end of 1972, the Iraqis had built a road through Kuwaiti territory leading to their station at the Gulf, and on March 20, 1973, the Iraqi troops occupied a Kuwait police post, Al-Samitah. When the Kuwaitis tried to stop them, the Iraqis shot at the poorly armed police gendarmes. Two Kuwaiti soldiers died and two were missing; one Iraqi soldier died as well.[73]

Meanwhile, Kuwait declared a state of emergency, ordered the border closed, and recalled its ambassador in Baghdad. The National Assembly supported the government policies: "the Assembly unanimously supports all measures which the Government has taken and is taking to safeguard Kuwait's national right." The chairman of the Assembly's foreign relations committee commented, "The state of relations between Iraq and Kuwait is like a time bomb."[74]

The Gulf states and Iran expressed their support for Kuwait, and other Arab states such as Egypt and Syria, the Arab League, and the PLO sought to settle the dispute through good-office mediation. However, the Iraqis added fuel to the flames when their foreign minister, Murtada Abd Al-Baqi, explained that "the whole of Kuwait is a disputed area. There is a document saying that Kuwait is Iraqi territory. There is no document which says it is not Iraqi territory." In referring to the islands of Warba and Bubiyan, the minister stated "we are not taking them from Kuwait, rather we are giving up Kuwait for the sake of the two islands." Iraq's purpose, according to the minister, "is that Iraq should be a Gulf state."[75]

Meanwhile, it was reported that certain Soviet naval units and U.S. Sixth Fleet units were moving towards the northern part of the Gulf, following urgent consultations between the Gulf states and the major powers.[76] In late 1973, in order to boost its military power, Kuwait decided to purchase from France 36 Mirage fighters worth $85 million.[77]

It has been alleged that Kuwait threatened to halt all cash grants to the confrontation states, and that Saudi forces moved to the Al-Hafr area on the Kuwaiti-Saudi border. Kuwait's use of its financial card, plus Soviet pressures on Iraq, convinced the Iraqis that they must negotiate. It was generally believed that the Iraqis had agreed to withdraw their troops from Al-Samitah before resumption of talks between the two parties. Saddam Hussein, the then Iraqi vice-president, visited Moscow one day after the incident, and upon his return the Iraqis changed their posture towards Kuwait.[78]

During a visit to Iraq by the then Kuwaiti heir apparent and prime minister, Jaber Al-Ahmad, in August 1973, he was plainly told that "Iraq would accept the de facto frontiers only if the islands of Warba and Bubiyan were either included within Iraqi territory or leased to it."[79]

Developments in the Gulf and the region, however, allowed Iraq to modify its stance. Since by 1975 Iraq had settled its Shatt Al-Arab dispute with Iran, by July 1977 the Iraqis agreed to withdraw their troops unilaterally from Kuwaiti territory. In other words, they now wished to appear as a moderate, status quo Gulf regime.[80] Domestic factors may also have tempted the Iraqis to change their behavior toward Kuwait. During the 1970s, Iraq lessened tensions with its neighbors and focused, instead, on domestic development.[81]

It seems that although small, powerless and vulnerable in comparison to its neighbors, Kuwait can employ its financial muscle and the leverage of Arab public opinion against a more aggressive neighbor. In fact, as the Iraqi newspaper *Ath-Thawrah* stated, Kuwait's aim was to show the Al-Samitah "incident as being much larger than it really is." It seems that the Kuwaitis knew in advance of the Iraqi moves, but had been unable to come to reasonable terms because of Iraqi intransigence.[82] Thus Kuwait's leverage with the Arab states and particularly the frontline states, and its reasonably good relations with the superpowers, helped it to achieve its immediate goal, Iraqi withdrawal from its military post. However, its long-term goal of settling the border issue remains to be achieved.

As a countermeasure to the Iraqi threats, in order to stymie Iraqi designs on the two islands and to create buffer zones with its two major neighbors, Kuwait initiated by the mid-1970s plans for two settlement cities in northern and southern Kuwait, for a causeway bridge between Bubiyan and the mainland, and for a settlement town in Bubiyan island. These projects serve as an integral part of a larger defense strategy.

Conclusion

The years between 1963 and 1979 witnessed the climax of Kuwait's power, as Kuwait effectively employed its financial potency to achieve its foreign policy goals.

Kuwait's economic development aid schemes reflected its humanitarian mission. Its political financial grants expressed its Arab identification and its centrist political ideology, which in turn reflected its underlying concern with state stability and military security. Kuwait's investment policies, designed to develop its capital surplus economy so as to guarantee its future revenues, demonstrated a combination of shrewdness, greed, haste, and venture, in essence commercial motives. But Kuwait also used its semiprivate investment institutions to extend its political influence in different countries and in certain Third World states. They were a quasi-official arm of Kuwait foreign policy. All in all, this financial-cum-political clout certainly has thus far sustained the state and made the Kuwaitis admired, respected, and on occasion envied around the world, particularly in the more impoverished Third World countries.

One note of caution: following their traditional mercantile patterns, Kuwaitis have acquired or held shares in an excessive number of sensitive oil, energy, and other kinds of investment ventures overseas, ventures that have generated public opposition in Western Europe and the United States and to a lesser extent even in Kuwait. In the long run, such investments could be counterproductive and vulnerable to sabotage. Kuwaiti investments might be exposed to freezing, higher taxes, nationalization, or mere expulsion. In pursuing such excessive adventures, Kuwait is actually outmaneuvering its own capabilities and outreaching its own strength. One reason for Kuwait's excessive financial aid and political commitment to Arab states and issues is that the elites who run financial institutions in Kuwait, private and public, are sympathetic to, or affiliated with, or the offspring of the nationalist generations of the 1920s and 1930s in Kuwait. Their personal attitudes and monopoly of the Chamber of Commerce and other financial institutions are reflected in Kuwait's overcommitments. Through financial, moral, diplomatic, and organization support to Palestinian causes, Kuwait was able to contain any major threats to its domestic stability from the large Palestinian community.

If the major shock of the Iraqi encroachment was the primary force driving expanded Kuwaiti aid and the Kuwaiti goal of securing allies and friends in the Arab world and beyond, then Kuwait can be said to have succeeded in one sense, and failed in another. Kuwait's success consists in the leverage it has achieved with Arab and regional states. Kuwait's commitment to their causes and its mediating roles in regional conflicts indicate its special position as a regional "leader," both financial and moral. This special position is most certainly due to Kuwait's financial might.

On the other hand, Kuwait has failed to achieve its national goals vis-à-vis Iraq. Despite Kuwait's unlimited generosity and friendly policies, mutual distrust has prevailed. Until both parties can agree on a solution to the border issue, Kuwaitis will continue to feel a deep-seated and historically justified fear towards their large, overbearing, and abusive neighbor.

Notes

1. *Aramco World Magazine*, vol. 36, no. 6 (November-December 1979), p. 26; see also Ragaei El-Mallakh and Mihseen Kadhim, "Arab Institutionalized Development Aid: An Evolution," *The Middle East Journal*, vol. 30, no. 4 (Autumn 1976), pp. 471–484; R. S. Porter, "Gulf Aid and Investment in the Arab World," in B. R. Pridham, ed., *The Arab Gulf and the Arab World*, pp. 189–213; and Maurice J. Williams, "The Aid Programs of the OPEC Countries," *Foreign Affairs*, vol. 54, no. 2 (January 1976), pp. 306–324.

2. All figures and tables adapted from Kuwait Fund for Arab Economic Development, *The Fund's Activities in the Developing Nations up to April 30, 1988* pp. 1, 3, 4, Pt. 2, p. 1, Pt. 6, p. 1, and other information provided to the author by the fund (February 6, 1989) and (June 30, 1989).

3. *Arab Report and Record* (May 1–15, 1966), p. 106.

4. For figures and data on the board's aid see General Board for the South and Arabian Gulf, *Services Extended by the State of Kuwait to the South and Arabian Gulf* (Kuwait: The Ministry of Foreign Affairs, July 1987), pp. 1–22. Figures on the budget were presented to the author by the General Board of the South and Arabian Gulf (July 1988).

5. Anthony Parson, "The Gulf States in the Eighties," *The Arab Gulf Journal* (April 1986), p. 13; for Kuwait's economic and financial position among the Middle Eastern states see Elias H. Tuma, "The Rich and the Poor in the Middle East," *The Middle East Journal*, vol. 34, no. 4 (Autumn 1980), pp. 413–437.

6. Information and data provided to the author by an anonymous source (November 3, 1988). The Kuwaiti decree was issued in March 27, 1964; see *The Middle East Journal*, vol. 18, no. 3 (Summer 1964), p. 333.

7. *Al-Watan Al-Araby* (May 17, 1983), p. 2.

8. "Financial Times Survey: Kuwait," *The Financial Times* (February 22, 1988), p. 15.

9. The statement is quoted in Walter J. Levy, "The Years that the Locust Hath Eaten: Oil Policy and OPEC Development Prospects," *Foreign Affairs*, vol. 57, no. 2 (Winter 1978/79), p. 297.

10. See "Inside the KIO," *Euromoney* (March 1988), p. 56, and "Inside Kuwait's Money Machine," *Institutional Investor* (August 1988), pp. 179–184.

11. *The Wall Street Journal* (October 6, 1981), p. 3.

12. *The Financial Times* (February 22, 1988), p. 18.

13. Information in this section is adapted from The National Bank of Kuwait, *Kuwait Interim Economic and Financial Report: Winter 1988* (Kuwait: NBK, Winter 1988), pp. 9–11; for the high estimate see "Inside Kuwait's Money Machine," *The Institutional Investor* (August 1988), pp. 179–184; and *The Economist* (August 22, 1987), p. 68. For the 1966 Committee see *Arab Report and Record* (January 1–15, 1966), p. 3, and (January 16–31, 1966), p. 7. For the $200 billion level, see "The Arabs Sweep Back into Spain," *International Management*, (December 1988), p. 57. KIO investment is estimated at more than $100 billion; see *Business Week*, (October

17, 1988), p. 48; U.S. Department of Commerce, *Foreign Economic Trends and their Implications for the United States; Kuwait, Key Economic Indicators* (Washington, D.C.: USGPO, prepared by American Embassy in Kuwait, January 1989), pp. 2–14; *Middle East Economic Digest* (July 8, 1988), p. 16 and (February 17, 1989), p. 20; *The Middle East* (December 1987), pp. 7–10; U.S. Department of State, *Background Notes: Kuwait* (Washington, D.C.: Bureau of Public Affairs, March 1988), pp. 1–8; Richard F. Nyrop, ed., *Persian Gulf States: Country Studies* (Washington, D.C.: USGPO, 1985, for the Foreign Area Studies); p. 102; U.S. Department of Commerce, *Business America* (April 10, 1989), p. 49; Gulf Economic and Financial Report, *Gulf Economic Outlook, 1989*, vol. 9, no. 1 (January 1989) (Bahrain: Gulf International Bank, 1989), p. 6; *Platt's Oilgram News*, vol. 67, no. 98 (May 22, 1989), p. 1; Dominic Lawson, "How to Hide $50 Billion," *The Spectator* (March 12, 1988), p. 16; *The Middle East and North Africa, 1972–1973*. 19th ed. (London: Europa Publications, 1972), p. 471; *The Middle East and North Africa, 1974–1975*. 21st ed. (London: Europa Publications, 1974), p. 470; The National Bank of Kuwait, *Kuwait and Gulf Cooperation Council: Economic and Financial Bulletin* (Kuwait: NBK, Fall 1987), p. 11; "Kuwait: Economy Adjusts to Sharp Drop in Oil Reserves," *IMF Survey* (March 23, 1987), p. 1; *The Economist* (March 26, 1988), p. 59, and *Al-Seyassah* (February 21, 1989), p. 8; Richard P. Mattione, *OPEC's Investments and the International Financial System*, p. 104; *Euromoney* (March 1988), p. 53; and H. Bowen-Jones, "The Gulf Today: An Overview of a Region in Recession," *The Arab Gulf Journal*, vol. 6, no. 2 (October 1986), p. 16. The Future Generation Fund was created by the parliament (Majlis Al-Ummah) in 1976, to protect future generations against unforeseeable drops in oil revenues, and requires that 10 percent of the annual oil income be added to the account, which should not be disposed of until the year 2001.

14. *Arab Report and Records* (December 1–5, 1974), p. 547; and *Middle East Economic Digest* (October 14, 1988), p. 10; and *Oil and Gas Journal* (April 24, 1989), p. 31. For the Kuwaitis' official statement, see The National Press Club, Saad Al-Sabah, Washington, D.C. (July 13, 1988). For Kuwaiti investment in the West see Sinclair Road and Averil Harrison, "Gulf Investment in the West: Its Scope and Implications," in B. R. Pridham, ed., *The Arab Gulf and the West*, (New York: St. Martin's Press, 1985), pp. 89–95. In mid-1989, Kuwait acquired 5.2% stake in Midland Bank at a price of $220 million, see *The Middle East Economic Digest* (June 23, 1989), p. 6.

15. "Kuwait Buys BP Stock like 'Marshmallows': An Unwelcome Suitor?" *The Christian Science Monitor* (January 15, 1988), p. 11; *Euromoney* (March 1988), p. 56; and *The Economist* (March 26, 1988), pp. 59–60.

16. *Al-Watan* (November 24, 1987), p. 2.

17. *The Christian Science Monitor* (January 15, 1988), p. 11; and "KIO's Lesson in Free-Market Capitalism," *Institutional Investor*, (November 1988), pp. 28–29.

18. The statement of the finance minister, Jassim Al-Khorafi, in *Al-Watan* (January 9, 1988), p. 8; for the British decision see *The New York Times* (June 10, 1988), p. 29.

19. *Middle East Economic Digest*, (August 17, 1984), p. 17; for KPI downstream activities in Europe, see Kuwait Oil Company, *The Kuwaiti Digest*, vol. 16, no. 2 (April/June, 1988), pp. 2–6; and John Roberts, *The Gulf, Integration, and OPEC: Overseas Downstream Activities*. Occasional Paper No. 4 (Boulder, CO: International Research Center for Energy and Economic Development, 1988), pp. 1–4, and 10–16; "Kuwait Petroleum Corporation Joins the Big League of Oil Majors," *South* (March 1984), pp. 54–56; Interview, Kuwait (April 11, 1988); *The Financial Times* (February 22, 1988), p. 15; *The Economist* (March 26, 1988), pp. 59–60; and *Al-Araby* (April 1989), pp. 68–91. In the fiscal year 1987/88, Kuwait Petroleum Corporation recorded

a net profit of K.D. 120 million ($412 million). This is a 70 percent rise above the 1986/87 profit of K.D. 70 million; see *Middle East Economic Digest* (May 19, 1989), pp. 26–27.

20. Richard P. Mattione, *OPEC's Investments and the International Financial System*, p. 114; and *The Spectator* (March 12, 1988), p. 18. In mid-1989, KFTCIC formed a German/Kuwaiti investment company to manage its investment portfolio in West German and other European firms, see *Middle East Economic Digest* (July 7, 1989), p. 6. For the activities of Kuwaiti investment firms see *Middle East Economic Digest* (July 28, 1989), p. 6, and (August 11, 1989), p. 7.

21. *The Christian Science Monitor* (January 15, 1988), p. 11; *Al-Majalla* (December 30, 1987), p. 37; "Madrid Awaits El Grande Bang," *Euromoney* (April 1988), pp. 147–152. For details of Kuwaiti investments in Spain see "The Arabs Sweep Back into Spain," *International Management* (December 1988), p. 57; and *Middle East Economic Survey* (April 17, 1989), p. B5; *Middle East Economic Digest* (March 10, 1989), pp. 30–31 and (May 19, 1989), p. 4. Torras Hostench, the principal Spanish affiliate of KIO, reported a pretax profit of some $42.4 million for the first quarter of 1989; see *Middle East Economic Digest* (May 19, 1989), p. 28.

22. *Foreign Broadcast Information Service (FBIS)*, JPRS Report, Near East and South Asia, "Near East" (hereafter cited as FBIS-JPRS) (April 11, 1988), p. 5; see also *Euromoney* (March 1988), p. 60.

23. Ministry of Planning, *Annual Statistical Abstract 1976* (Kuwait: October 1976), p. 188; Ragaei El-Mallakh, *Kuwait: Trade and Investment* (Boulder, CO: Westview Press, 1979), p. 235; and for other investments, pp. 229–233 and 235–240. For public and private investment in the U.S. see *The Wall Street Journal* (October 5, 1981), p. 35; *Middle East Economic Digest*, Special Report (May 1982), p. 32; *Middle East Economic Digest* (August 20, 1982), p. 28; "Kuwait's Drive to Be Oil's Eighth Sister," *Business Week* (January 11, 1982), pp. 36–37; "Why Kuwait Wants a U.S. Oil Partner," *Business Week* (October 19, 1981), pp. 42–43; G. Alen Petzet, "Kuwait to Buy Santa Fe for $2.5 Billion," *Oil and Gas Journal* (October 12, 1981), pp. 56–57. U.S. Department of Commerce, International Trade Administration, *International Direct Investment: Global Trends and U.S. Role*, 1988 edition (Washington, D.C.: USGPO, 1988), p. 40 put Kuwait's direct investment in the U.S. at $3.8 billion at the end of 1986; Kuwait's oil investments are $2.5 billion in Santa Fe International Corporation; $150 million in Andover Oil Co.; $350 million in Occidental Geothermal, Inc., and $190 million in Keydril Co., pp. 142–145; for the Kiawah sale see Roger Lowenstein, "U.S. Investors Buy Kuwaitis' Resort in South Carolina," *The Wall Street Journal* (July 1, 1988), p. 4; *Facts on File*, vol. 41, no. 2134 (October 9, 1981), p. 732; *The Wall Street Journal* (October 6, 1981), p. 3; and *Middle East Economic Digest* (December 18, 1981), p. 22.

24. *The Wall Street Journal* (October 6, 1981), p. 3.

25. U.S. Congress, House, Hearings, Subcommittee, Committee on Government Operations, *Federal Response to OPEC Country Investments in the United States, Part 2—Investment in Sensitive Sectors of the U.S. Economy: Kuwait Petroleum Corp. Takeover of Santa Fe International Corp.*, 97th Congress, 1st Session, October 20, 22, November 24, and December 9, 1981 (Washington, D.C.: USGPO, 1982), P. 116.

26. Saud Nasir al-Sabah, *A Kuwaiti View of Middle Eastern and International Affairs*, p. 32.

27. *Facts on File*, vol. 4, no. 2146 (December 31, 1981), p. 975; Santa Fe International had overseas operations in various countries. It produces some 13,000 b/d in the North Sea, and its portfolio in the North Sea concession is thought to be wort' $400 million; see *The Spectator* (March 12, 1988), p. 18.

28. Shakib Otaqui, "Kuwait," *The Middle East Review* (1986), p. 133.

29. See the statement of Fahad al-Rashed, managing director of Kuwait Investment Authority, in *Al-Watan* (December 3, 1987), p. 5; and CBS, *60 Minutes* (February 14, 1988). In 1987, Kuwait acquired some $845 million worth of direct investment outlays in the U.S., $227 million of this amount was invested in the banking sector, see U.S. Department of Commerce, Bureau of Economic Analysis, *Survey of Current Business*, vol. 69, no. 5 (May 1989), p. 26.

30. Martin and Susan Tolchin, *Buying into America: How Foreign Money is Changing the Face of Our Nation* (New York: Times Books, 1988), p. 7. It was estimated that Kuwait might have lost $5 billion of its investment as a result of the 1987 October New York stock crash; see *The Middle East* (December 1987), pp. 7–10; and *The New York Times* (November 3, 1987), p. D25.

31. Shireen Hunter, *OPEC and the Third World*, p. 75; and Richard P. Mattione, *OPEC's Investments and the International Financial System*, p. 123.

32. *Al-Majalla* (December 30, 1987), p. 35; *Euromoney* (March 1988), p. 60; a statement by the finance minister in *Al-Watan* (January 9, 1988), p. 8; and *Middle East Economic Digest* (April 21, 1989), p. 2. For Kuwait's downstream investments in Asia and Australia see "Kuwait Oil Industry: Tomorrow the World," *The Economist* (June 24, 1989), pp. 68–69.

33. Richard P. Mattione, *OPEC's Investments and the International Financial System*, p. 180; *Keesing's Record of World Events*, vol. 33 (November 11, 1987), pp. 35545; see also *Middle East Economic Digest* (December 18, 1981), p. 22 and (July 8, 1988), p. 17; and *Oil and Gas Journal* (May 22, 1989), p. 48.

34. For Kuwait's rank in international banking see *The Banker* (July 1988), p. 122 (July 1987), pp. 87–89; for Arab bank ratings see *Euromoney* (November 1987), pp. 155–158 (November 1988), pp. 145–148, and 151–157; for creditworthiness see *Institutional Investor* (March 1989), p. 188. See also Andrew Cunningham, "The Challenge Facing Kuwaiti Banking," *Middle East Economic Digest* (May 26, 1989), pp. 6–7.

35. Rashed Al-Rashed, "Al-Tawasout Fil Siyassat Al-Kuwayt Al-Kharijiya," (Mediation in Kuwait Foreign Policy), a lecture given at a training course, Department of Political Science, University of Kuwait (April 1, 1984), p. 5.

36. *Keesing's Contemporary Archives* (October 9–16, 1965), p. 21002; and Hussein A. Hassouna, *The League of Arab States and Regional Disputes*, p. 190.

37. Abdullah Yacoub Bishara, "Dawr Al-Umam Al-Mutahida Fi Istiqlal Al-Bahrain," (Role of the United Nations in the Bahraini Independence) *Journal of the Gulf and Arabian Peninsula Studies*, vol. 2, no. 7 (July 1976), pp. 235–241; and Sulaiman Majid Al-Shaheen, "Al-Tafawoudh Fil Siyassat Al-Kuwayt Al-Kharijiya," (Negotiations in Kuwait Foreign Policy), a lecture given at a training course, Department of Political Science, University of Kuwait (April 15, 1986), pp. 13–14. For the Shatt Al-Arab dispute see *Arab Report and Record* (May 1–5, 1969), p. 180.

38. Hussein A. Hassouna, *The League of Arab States and Regional Disputes*, pp. 202–203.

39. The British Broadcasting Corporation (BBC), *Summary of World Broadcasts, Part 4, The Middle East and Africa* (hereafter cited as SWB), ME/3494/A11/A17 (September 29, 1970).

40. Sulaiman Majid Al-Shaheen, "Negotiations in Kuwait Foreign Policy," pp. 14–17; and Rasheed Al-Rasheed, statement in *Al-Watan* (October 31, 1984), p. 4.

41. See *Al-Watan* (January 31, 1989), pp 1, 19, and (February 4, 1989), pp. 1, 21; *Al-Seyassah* (February 5, 1989), pp. 1, 11, 20; *Al-Qabas* (January 30, 1989), pp. 1, 23; *Asharq Al-Awsat* (February 20, 1989), pp. 1–2, and (February 22, 1989), pp. 1–2; *Al-Anba* (February 8, 1989), pp. 1, 30; and *Al-Rai Al-Aam* (February 22, 1989),

p. 22. See the lecture by Abdul-Hamid Al-Boejan, Director of Arab Countries in the Ministry of Foreign Affairs, on Kuwait's role in Lebanon, *Al-Watan* (June 1, 1989), p. 13; *Al-Qabas* (June 1, 1989), p. 4; and *Al-Anba* (June 1, 1989), p. 3. It was reported that Kuwait played a constructive role in building contact between the Sudanese authorities and John Garang, the Sudanese People's Liberation Army Chief; see *Al-Qabas* (June 1, 1989), p. 21; and *Al-Anba* (June 1, 1989), p. 1.

42. Sulaiman Majid Al-Shaheen, "Negotiations in Kuwait Foreign Policy," p. 10.

43. Sulaiman Majid Al-Shaheen, pp. 18–19.

44. *Al-Watan* (March 2, 1986), p. 13; *Al-Qabas* (August 11, 1982), p. 1; and Abd Al-Aziz Husayn, *Al-Mujtame 'Al-Araby Bil Kuwayt*, pp. 110–111. For an analysis of the role and influence of Palestinians in Kuwait see Bilal Al-Hassan, "Filistineyeen Fil Al-Kuwayt: Dirasat Ehsaeyeeh," *(Palestinians in Kuwait: Statistical Study)* (Beirut: Palestine Liberation Organization, Research Center, February 1974), pp. 7–122.

45. *Al-Watan* (March 2, 1986), p. 13.

46. *Al-Qabas* (August 11, 1976), p. 2.

47. *Al-Qabas* (March 7, 1983), p. 5.

48. *Al-Qabas* (March 5, 1983), p. 4.

49. *Al-Rissalat* (June 6, 1967), p. 3. For Arab and internal pressures inside Kuwait, see Anthony H. Cordesman, *The Gulf and the Search for Strategic Stability: Saudi Arabia, the Military Balance in the Gulf, and Trends in the Arab-Israeli Military Balance* (Boulder, CO: Westview Press, and London: Mansell Publishing Ltd., 1984), pp. 568–581; and *Al-Rai Al-Aam* (June 28, 1967), p. 4.

50. Interview with a French television reporter, printed in *Majalat Al-Kuwait* (July 16, 1967), p. 4.

51. Don Peretz, "Middle East Oil and Changing Political Constellations," in Russell A. Stone, ed., *OPEC and the Middle East: The Impact of Oil on Societal Development* (New York: Praeger, 1977), p. 22, and Mordechai Abir, *Oil, Power and Politics* (London: Frank Cass, 1974), p. 13.

52. *Arab Report and Record* (September 16–30, 1973), p. 412; and SWB, ME/4239/ i (March 8, 1973).

53. For the activities of the Israel Boycott Office in Kuwait, see *The Middle East Journal*, vol. 14, no. 4 (Autumn 1960), p. 449. The director of the Israel Boycott Office stated that "Kuwait is one of the few Arab countries abiding strictly by the regulations and principles" of the Arab boycott; see *Al-Watan* (February 4, 1989), p. 5.

54. More than 16 Kuwaiti soldiers were killed during the war of attrition between Egypt and Israel; see *Arab Report and Record* (June 16–30, 1970), p. 357; and *Middle East Journal*, vol. 24, no. 4 (Autumn 1970), p. 495. The Kuwaiti troops were withdrawn in December 1–9, 1974, see *Arab Report and Record* (December 1–16, 1974), p. 546.

55. *The Middle East and North Africa 1988*, 34th ed. (London: Europa Publications, 1987), p. 522; and Girgis B. Ghorbal, "OPEC: Its International Economic Significance, 1974–75," in Russell A. Stone, ed., *OPEC and the Middle East*, p. 79. It is ironic that by the late 1980s Kuwait was pushing so hard to change its OPEC's production quotas as high as it could, see *The Wall Street Journal* (June 12, 1989), pp. A1, A4.

56. United Nations, *General Assembly Plenary Meetings*, 29th Session, 2249th meeting (September 30, 1974), p. 309.

57. *Facts on File* (August 17, 1979), p. 605.

58. *Facts on File* (August 8, 1980), p. 592, and (October 10, 1980), pp. 761–762.

59. *The Washington Post* (August 16, 1983), pp. A7–A8, and (August 15, 1983), p. 1.

60. *Al-Qabas* (August 20, 1983), p. 4.

61. *Al-Qabas* (October 5, 1984), p. 19 and (March 2, 1985), p. 5; *Al-Watan* (January 8, 1985), p. 2; and information provided to the author by an anonymous source, (November 3, 1988).

62. *Al-Hadaf* (Kuwait) (March 11, 1965), p. 5; *Al-Qabas* (May 25, 1982), p. 2; and *Facts on File* (January 24, 1986), p. 32.

63. *Facts on File* (December 31, 1987), p. 1.

64. *Al-Watan* (December 21, 1988), pp. 1, 9, and (January 4, 1988), p. 2.

65. *Al-Qabas* (January 1, 1982), p. 6.

66. *Al-Watan* (January 20, 1988), p. 1. For the Palestinian community professional organizations in Kuwait see Laurie A. Brand, *Palestinians in the Arab World: Institution Building and the Search for State* (New York: Columbia University Press, 1988), pp. 107–148.

67. For the 1982 incident, see *Al-Taliat* (March 31, 1982), p. 12; and Lawrence Zirig, *The Middle East Political Dictionary*, pp. 113-114. For the 1988 incident, see *The Middle East Journal*, vol. 42, no. 3 (Summer 1988), p. 469. For a recent review of Palestinians in Kuwait see Alan Cowell, "For the Palestinians in Diaspora, Vision Fades but Won't Die," *The New York Times* (March 24, 1989), pp. A1, A6. Cowell claims that the number of Palestinians in Kuwait is between 350,000 to 380,000 and constitutes the biggest Palestinian concentration outside Israel, the occupied territories, and Jordan. Some 2,000 or so Palestinians have been granted Kuwaiti citizenship.

68. *Arab Report and Record* (June 1-15, 1969), p. 238, and (July 1–15, 1969), p. 281.

69. Majid Khadduri, *Socialist Iraq: A Study in Iraqi Politics since 1968* (Washington, D.C.: The Middle East Institute, 1978), p. 154.

70. Majid Khadduri, *Socialist Iraq*, p. 155; and *The Economist* (April 17, 1973), p. 29.

71. Robert Litwak, *Security in the Persian Gulf II: Source of Interstate Conflict*, p. 29.

72. Majid Khadduri, *Socialist Iraq*, p. 156.

73. Majid Khadduri, *Socialist Iraq*, p. 156; Adeed Dawisha, "Invoking the Spirit of Arabism: Islam in the Foreign Policy of Saddam's Iraq," in Adeed Dawisha, ed. *Islam in Foreign Policy* (Cambridge: Cambridge University Press, 1983), p. 116; *Al-Rai Al-Aam* (March 26, 1973), p. 3; SWB, ME/4250/i (March 21, 1973); and *London Times* (March 21, 1973), p. 1.

74. SWB/ME/4250/A/5 (March 21, 1973); and *Arab Report and Record* (December 1–15, 1974), p. 546.

75. The Iraqi foreign minister's interview with the Lebanese magazines *As-Sayyad* and *Al-Nahar*; see Foreign Broadcast Information Service, *Daily Report: Near East and Asia* (hereinafter cited as FBIS) (April 4, 1973), p. C2 and (March 27, 1973), p. C1. For Saudi support in 1973, see Nadav Safran, *Saudi Arabia: The Ceaseless Quest for Security* (Cambridge and London: The Belknap Press of Harvard University Press, 1985), pp. 126, 138, and 212.

76. FBIS (April 20, 1973), p. B7, and (April 5, 1973), p. B7; and *Al-Rai Al-Aam* (April 5, 1973), p. 1.

77. *Al-Rai Al-Aam* (November 27, 1973), p. 2, and FBIS, (February 11, 1974), p. C1.

78. FBIS (March 30, 1973), p. B2 and (March 30, 1973), p. E1; *The New York Times* (March 31, 1973), p. 10; *Al-Rai Al-Aam* (April 5, 1973), p. 1; and Anne M. Kelly, *The Soviet Naval Presence during the Iraq-Kuwait Border Dispute: March-April 1973* (Professional Paper #122, June 1974, Center for Naval Analyses), pp. 9–11.

79. Majid Khadduri, *Socialist Iraq*, p. 157; for the joint Kuwaiti-Iraq communiqué, see *FBIS* (August 23, 1973), pp. C2–C4.

80. Majid Khadduri, *Socialist Iraq*, p. 159; and Robert Litwak, *Security in the Persian Gulf II*, pp. 31–32.

81. David E. Long, *The Persian Gulf: An Introduction to Its People, Politics, and Economics* (Boulder, CO: Westview Press, 1976), p. 60.

82. For the text of the official Iraqi revolutionary Bath newspaper "Ath-Thawrah" article, see *FBIS* (March 23, 1973), p. C5; Interviews, Kuwait (March 29, 1988).

4

Ambivalence
and Tilting (1979–1986)

The regional developments of the late 1970s and the 1980s were not good omens for Kuwait. The Islamic revolution in Iran and the subsequent Iran-Iraq war had, still have, and probably will continue to have a profound impact on Kuwaiti politics. These and later events exposed the fragility of Kuwait's domestic structure and redefined its external outlook. Indeed, after a long period of internal security and external pragmatism, Kuwait reached the threshold of turmoil. For the first time since the foundation of the state, the hidden strains of communal life tested its structure and the society became more polarized. The country was engulfed in bombings and terrorist acts unprecedented in its history, acts for which the political regime found itself unpreprepared.

Externally, Kuwait's balanced, centrist foreign policy in regional affairs began to change. Its priorities changed to domestic and regional security; its direction began to tilt toward the moderate status quo regimes.

In this period Kuwait and the other Gulf states searched for security, stability, and national unity. In Kuwait, this search meant returning to parliamentary life, cracking down on the Shiites, joining a military "entente" (the Gulf Cooperation Council), realigning with Iraq, and finally inviting superpower protection in the Gulf through reflagging or chartering arrangements for its oil tankers (see next chapter).

The Islamic Revolution in Iran

Despite Kuwait's public opposition to the shah of Iran's stature as the guardian of foreign interests and powers in the Gulf, the shah was nevertheless, on balance, a supporter to Kuwait. He gave Kuwait room to maneuver in its dealings with the regional powers, as well as a sense of confidence that allowed it not to acquiesce to Iraq's wishes in the crises of 1961 and 1973, or to give in to other regional pressures. Iran's shah neutralized Kuwait's stronger neighbors. A case in point was the Kuwaiti government's reluctance, despite public outrage, to break its relations with Iran when the latter occupied the three Arab islands in the lower Gulf in late 1971. Kuwait merely and symbolically recalled its ambassador from Teheran. By the same token, Iran benefited from Kuwait's good relations with the so-called radical camp. When an Iranian F-14 was shot down over South Yemen, Iran requested that Kuwait mediate the release of the pilot and the return of the plane, the pilot, and the body of the co-pilot, who died in the crash.[1] In the late 1970s, during the shah's absence, Kuwait found itself caught between the two competing forces of Iraq and Saudi Arabia, and exposed to their demands and pressures.

Events in Iran in late 1978 and early 1979 therefore created a political "paranoia" inside Kuwait. For Iran had become a newer, larger Cuba, a source of religious and revolutionary contagion. The reactions of the government and the public were different, perhaps even diametrically opposed. The social fabric experienced far-reaching convulsions, indeed shock waves. The national harmony was shattered.[2]

Although the official reaction was ambivalent and lukewarm—the government stated that the events in Iran were internal in nature and should be dealt with in the Iranian context (i.e., they were none of Kuwait's business)—in fact, the Kuwaitis were equally anxious not to become involved and not to antagonize the shah. The authorities declined to admit Ayatollah Khomeini into the country in October 1978, and he was turned back at the border post on the Iraqi frontier. This act, in retrospect, may have paradoxically contributed to the worldwide publicity and prominence he received when he left for France. Khomeini may have indeed carried throughout his lifetime a personal animosity toward Kuwait.

In reality, the changes in Iran marked the beginning of a direct threat to the traditional status quo regimes of the Gulf. Despite their public pronouncements, the shah was able with Western armaments to keep the Gulf stable and secure from external intervention. The new Iranian regime's proclamation of disengagement in protecting the Gulf from outside forces aggravated the Gulf states' burden. The Iranian authorities contemptuously referred to the Gulf regimes as "mini-shahs," and Khoemeini described the traditional ruling families of the Gulf as practicing "the American Islam," or "the golden Islam."[3] More seriously, the demise of the shah's regime was viewed by the Kuwaiti government as the end of regional stability and internal contentment.

Kuwaiti public reaction to events in Iran was, in contrast, joyous and supportive. The Kuwaitis initially admired and felt proud of the Iranians for their courage and determination to topple one of the most tyrannical regimes of the region. Moreover, the collapse of the shah signaled the abilities of the indigenous people to overthrow the vestiges of foreign-supported regimes. The changes in Iran were a blow to the United States, which has been seen as the main enemy of Arab and Moslem nations and the supporter of Israel. The religious elements, both Sunni and Shiite, viewed the Iranian revolution as proof that Moslem nations could overthrow secular anti-Islamic regimes. It gave the beleaguered fundamentalist movements in the area the psychological boost and the political support they needed. In fact, Iran was seen as a model or prototype of popular Islam, genuine Islam based on Quranic principles and the people's rule.[4]

Developments in Iran had immeasurable impact on the Shiite groups in Kuwait in particular. In general, the merchant class was skeptical, seeing dire implications in the situation in Iran. The merchants' cultural affinities were with the shah and his protégés, and their commercial interests would be harmed. Locally, their booming business might be affected if local tension were incited. But the overwhelming majority of the Shiites, who are mostly middle-class, were sympathetic with their brethren in Iran. The changes in Iran fostered a new assertiveness, pride and consciousness among most Shiites, who as a minority have historically felt themselves to be down-trodden, underprivileged, and subordinated to the Sunni majorities in the Gulf states.[5]

Unlike their parents and older generations, who tended to be submissive and acquiesce in the status quo, the new generation of Shiites seek to be treated as equals, with the same rights, privileges, and obligations as the Sunnis. Most of the Sunnis, however, particularly those of Wahhabi and fundamentalist affiliations, look at Shiites as "inferior," "less godly," "less loyal," and "untrustworthy"—in short, a fifth column for Iran. In essence, mutual distrust between the two sects is deeply ingrained in their history of conflicting claims over the Caliphate of the Moslems. In addition, Arab nationalists view Iranian Shiism as a form of tainted Islam, a cover behind which hides Persian nationalism—historically a mortal enemy of the Arab nation.

The new Shiite consciousness shocked and dismayed the Sunnis and the political regime, since the Shiites had always been loyal and "submissive." The new consciousness identifies Kuwaiti Shiites' kinship with Shiites in Iran. Thus the social division between the two sects in Kuwait took a political dimension, and the issue of Shiism was politicized. It was at first thought that the only Shiite legal body in Kuwait, *Al-Jamiat Al-Thakafiat Il-Ijtimiah* (the cultural and social society) could form a nucleus to integrate Kuwaiti Shiites as a major political force. However, since the society was run by the Shiite fundamentalists and became a proxy of revolutionary Iran, and since the majority of Kuwait's Shiites are loyal citizens, the society proved to be a source of disintegration and friction.

The Kuwaiti Shiites' grudges are not a new phenomenon. They date back to the short-lived representative assemblies of the 1920s and 1930s, which excluded the Shiites from participation and did not consider them as full-fledged Kuwaiti citizens. Yet the Shiites have always been supporters of the royal family against antiregime factions. There is a kind of schizophrenia within Kuwait; Shiites of Persian stock are not accepted as Arabs, either because they themselves have been reluctant to assimilate or because the Sunni Arabs have been reluctant to accept them as full-fledged Arabs even though they are accepted as Kuwaiti citizens. Kuwaiti Sunnis of Persian stock, on the other hand, who were considered outcasts until the 1960s, have now become accepted as Arab Kuwaitis. In fact, some Arabs think that Shiites of Persian origin refused to assimilate because they felt superior, as Indo-European Aryans to the Arab "Semites." Additionally, the pride of the old Persian glory makes the assimilation process much more complicated. On the other hand, the nationalists distrust the Shiites because of the latter's support for the regime.

The triumphs of Shiism in Iran against the shah and the United States fueled a Shiite consciousness in the Gulf in general and in Kuwait in particular. The Shiites' victory was unprecedented in their contemporary history, with its memories of submissiveness, and acquired a symbolism comparable only to Imam Hussein's martyrdom in Karbala.

The political system had in recent years ignored or underestimated the differences and antagonism between Sunnis and Shiites, and had tried to ignore discrimination and prejudice. It is true that in Kuwait discrimination against Shiites is much less marked than in the rest of the Gulf states. Indeed, it is not discrimination in the classical sense, but rather a lack of trust in the Shiites' word and behavior. Lately, jobs in the armed forces, security, and other fields have been off-limits to them, for example. But the problem, unfortunately, is much deeper than this; its origins go back to the historical split in religion, a split that never healed, thereby creating two separate communities, each with its own customs, habits, courts, manners, etc. To most Sunnis, the Shiites are renegades and rebels who cannot be trusted until they become Moslems, i.e., Sunnis. In effect, there is no organized discrimination but rather tacit and sometimes officially tolerated relative discrimination.

Moreover, since the new regime in Teheran considered itself anti-Israel and offered the Palestinians moral, political, and financial support, the traditional regimes of the Gulf, including Kuwait, feared Palestinian-Iranian-local Shiite conspiracies, and were keen in taking measures to prevent them.[6]

Meanwhile, a new, less potent external threat to the Gulf states emerged from the Soviet invasion of Afghanistan. The Kuwaiti reaction was less emotional and more pragmatic than that of the other Gulf regimes, which feared the communist ideology and Soviet penetration through the Afghani back door. Kuwait's foreign minister, Sabah Al-Ahmad, stressed Kuwait's mutual distrust of both superpowers: "while objecting to the use of force by the U.S. in the region, Kuwait also stresses its opposition to Soviet involvement in Afghanistan."[7] He also called for a "peaceful and just solution" based on the UN resolution, which emphasized "the withdrawal of foreign troops . . . the right of . . . self-determination and the establishment of a political system . . . without any foreign intervention."[8]

Kuwait was thus able to advance its Islamic foreign policy without endangering its pan-Arabist orientation and global centrism. Kuwait took a number of actions to support Pakistan economically, through aid and through the establishment of joint ventures to strengthen its capabilities to halt the communist advances (see Chapter 3). Furthermore, Kuwait tolerated and indeed encouraged private institutions' economic, medical, and humanitarian aid to the Afghan refugees and the Mujahedeen resistance. The powerful fundamentalist elements in Kuwait provided sanctuary to the Mujahedeen supporters, and it was even reported that some Kuwaitis had fought alongside the Mujahedeen in Afghanistan, and died there.[9]

This balanced policy satisfied both the nationalist and the fundamentalist forces domestically, and reflected the Islamic dimensions of the regime's foreign policy. In addition, it showed Kuwait's noncommittal policies toward the superpowers.

In response to the regional changes, the political regime in Kuwait began a domestic policy of "guns and butter," or a "reformist" approach toward the population.[10] In February 1980, the government set up a 35-member committee to propose the revision of the constitution and called for the election of the National Assembly, which had been suspended since the summer of 1976. However, the government gerrymandered the electoral precincts, thus eliminating large Shiite and nationalist representation, and conversely increasing the progovernment traditional elements in the assembly. As a result of the 1981 election, Shiites won four of the fifty seats in the assembly (and one became a minister), as compared to ten in the last (1975) election. Their power was diminished over sixty percent compared with their leverage in the earlier assembly. In fact, the Shiite landslide in the 1975 election had caused the government to institute a tradition of appointing one Shiite minister to each cabinet.

Moreover, the government reorganized the internal police force as a result of its new security concerns. Twenty-six high-ranking police officers went into early retirement in fall 1979, and the regime gradually demoted or eliminated the Shiites from sensitive security and military positions.[11] Henceforth, the upper echelon of the security forces was to be composed entirely of reliable loyalist elements.

The first test of the government challenge to the Shiites came in September 1979, when, apparently in conjunction with other Gulf states, Kuwait stripped Sayed Abbas Mohri, Khomeini's special spiritual representative in Kuwait, of his citizenship, and eventually expelled him and eighteen members of his family.[12] In addition, the passports of three prominent Shiites were withdrawn. They were charged with stirring up unrest among the Kuwaiti Shiites by holding political meetings in a mosque.[13] An Iranian newspaper, referring to Mohri's ouster, declaimed that the spread of Islamic revolution cannot be suppressed by threats, expulsions, etc.[14]

The Iranian revolution gave the Kuwaiti Shiites, and to a lesser degree the nationalists and the Palestinians, a way to express their grievance in an open, public forum. The government therefore feared that these events might be a prelude to domestic uprisings. As a result, it moved swiftly to erode the grassroots of their gatherings. Later on, the government banned private meetings of more than twenty persons, in order to prevent any possible political agitations.

The result of these policies was, among other things, an alarming pattern of political unrest in Kuwait. Violence and protests reached an apex (see Appendix C). In 1978, two cases of political unrest were reported, in 1979, four, and in 1980, seventeen, of which eleven had Iranian connections. Some observers downplayed these activities as "the passage to terror."[15] On November 12, 1980, for the first time ever, Iran directly attacked a Kuwaiti border post: two Iranian aircraft bombed the post at Abdali.

As internal stability worsened in the mid-1980s and as Kuwaiti Shiites began to be involved in a series of bombings, the security forces began to raise slogans such as "every citizen is on the watch," and set up new neighborhood watch groups in the country.[16] Some observers feared that these groups might serve as "collective vigilantes." Moreover, as a precautionary measure, hundreds and thousands of undesirable expatriates were expelled from the country in the 1980s. By November 1987, some 26,898 people had been deported for security reasons.[17]

In a reflection of Kuwait's dual policy to contain domestic unrest and eradicate its external roots, and to build better working relations and maintain a bridge of official contact with Teheran, the Kuwaiti foreign minister, Sabah Al-Ahmad, was the first Gulf state foreign minister to visit Teheran in July 1979. The purpose of the trip was ostensibly to congratulate the new regime in Teheran, to discuss Gulf security, and to improve Arab-Iranian relations.[18] The foreign minister expressed the belief that the visit would make "our relations . . . better than today."[19] Some observers, however, speculated that the Kuwaiti delegation came back disappointed at its talks with Iranian officials.[20] Meanwhile a "people's delegation," most of whose members were Kuwaiti Shiites, visited Iran to congratulate the new regime.

As a further sign of goodwill, in the early 1980s Kuwait sent humanitarian aid (medicine and food) for the victims of floods in southern Iran. In addition, Kuwait agreed in 1980 to supply Iran with refined oil products, especially kerosene, and to establish oil and technical cooperation between the two countries.[21]

Kuwait continued to emphasize diplomacy as a channel for influencing Iran's attitude toward the Gulf states. In April 1980, the Iranian foreign minister, Sadeq Qotbzadeh, visited Kuwait, but it seems that little if any change resulted from the visit, though it kept diplomatic dialogue open between the two neighboring states. And despite American pressures to impose economic sanctions on Iran during the hostage crisis, when Kuwait was a member of the Security Council, Kuwait "opposed" an economic boycott, "condemned" the American rescue mission in Iran, and "deplored" the freezing of Iranian assets.[22]

The Iran-Iraq War (1980–1988)

Despite its initial reservations towards the new Islamic theocracy in Iran, Kuwait had sought to find a means of dialogue or a modus vivendi with Teheran. Teheran's emphasis on exporting the Islamic revolution to the Gulf notwithstanding, Kuwait could not afford a confrontation with any of its neighbors. Kuwait's rulers had thought that the revolution could confine its slogans and influences to its own boundaries and be able to coexist with the traditional Gulf regimes. However, domestic insurgency and turmoil weakened the ability of the central government in Teheran to deal effectively with its neighbors. The sudden war between Iran and Iraq reshifted the focus of the Iranian government. Kuwait was surprised by the magnitude of the all-out Iraqi conventional attacks on Iran. Iraq's prior consultations with the Gulf regimes concerning its relations with Iran had not been a sufficient signal of things to come. The war's importance to Kuwait became obvious when the Kuwaiti foreign minister, Sabah Al-Ahmad, who was en route to the annual UN General Assembly meetings in New York, returned home, thus forfeiting Kuwait's main speech to the United Nations in 1980.

The Iran-Iraq war was viewed in different ways within Kuwait.[23] On the positive side, the war had diverted the attention of two hostile states away from Kuwait. The traditionally hostile state of Iraq would have to shift its emphasis to other fronts and issues, and the war's consequences might weaken and subdue it altogether, while the newly hostile regime of Iran was engaged in a war that might drain its revolutionary fervor. Nevertheless, the war would have dire consequences for Kuwait. First, the war zone was less than 150 miles from the center of Kuwait City, and bombardment echoes and smoke could be heard and seen in Kuwait. The war dampened an already depressed national mood and social relationships. Second, any position that the government took would eventually alienate a domestic constituency, and perhaps regional forces as well. Third, Kuwait's well-being and economic prosperity depended in part on the re-export of commerce with the two combatants and on smooth shipment of its oil crude. In fact, it has been reported that Kuwait's trade shrank by one-third as a result of the war. Finally, the war could have had unpredictable, but potentially dire spill-overs into Kuwait and the Gulf region. The worst-case scenario of a domino theory began to appear possible in 1982, after the Iranians expelled the Iraqis from Iranian territories and pursued them into Iraqi territories. The Gulf states feared that if Iraq fell, the rest of the Gulf states might follow in its steps, and foremost among these states would be Kuwait. Iraq was viewed as the front line against Iranian inroads, with Kuwait next in line.

Kuwait therefore faced critical choices and walked a delicate tightrope. It officially maintained "strict" neutrality, while unofficially and covertly being sympathetic toward and supportive of Iraq in a variety of ways.

Kuwait stuck to its 1972 and 1978 transit agreements with Iraq, thus allowing commercial and "military" equipment to be transshipped through Kuwaiti ports to Baghdad. The agreement justified Kuwait's role, and the Iraqi use of piers in Shuwaikh and Shuaiba ports mitigated Iraqi demands for deep-water facilities. In addition, under Iraqi pressure and as part of the Gulf states' subsidy to the Iraqi war effort, Kuwait extended a total of $13.2 billion in noncollectable "financial-political" subsidies between 1980 and 1988 (see Chapter 3). Of this amount, $6 billion was in direct cash forms. Moreover, when Syria shut the Iraqi oil pipelines through its territories in late 1982, Kuwait and Saudi Arabia agreed to sell some 300,000–350,000 barrels per day of oil from their neutral zone on behalf of Iraq.[24] From 1983 to 1988, it was estimated that Kuwait's share from this "war relief subsidy" reached some $7.2 billion. In addition, it was reported that the Kuwaiti government compensated Kuwaiti merchants for works carried and unpaid for in Iraq, and that Kuwait paid up to 10 percent of the Iraqi contractual obligations to British companies.[25]

Further signs of a Kuwaiti tilt toward Iraq were evident in the vituperative tone of propaganda and media warfare. Kuwaiti newspapers and other media were quite uncategorically biased in favor of Iraq and tended to give a one-sided interpretation of the war and its developments. It is conceivable that the favorable climate of opinion in the Kuwaiti press towards Iraq was the product of conviction and Arab nationalism, but it is also possible that the Kuwaiti press was either intimidated by fear of reprisals or bribed.

Kuwait's unequivocal siding with Iraq took on a new dimension, however, when Kuwaiti merchant and oil ships became prey to Iranian attacks. The first known Iranian attack on Kuwaiti ships occurred right at the start of the war, in September 1980 (see Appendix C). However, the most far-reaching attacks were against Kuwaiti oil tankers in May 1984. As a result, on May 21, 1984, the GCC states complained to the UN Security Council against Iranian attacks on commercial ships en route to and from the ports of Kuwait and Saudi Arabia. The council passed a resolution reaffirming "the right of free navigation in international waters for shipping en route to and from all states not parties to the hostilities." By end of 1987, eleven vessels under the Kuwaiti flag had been attacked by Iran.[26]

But Kuwait's worst nightmares came true in February 1986, when Iran occupied the Faw peninsula, less than 10 miles away from Kuwaiti territory. This action posed for the first time a direct Iranian military and political threat to Kuwait, worsening its "siege mentality." After the occupation of the Faw, the speaker of the Iranian parliament, Hasheimi Rafsanjani, proclaimed, referring to the Gulf states' subsidies, that Iran would not continue to "tolerate the berthing of ships at your ports with military hardware for the Iraqi regime." His warning to Kuwait was explicit: "we figured it was necessary for them to see our troops across the waters."[27] Despite the official Iranian assurances that "Kuwait would not become embroiled in its war with Iraq provided that it maintain military neutrality,"[28] Kuwait's foreign minister, Sabah Al-Ahmad, echoed Kuwait's real fear: "the Iranians are not far from Kuwait. Go to Bubiyan and you can see them with your own eyes. This situation of course forms a danger to Kuwait."[29]

The pattern of Kuwait's political, financial, media, and other popular support for Iraq upset Iran and alienated a large segment of the Shiite community in Kuwait. Iranian harassment, intimidation, and attacks on Kuwait and Kuwaiti interests in order to destabilize the country jumped drastically. Iran utilized a network of Arab and Kuwaiti sympathizers to carry out threats and actual violent attacks against Kuwait. Up to this point, Kuwait's domestic life had been tranquil and peaceful over a span of eighteen years (1961–1978); with the revolution and the war, political protests, sabotage, and violence rose at an alarming rate.

A total of 170 politically motivated protests and violent acts were reported in the period 1961–1988, not to mention several cases involving, among other things, underground distribution of leaflets against state security (see Appendix C). Between 1961 and 1978, only thirty-three cases of political violence took place, or 1.8 cases per year; whereas between 1979 and June 1989, 137 cases were reported, or an average of 12.45 cases per year—over a sixfold increase. The peak of violence occurred in 1987 (26 cases, or 15.29 percent of the twenty-eight year total). One reason for this increase, besides local dissension and the Iran-Iraq war, was the Iranian response to Kuwait's alignment with and invitation to the superpowers to protect its oil tankers (see next chapter). The 1980s cases showed the emergence of Kuwaiti conspirators as well as victims. In all, between 1961 and June 1989, 43 people died and 177 persons were wounded in political violence in Kuwait. In the period 1961–1978, seven died and five were injured; while in the period 1979–1989, thirty-six were killed and 172 were wounded. In addition, on several occasions, either an undetermined number or "several dozen" people were wounded.

Of these incidents, one of the most dramatic was the December 12, 1983, set of attacks against the American and French embassies and five Kuwaiti economic facilities. Five people died, and 63 were wounded. The pro-Iran Islamic Jihad claimed responsibility. Seventeen people, mostly Iraqi Shiites, were arrested in connection with these incidents.[30] Kuwait's crown prince and prime minister, Saad Al-Abdullah, vowed to punish those responsible and to "purify the country of all suspects who exploited its hospitality."[31] The most serious attack, however, was the May 25, 1985 assassination attempt on the motorcade of the Kuwaiti Amir, Jaber-Al-Ahmad. Three people died, and fifteen more were wounded. The Islamic Jihad claimed responsibility for this senseless attack. A number of Iraqi Shiites were arrested and charged with this act.

But the most daring threat to the security of the state was the widely publicized hijacking of the Kuwaiti airliner *Al-Jabriyah*, in April 1988, in which two Kuwaitis were cold-bloodedly murdered. The plane zigzagged to three countries for 17 consecutive days. The hijackers' identities remain unknown, though they claimed Iranian support.[32]

Several acts of violence during the 1980s were the work of an obscure group, the "Revolutionary Organization-Forces of the Prophet Mohammed in Kuwait."[33] It seems that these acts were committed with the support of outside powers. And given the displeasure of the Iranians and their supporters with Kuwaiti aid to Iraq, it is highly probable that most of the 1980s violence had moral and logistical support either from the Iranian government or from the revolutionary forces.[34]

There are a number of explanations for the pattern of political protests and violence between 1961 and 1988. The scope and intensity of violence increased dramatically after the Iran-Iraq war in 1980. The early violent incidents were related to inter-Arab political clashes and Palestinian feuding, whereas the later cases were related to Kuwait's position and policies vis-à-vis regional conflicts and its internal problems. It is estimated that a Palestinian group, headed by Abu Nidal (Sabry Al-Banna), committed five acts of terrorism in Kuwait during the period 1973–1986. The 1960s cases involved Kuwaiti Sunni members of Arab nationalist movements. They were charged, tried, imprisoned, and eventually pardoned.[35] The 1980s cases involved Kuwaiti Shiites who were sympathetic to Iran and members of the Shiite fundamentalist elements. Most were arrested, charged, and tried. But, the involvement of Kuwaiti Shiites further polarized an already strained society. Public support for the two combatants of the war was based more or less on sectarian and ethnic background: the Sunnis and Arabs supported Iraq, while the Shiites and some Kuwaitis of Persian stock supported or sympathized with Iran. The Shiites, because of their support for non-Arab Iran and their involvement in terrorist acts, were viewed as a fifth column, an untrusted, unloyal minority that cared little for the survival of the state or, indeed, of the Arab nation.[36] Needless to say, the Kuwaiti mass media played a major role in whipping up emotional frenzy and mass hysteria.

Some of the terrorist acts targeted Kuwait's economic and industrial infrastructure, such as oil refineries, etc. An example is the May 22, 1987, sabotage at Kuwait's huge $5 billion Al-Ahmadi oil refinery. Kuwait's oil minister, Ali Al-Khalifa, explained Kuwait's fear of subversion at oil installations: "Oil fields are both extremely difficult to defend and, once attacked, extremely difficult to operate afterward."[37] Clearly, in this case, the terrorists' aim was not only to cripple the financial and economic capabilities of the state but also to destroy lives, as water desalinization plants and generation of electricity are dependent on these refineries.

A number of these attacks were meant to cause indiscriminate human suffering, such as the July 11, 1987, bombing at popular seafront cafes, in which dozens of people were killed and wounded. The goal of this and similar acts was perhaps to put popular pressure on the government to modify its policies on certain issues. Kuwait's foreign minister, Sabah Al-Ahmad, acknowledged that "Kuwait . . . had been repeatedly exposed to the war fall-out," and moreover, that it had "been subjected to a series of . . . blind terrorist attacks." On the other hand, the foreign minister downplayed the series of bombings in Kuwait: "The incidence of bombings has become a symptom of the modern world's epidemic. They will not affect life in Kuwait."[38] The evolution of the terrorist acts during the 1980s leads one to believe that they demonstrated disapproval of Kuwaiti policies by a fraction of the people, rather than reflecting substantive ideological cleavages. Terrorism did not fundamentally alter the minds and behavior of the people who continued to display their characteristically passive and fatalistic attitudes and mannerisms. It did, however, alter the reactions and responses of the government, which became more forceful than its traditional paternalistic patterns. Finally, contrary to the assumption that external threats would unify the internal forces, the 1980s challenges to Kuwait unfortunately fragmented the citizens into opposing factions.

A number of plausible explanations might justify the Kuwaiti position vis-à-vis the Iran-Iraq war. The regime was fearful of an Iranian victory that might undermine the status quo regimes and might involve Islamic fundamentalism. Second, Kuwait's Arab identification seemed to necessitate concrete help to the besieged regime in Baghdad; Islamic values and identification with Iran became secondary considerations. Third, concern over regional and external factors subordinated concern over local Shiite reaction. The government's calculations concerning the broader regional implications of an Iranian Islamic victory were nightmarish to say the least. This factor alone outweighed any other considerations. It was assumed that domestic Shiite reaction could be checked and contained, whereas an Iranian victory would be beyond even several nations' capabilities to control. In fact, in the event that an Iranian victory should take place, some Middle Easterners feared that a Fertile Crescent of Shiism would be created by the forced unification of Iran-Iraq-Syria and Lebanon. Fourth, the overwhelming majority of the Sunnis in Kuwait, particularly those with economic influence, supported Iraq. In general, the Shiites have had minor influence on decision-making in Kuwait compared with the Sunnis, since they "have rarely been able to advance into powerful political offices, to gain a voice in making key national decisions, or hold sensitive jobs."[39] In fact, the authorities' preoccupation with the Shiite issue has, in the words of one expert, prevented them from addressing "the much broader and more serious challenge posed by the growing reassertion of Popular Islam in general."[40] As a result Sunni fundamentalist movements, with some official blessing, had an almost free hand in conducting a campaign of influence, "brainwashing," and intimidation among the population. In fact, as they became more powerful they began to interfere in the arena of individual behavior, prescribing both rewards and punishments within the political system.

Lastly, the Kuwaiti regime assumed that in secular Iraq it would be dealing with the relatively predictable, increasingly pragmatist regime of Saddam Hussein, whereas the theocratic Khomeini regime was made up of unpredictable ideologues. Thus the Kuwaitis hoped that in one stroke they would be able to court the Iraqi regime and, once the war was over, settle the border issue. Domestically, aid to Iraq would satisfy the demands of Arab nationalists, fundamentalist Sunnis, and the powerful Chamber of Commerce members. The commercial interests were looking forward to receiving contracts after the war, or to being reimbursed for unpaid contracts; the Iraqi first deputy premier, Yassin Ramadan, warned foreign companies that those which "showed reluctance," and "fell short in their commitment to Iraq . . . [have] damaged their own interests as they will miss future opportunities."[41]

State survival meant redefining priorities and realigning the nation, even with a former antagonist. After all, the war had perforce readjusted the priorities of Kuwaiti foreign policy to national security issues; i.e., internal security and the security of the Gulf. In fact, there has been a sort of "retrenchment" in Kuwait's activity in larger inter-Arab affairs, in comparison with the 1960s and the 1970s. These developments elevated Gulf politics as the core of Kuwait's foreign and domestic policies, whereas other inter-

Arab relationships were marginalized. At this stage, the primary foreign policy goal was the state's survival and its military security.

Despite Iranian intimidation and Kuwait's "alliance" with Iraq, Kuwait and the GCC states tried unsuccessfully to mediate the war between Iran and Iraq. On May 16 and 17, 1983, the Kuwaiti and UAE foreign ministers visited Teheran and Baghdad. However, this effort proved fruitless, partly because Iran feared that Kuwait was about to hand over the Warba and Bubiyan islands to Iraq.[42] An Iranian newspaper claimed that if Bubiyan went to Iraq, then Failaka should go to Iran.[43] Iraq, on the other hand, feared that the Gulf states would try to maintain a close dialogue with Iran, leaving Baghdad to fight individually. In point of fact, many Arab states in the lower Gulf have had a business "bonanza" with Iran during the war years.

But despite Kuwait's official nonbelligerency, it was by virtue of its assistance a de facto or functional ally of Iraq. In short, Kuwait was "making loans to Iraq, allowing Iraqi aircraft to penetrate Kuwaiti airspace on their way to attack Iranian shipping and allowing weapons and munitions destined for Iraq to pass through its ports."[44] The Kuwaiti foreign minister, Sabah Al-Ahmad, admitted that Iraqi aircraft overflew Kuwaiti territories in Khor Abdullah for 20 seconds.[45] Some Kuwaiti officials rationalized Kuwait's aid to Iraq as required by the Arab Defense Pact.[46]

In fact, the Iranians repeatedly warned the Arab states, through diplomatic channels, public media, Friday sermons, subversion, and direct attack, that support to Iraq in any form was tantamount to declaring war against Iran. On March 30, 1987, Iran sent a special emissary to Kuwait to discuss bilateral issues, the Iran-Iraq war, and above all the maltreatment of Kuwaiti Moslems (i.e., Shiites).[47] The emissary was requested to leave the country and stop meddling in Kuwait's internal affairs, since these Shiites were citizens of Kuwait. Besides the direct pressures, it was alleged that Iran had asked the United States through the Iran-Contra affair to put pressure on Kuwait to release 17 Shiite terrorists who were imprisoned in Kuwait, charged with the December 1983 bombings. The Kuwaiti foreign minister, Sabah Al-Ahmad, reacting to these rumors, stated in January 1987, "We were never asked and if we had been asked we would have refused because it's an internal matter."[48]

The Gulf Cooperation Council (GCC)

Kuwait realized that for small, powerless political units, coordination and cooperation are perhaps among the best means of survival in a turbulent political world. Therefore, it embarked on and indeed propagated a policy of "cooperation" among the regional states of the Gulf, but more in diplomacy than in military affairs. After Britain announced its plans to withdraw from the Gulf by the early 1970s, Kuwait was instrumental in settling the Bahraini issue and in creating the United Arab Emirates. Kuwait emphasized all along that the security of the Gulf region is the Gulf states' responsibility, and vehemently objected to outside interference in the security of the littoral states. During the shah of Iran's visit to Kuwait in November 1969, mutual cooperation was pronounced as a goal and there was call for continued stability in the region.[49] In a 1981 speech before the United Nations General Assembly, Kuwait's foreign minister, Sabah Al-Ahmad, reiterated that "the responsibility of the security and protection of the Gulf lies with the Gulf states alone . . . [Kuwait opposes] policies which try to make people believe that the area needs some kind of foreign military presence, whether it be so-called [Rapid Deployment] Force, or in the form of military facilities in certain areas."[50]

In the mid-1970s the Kuwaiti ruler, Jaber Al-Ahmad, then crown prince and prime minister, advocated that a venue be created for collective work with the rest of the Gulf states. In May 1976, he called for Gulf unity, "in order to achieve cooperation in the fields of politics, economics, education, and information. To find a kind of union or unity built on just and solid bases for the sake of the people of the Gulf and the security of the region."[51] The Kuwaiti statement became a major guideline for subsequent political moves toward cooperation.

Many bilateral and multilateral agreements between the various Gulf states were concluded in the 1960s and 1970s in the fields of economics, politics, and social and cultural affairs. An important meeting took place in Muscat in 1976 among the foreign ministers of the eight Gulf states, to discuss the issue of Gulf regional security, but little progress was reported, primarily because of divergences particularly between the Iranians and the Iraqis.[52] Some tangible cooperative enterprises were achieved in nonpolitical fields, such as the creation of a Gulf Marine Environmental Protection Agency and the Arab Gulf States Educational Organization.

Yet, as pressure mounted and regional politics took different turns, Kuwait, being sandwiched between the two combatants of the Iran-Iraq war, realized that it could not individually protect itself against external threats, let alone internal subversion.[53] The revolution in Teheran and the Gulf war set in motion an accelerating coordination among the traditional status quo regimes of the Gulf, left little room for doubts or reservations about the viability of collective security, and institutionalized the informal cooperation. Thus the Gulf Cooperation Council (GCC) was born out of both a genuine desire for coordination and the exigencies of realpolitik, to shield the member states as well as their societies from unconventional threats.

In December 1978, Kuwait's crown prince and prime minister, Saad Al-Abdullah, paid a visit to the six Gulf Arab states to "discuss means of Gulf cooperation," in light of the absence of Egypt in inter-Arab politics, the instabilities in Iran, and the increased significance of the Gulf region to the world. A number of bilateral visits and meetings between officials from Kuwait and the other Gulf states ensued. The foreign ministers of the six Arab states met at Taif, Saudi Arabia, October 14–16, 1979. The meeting reportedly discussed "mutual defense and political stability" as a result of Iranian threats to the six states and possible threats to the lifeline of their stability and prosperity: oil shipping routes.[54]

After extensive consultations, on February 4 and March 8, 1981, the foreign ministers of Bahrain, Kuwait, Oman, Qatar, Saudi Arabia, and the United Arab Emirates met in Riyadh and Muscat respectively to make final plans for the GCC. On May 25, 1981, the Gulf Cooperation Council was officially set up by the heads of the six Gulf states in their meeting in Abu Dhabi, out of "recognition that special relationship, similar characters, and political identification bind [these states] together. Its goal is to generate coordination in all fields of economic and social spheres, and to achieve coordination, integration and linkages in all fields."[55]

Structurally, the new organization is made up of the Supreme Council, which consists of the heads of the states; the ministerial council, which is composed of the foreign ministers of the GCC; and the Secretariat-General, which handles the day-to-day administration of the regional organization.

In fact, the traditional states' cooperation goes back a long way before such formal agreements. It was reported that Kuwait dispersed some of its 36 A4-H Skyhawk fighter bombers to Saudi Arabia, Bahrain, and the UAE in the aftermath of the Iraqi threats to Kuwait in 1973. Likewise, Saudi Arabia dispatched thousands of its troops to the Kuwaiti-Saudi border to bolster Kuwait's defenses that year. These patterns unequivocally represented the beginning of an informally operative Gulf security system, without formal agreements.[56]

Contrary to public expectation, one of the first substantive acts of the GCC was to develop mutual defense structures including "rapid development force, air defense, transport and procurement. This was reinforced by internal security pacts" between Saudi Arabia and all Gulf states except Kuwait. Kuwait declined because of public outrage and protests from the National Assembly, which feared that the intrusion of Gulf states security forces into Kuwait might harm Kuwait's unique political and cultural system and jeopardize its balanced policies towards other regional states.[57] Initiatives had been taken towards a collective air defense system based on Saudi Arabia's AWACS radar and C-3 capabilities, from which Kuwait had already benefited on an ad hoc basis.[58] Joint military exercises among the six states augmented: in November 1983, air maneuvers involving Kuwaiti and Saudi troops; in February and April 1984, Oman-UAE air force exercises; in April 1984, Kuwaiti-Bahraini-Qatari-Saudi air exercises; in January 1985 Kuwaiti-Qatari naval exercises; in March 1985, Kuwaiti-Omani air maneuvers; in April 1985, Saudi-Kuwaiti naval exercises, and in November 1988, joint GCC states' air maneuvers in Kuwait. Moreover, in mid-1983 the GCC created a joint strike force, the "Peninsula Shield," its "symbolic" rapid deployment force of 10,000 troops stationed in Hafr al-Batin in northeastern Saudi Arabia and earmarked from the six states.[59]

Kuwait's desire to be involved in a military "alliance" with the Gulf states emanated not only from growing political threats to its existence, but also from a realistic assessment of its actual military capabilities. Kuwait began to realize that its small, relatively powerless armed forces were not capable of dealing with the stronger, more zealous forces of its larger neighbors, particularly Iran and Iraq. Kuwait's meager military forces consisted of 600 men by the mid-1950s; 2000–2500 by 1961, the year of independence; 7000–8000 in 1966; 10,000–12,000 by 1979; and approximately 15,000 to 18,000 by the end of 1988. Some 7,000 to 10,000 paramilitary troops (national guards and police) complement these forces, in addition to some 5,000 to 7,000 reserves. The total number of reserves and paramilitary is roughly 15,000 to 17,000 persons.[60]

Kuwait's concern about its military capabilities, both quantitatively and qualitatively, became a focal point in the mid-1970s, as a result of Iraqi threats and as a part of total national development schemes. Kuwait initiated a three-pronged military expansion and modernization policy: military conscription, the first such program in a Gulf Arab state; construction of new military facilities; and acquisition of modern military hardware. The first seven-year Defense Development Program, enacted by the National Assembly in 1976 and budgeted at some $1.5 billion, set military service periods at 9 to 18 months, depending on the level of education attained by the draftees; called for the establishment of a naval base and a military college; and authorized arms purchases from a variety of sources. In order to implement the plan, beginning in March 1978, the government built a new military complex outside Kuwait City at a cost of over $100 million, its first naval base at a cost of about $30 million, and two air force bases.[61]

Kuwait's commitment to its military infrastructure has mushroomed. Since the 1970s the regime's commitment to the defense sector has been expressed through two fiscal means, the regular annual budget and the extra supplementary budget. The former includes salaries, wages, services, transport, construction, and the purchase of goods and arms, whereas the latter is intended solely for military procurement, and has been requested on an intermittent basis. In the past the arms budget was relatively stable; it rarely took an enormous leap. The annual military budget has increased from $21.9 million at the time of independence in 1961/62 to an estimated $1.5 billion by 1988/89 (all figures are given at the 1987 exchange rate; see Table 4.1). The total of military budgets from 1961/62 through 1988/89 is $11.86 billion, with an average yearly expenditure of $423.77 million. Military expenditures jumped dramatically in fiscal year 1975/76, after the Iraqi crisis of 1973, from $148.5 million to $247.0 million, a rise over 60 percent; and again in 1980/81 and in 1986/87, because of Iranian threats, from $531.6 million to $731.6 million, and from $1.0 billion to $1.4 billion, an increase of 72.6 percent in each case. Military outlays made up some 1.0 percent of GNP in 1961/62, 8.3 percent in 1972/73, 9.2 percent in 1986/87, and about 8.1 percent in 1988/89. Since the first government request for additional funds to cover military purchases was made in 1973, a number of supplementary budgets have been approved: $1.5 billion in 1973, $2.8 billion in 1976, $1.5 billion in 1977, $1.8 billion in 1981, and $5.5 billion in 1988.[62] The total supplementary military allocations reached $13.1 billion. If one adds these additional funds to the regular military budgets since 1961, Kuwait's total military spending reaches some $24.96 billion or an average of $891.63 million per year since independence.

TABLE 4.1 Military Budgets (Including National Guards) Fiscal Years 1961/62-1988/89

	Kuwaiti Dinars (Million current)	ME/ GNP	$ Million (1987 current)	Armed Forces (000)	Armed Forces per 1000 people
1961/62	6.1	1.0	21.9	2	6.2
1962/63	6.8	1.1	24.4	2	5.4
1963/64	13.2	1.8	47.5	2	5.1
1964/65	12.5	1.9	45.0	2	5.0
1965/66	10.5	1.9	37.8	8	17.0
1966/67	13.00	1.9	46.8	8	16.3
1967/68	21.09	2.9	75.9	8	14.5
1968/69	24.00	2.9	86.3	10	16.6
1969/70	25.69	2.8	92.4	10	15.3
1970/71	26.00	8.9	93.5	10	13.5
1971/72	30.39	8.2	109.3	14	17.9
1972/73	32.04	8.3	115.3	14	17.5
1973/74	38.74	8.1	139.4	14	15.6
1974/75	41.29	6.2	148.5	15	16.7
1975/76	68.70	7.2	247.1	15	15.6
1976/77	93.08	6.6	334.8	15	15.6
1977/78	105.48	7.3	379.4	10	9.1
1978/79	93.95	6.6	337.9	11	8.3
1979/80	134.21	4.9	482.8	12	8.5
1980/81	147.79	4.7	531.6	12	8.6
1981/82	203.43	5.1	731.8	13	8.4
1982/83	243.66	7.2	876.5	13	8.7
1983/84	258.11	5.4	928.5	15	8.3
1984/85	275.67	7.5	991.6	15	9.2
1985/86	282.02	6.3	1014.5	16	9.4
1986/87	283.21	9.2	1018.7	16	8.8
1987/88	390.00	8.6	1402.9	16	8.5
1988/89	425.00	8.1	1503.7	18	9.2
Totals*	3,305.65		11,865.8		

*The FY 1989/90 military budget is K.D. 327.71 million ($1,159.4 million), see *Al-Kuwait Al-Youm* (June 28, 1989), p. 5. The amount is not included in the total.

Sources: Adapted from Stockholm International Peace Research Institute, SIPRI, *World Armaments and Disarmament: SIPRI Yearbook 1977*, pp. 228-229, 230-231; SIPRI, *World Armaments and Disarmaments, SIPRI Yearook 1980*, pp. 26-30; Ministry of Planning, *Annual Statistical Abstract 1987*, p. 272; *Annual Statistical Abstract 1982*, p. 242; *Annual Statistical Abstract 1977*, p. 218; *Statistical Yearbook of Kuwait 1974*, p. 144; *Statistical Abstract 1970*, p. 148; *Annual Statistical Abstract 1976*, p. 181; *Statistical Abstract 1966*, pp. 99-100; International Institute for Strategic Studies, *The Military Balance 1987-1988*, p. 103; and *The Military Balance 1988-1989* (London: IISS, 1988), pp. 105, 225; and other sources.

Through military relationships, Kuwait has been able to reinforce its noncommittal stance toward the superpowers. Military links have reflected, in large part, the regime's "centrist" tendency to stay clear of close identification with either superpower and to build some leverage with both parties. Kuwait was, until very recently, the only GCC state that maintained a reasonable relationship as well as leverage with the Soviet Union in the spheres of politics, finance, and military affairs, albeit on a lower scale than that of its relations with the West. In fact, Kuwait's foreign minister, Sabah

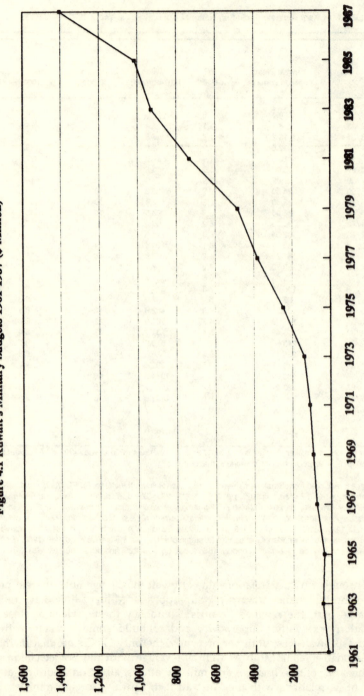

Figure 4.1 Kuwait's Military Budgets 1961-1987 ($ Million)

TABLE 4.2 Arms Transfers to Kuwait (1964–1986) (Current $ Million)

	Total	Soviet Union	USA	France	Britain	West Germany	Italy	Others
1964–74	68	--	6	--	60	--	--	2
1975–80	850	50	390	130	220	20	30	10
1981–86	1,200	220	230	420	20	210	80	20
Total*	2,118	270	626	550	300	230	110	32

*Kuwait arms import in 1983-1987 was estimated at $1,275 million, see ACDA, *World Military Expenditures and Arms Transfers 1988*, p. 113.

Sources: Adapted from U.S. Arms Control and Disarmament Agency, *World Military Expenditures and Arms Transfers 1987*, p. 129; *World Military Expenditures and Arms Transfers, 1986*, p. 145; *World Military Expenditures and Arms Transfers, 1985*, p. 134; *World Military Expenditures and Arms Transfers 1972-1982*, p. 97; *World Military Expenditures and Arms Transfers 1971-1980*, p. 119; *World Military Expenditures and Arms Trade 1963-1973*, p. 70; *World Military Expenditures and Arms Trade 1970-1979*, p. 129; and *World Military Expenditures and Arms Transfers 1967-1976*, p. 158.

Al-Ahmad, visited Moscow in April 1981, a month before the birth of GCC. It was reported that he had the "mandate" of the GCC, including Saudi Arabia, to open up dialogue with the Soviet Union, and to show that the GCC was not a U.S.-designated military pact.[63]

In the period 1964–1986, over $2.1 billion worth of arms was transferred to Kuwait from the major arms suppliers (see Table 4.2). The Soviet Union transferred $270 million (12.7%); the United States $626 million (29.5%); France $550 million (25.9%); the United Kingdom $300 million (14.1%); West Germany $230 (10.8%); Italy $110 million (5.1%); and others (including Argentina, Singapore, and South Korea) $32 million (0.15%).

Although Britain traditionally had been Kuwait's sole supplier of arms, it was gradually supplanted by other competing arms suppliers; still, the 1977 military development plan involved the purchase of some 150 Chieftain tanks at the price of $200 million. By early 1989, Kuwait signed an agreement to buy 16 British-made Short Tucano jet/trainer aircraft, at an estimated cost of $24 million.[64]

But the first tangible Kuwaiti-Soviet military rapprochement took place in August 1976, when Kuwait concluded a $300 million deal to purchase air-to-air and ground-to-air SAM-7 missiles, advanced artillery, tanks, and antipersonnel weapons.[65] In August 1984, the two states signed another contract worth some $325 million for an air defense system. In summer 1988, Kuwait signed a third arms agreement, in part to offset a planned major purchase from the United States. This deal included the purchase of 245 BMB2 Soviet armored personnel carriers, and was estimated at $300 million. By late May 1989, Kuwait signed a contract for "advanced military equipment" with Yugoslavia. It was presumed that this contract involved the purchase of 200 Soviet-designed M-84 main battle tanks, 15 command tanks, and 15 recovery vehicles, built in Yugoslavia and valued at $800 million, to replace French AMX-30 and Chieftain tanks.[66]

The first Kuwaiti-Soviet deal created some discomfort domestically and regionally. There were accusations that Kuwait was open to Marxist indoctrination through military training of its nation as well as opening the door to a possible Soviet advisory capacity in Kuwait's military infrastructure.[67] More importantly, the Saudis' opposition to Soviet penetration into the Peninsula through Kuwait prompted them, among other things, to occupy the Kuwaiti islands of Qaru and Umm Al-Maradim off the Saudi-Kuwaiti coast in summer 1977.[68] This incident, like many others, was denied by the Kuwaitis, and was resolved through the influential channel of communications between the two royal families.[69] And the Kuwaiti-Soviet military package was revised so that the Kuwaitis would receive their training on the new equipment in Egypt, Syria, and Kuwait itself from Egyptian advisors.

Subsequent military agreements permitted a small number (five to ten) of Soviet experts to train the Kuwaitis in Kuwait and periodically visit Kuwait to check on the equipment.[70] Likewise, Kuwaiti military officers, particularly in the air-defense system, were sent to the Soviet Union to receive their training. In general, the Kuwaiti-Soviet relationship has seemingly paid some dividends. In early 1987, it was reported that the Soviet Union had approached Iran with a request to halt attacks on Kuwait and to respect Kuwaiti independence and sovereignty.[71]

However, the Kuwaiti goal of balanced arms purchases from the United States faced political snarls in the pro-Israeli U.S. Congress, a typical fate for deals with the Arab world. As part of a military modernization scheme, in the 1970s a team of American defense experts visited Kuwait and proposed a plan to develop its military capabilities. The United States proposed to sell Kuwait arms worth more than $750 million, consisting of improved antiaircraft Hawk missiles, A-4 fighter aircraft, and cargo aircraft. Kuwait's desire to purchase arms from the United States was seen in Washington as "a political gesture and, as such, . . . sympathetic of Kuwait's desire for closer cooperation with the United States."[72]

In addition, in the early 1980s, Kuwait requested to purchase Stinger antiaircraft missiles worth more than $82 million. In order to soothe congressional objections, Kuwait's foreign minister, Sabah Al-Ahmad, explained his country's domestic needs: "some people think we want the Stingers in order to fight Israel. But we want them only in self-defense."[73] When Congress turned down the Stinger request, Kuwait turned to the Soviet Union, although it made some modest military contracts with the United States. For instance, Kuwait sent some 150 cadet pilots to the U.S. for training at a cost of up to $78 million, and asked Washington to set up a pilot training school in Kuwait.[74] American military training and perhaps indoctrination seems to have had considerable influence on the Kuwaiti military establishment. By early 1988, it was estimated that more than 3,000 Kuwaiti military personnel (or more than 15% of the total) have participated in the Pentagon training.

By mid-1988, in spite of some opposition in Congress, Kuwait and the United States had agreed on a package deal worth $1.9 billion, the biggest arms deal Kuwait had ever signed. Kuwait's crown prince and prime minister, Saad Al-Abdullah, paid a visit to Washington in July 1988 to "lobby" and "pressure" the Congress to approve the deal. He even used a veiled threat: "don't be surprised, when you hear tomorrow, next week, next month, if Kuwait buys military equipment [elsewhere]."[75] The agreement included the delivery of 40 F/A-18 "Hornet" fighter-bomber aircraft; 200 air-to-air "Sparrow" missiles; 120 air-to-air "Sidewinder" missiles; 40 "Harpoon" air-to-ship missiles; 300 "Maverick-G" heat-seeking air-to-surface missiles; 400 laser-guided bombs, and 200 cluster bombs. The delivery will begin by 1991 and be consummated by 1994; to mitigate Israeli fear, the aircraft will not be provided with air refueling capabilities. In early 1989, the U.S. administration was seeking congressional approval to sell Kuwait 200 M1-A1 Abrams main tanks, seven rocket artillery systems, and 1,500 TOW anti-tank missiles. The estimated cost of the tanks alone was $500 million.[76]

Kuwait also purchased arms from France. For example, in 1983 Kuwait and France agreed on an arms contract surpassing $300 million that included "Mirage F-1" aircraft. By the end of 1984, it was reported that Kuwait had agreed to purchase up to $610 million worth of arms and supplementary civilian materials worth $380 million from France. By late 1988, Kuwait was engaged in a "delicate phase" of negotiations to conclude an agreement to purchase 40 Mirage-2000 fighter/bombers, estimated at $1.7 billion.[77] Likewise, by mid-1988, it was reported that Kuwait was negotiating with China to purchase missiles with a range of 720 miles.[78]

Kuwait's policy in arms procurement was a diversification of the sources, thus allowing the purchase of weapons without pressure for political agreements or concessions to either of the superpower suppliers.[79]

These military purchases and other deals have created a reasonably good stockpile in the Kuwaiti armed forces weapons system (Table 4.3). Kuwait's defense forces consist of three major divisions: the army, the air force, and the navy. The army is the oldest branch and the navy, established in the 1970s and operational by the mid-1980s, is the most recent.

The army is made up of some 13,000 to 16,000 soldiers. There are 2 armored brigades, each with 2 armored regiments, and 1 artillery battalion. One of the brigades is mechanized, and the other has 2 mechanized regiments. One of these brigades consists of mechanized infantry, with 1 armored and 3 mechanized infantry/commando regiments, and 1 artillery battalion. Finally, the army has one artillery brigade, with 1 self-propelled artillery regiment and 1 surface-to-surface missile battalion.[80] It possesses over 275 late-model British-made battle tanks (70 Vickers MK-1, 40 Centurion, and 165 Chieftain-5), in addition to 100 Saladin and 90 Ferret armored fighting vehicles, some 200 M-113s, and 130 Saracen armored personnel carriers. The artillery is made up of 40 AMX MK F-3 155m self-propelled French guns, 36 M-109 A-2 self-propelled American howitzers, and 12 Frog-7 Soviet surface-to-surface missile launchers (range 44 miles). The surface-to-air missile

DOUGLAS COLLEGE LIBRARY

TABLE 4.3 Kuwaiti Major Arms Acquisitions

Number	Major Equipment	Equipment Description
ARMY		
70	MK-1 Vickers	Tanks
40	Centurion	Tanks
165	Chieftain-5	MBT
100	Saladin	ARV
90	Ferret	AFV
200	M-113	APC
130	Saracen	APC
62	V-300 Commando	APC
40	AMX MK F-3, 155 mm	Artillery guns, SP
100	Fahd	APC
36	M-109 A2	Howitzers, SSM
12	FROG-7	Launchers, SSM
N/A	120 mm	Mortars
4000	BGM-71A Tow/ Improved	ATGW including 56 M-901 SP
N/A	SA-6	Portable SAM
N/A	SA-7 Grail	Portable SAM
N/A	SA-8 Gecko	SAM (land/mobile)
AIR FORCE		
24	A-4KU Skyhawk	FGA
3	TA-4KU Skyhawk	FGA
32	F-1CK Mirage	Fighter/Interceptor
2	F-1BK Mirage	Trainer
12	Hawk	Counter-insurgency training
20	IA-58A Pucara	Counter-insurgency training
2	DC-9	Transport
4	L-100-30	Transport
1	L-100-20	Transport
1	C-130	Transport
2	DHC-4	Transport
12	SA-342K Gazelle	Attack/antitank with HOT missiles (Helicopters)
6	AS-332 Super Puma	Attack (Helicopters)
10	SA-330 Puma	Transport (Helicopters)
9	BAC-167 Strike- master	Training
7	SA-342	Training (Helicopters)

TABLE 4.3 (Continued)

Number	Major Equipment	Equipment Description
On Store		
12	BAC Lightnings	Fighter/bombers
4	HS Hunter	Fighter/bombers
Air Defense		
6	Batteries	SAM with 12x12 Improved Hawk
2	Batteries	SAM with SA-8 Gecko
N/A	R-550 Magique	AAM
78	Super R-530	AAM
N/A	AIM-9 Sidewinder	AAM
24	AM-39 Exocet	AShM
N/A	Armat	Antiradar missiles
N/A	AS-11/-12	ASM
1	Amoun	Air defense (a radar system, two 35mm guns, and 2 anti-aircraft missile launchers)
N/A	Sakr Eye	SAM portable
NAVY		
6	Al-Boom NC-45/ Lursen	Fast attack crafts, with 2 x MM-40-Exocet SSM
2	Al-Istiqlal-FPB/57 Lursen	MM-40 Exocet SSM
50		Patrol craft, 15 armored
4	LCM/loadmaster	Amphibious mechanized landing craft
6	LCU/Loadmaster	Utility landing craft
3	320-tons	Support ships
96	MM-40 Exocet	SSM

Sources: Adapted from The International Institute for Strategic Studies, *The Military Balance 1987-1988* (London: IISS, 1987), pp. 103-104; and Stockholm International Peace Research Institute, *SIPRI Yearbook 1987: World Armaments and Disarmaments 1987* (Oxford: Oxford University Press, 1987), pp. 387-388, ILSS, *The Military Balance 1988-1989*, p. 105; U.S. Congress, House, *Proposed Arms Sales to Kuwait*, p. 34; and *Middle East Economic Digest* (July 8, 1988), p. 17.
N/A = Not Available.

battery consists of Soviet SAM, SA-6, SA-7, and SA-8 Gecko missiles. In late 1988, the army also had on order British Scorpion light tanks and improved TOW and SAM missiles.

The air force consists of 2200 men. It has 18 armed helicopters and 70 combat aircraft. The aircraft capabilities consist of 2 squadrons of fighters with 24 A-4KU and 3 TA-4KU American Skyhawks, and one squadron of 32 French F-1CKs and 2 F-1BK Mirages. One squadron of 12 British Hawk jets is used for training and counterinsurgency. It has been reported that in the early 1980s Kuwait procured some 20 IA-58A Argentine Pucara counterinsurgency planes worth $120 million.[81] The air transport arm has 2 DC-9s, 4 L-100-30s, 1 L-100-20, 1 C-130, 2 DHC-4, 3 squadrons of helicopters, 12 SA-342K French Pumas, and 6 AS-332 Super-Pumas, equipped with Exocet anti-ship missiles. The air defense wing uses 9 BAC-167 British Strikemasters and 7 SA-342K French Gazelle helicopters for training purposes.

The air defense system consists of 2 surface-to-air missile battalions, 1 (6 batteries) with 2x12 Improved Hawk missiles; and 1 (2 batteries) with SA-8 Gecko missiles. Among air-to-air missiles there are 78 Matra Super R-530s, some R-550 French Magiques, and an undisclosed number of AIM-9H American Sidewinders. Air-to-surface missiles are French AS-11/-12S, and air-to-ship missiles comprise 24 AM-39 French Exocets and an undetermined number of Armat antiradar missiles.

The navy is a recent entrant to the defense infrastructure. Before the 1980s, the navy was a coast guard force attached to the ministry of the interior and dealt mostly with the protection of the Kuwaiti coast and prevention of illegal penetration into Kuwait. As part of the armed force modernization program, a naval base was erected south of Kuwait city. By the mid-190s, the force was operational and functional, though it barely exceeded 2,100 men. The navy's weapon system consists of 8 German-made fast attack craft (6 Al-Boom Lurssen TNC-45, and 2 Al-Istiqlal Lurssen FPB-57), 4 supplied with MM-40 French Exocet surface-to-surface missiles, in addition to 10 amphibious landing craft, 4 loadmaster mechanized landing craft, and 6 utility landing craft, all British-made. The coastal patrol has 50 ships, 15 of which are armored, and three 320-ton support ships. Marine forces consist of two battalion commandos. It was reported that by summer 1987 Kuwait had received four 55-meter South Korean missile patrol boats with anti-ship missiles, helicopter pads, and a Hovercraft docking facility.[82] As of late 1988, the navy had on order 20 Magnum Sedan patrol craft; 6 SRN-6 hovercraft; some SA-365N French Dauphin II helicopters, and 96 MM-40 surface-to-ship and ship-to-ship Exocet missiles. By mid-1989, Kuwait had placed numerous orders of military hardware for its defense forces from a variety of sources (see Table 4.4).

A major component of Kuwait's defense strategy is the paramilitary forces, which have been beefed up in recent years because of the political and security situation in the country. Besides the regular police force, which has been supplied with the latest antiriot control equipment, the national guard, border guard, palace guard, and reserve forces, with an estimated manpower between 15,000 and 17,000 men, form an integral part of the state defense and security system. The interior ministry's budget has increased in volume from K.D. 8.7 million in 1963/64 to K.D. 13.2 million in 1965/66, K.D. 20.2 million in 1970/71, K.D. 49.6 million in 1975/76, K.D. 79.4 million in 1980/81, and K.D. 137.8 million in 1985/86, an expansion of over 100 percent in the last two decades, and an increase of over 57 percent in the period 1980/85 alone. Meanwhile, the national guard budget has risen from K.D. 11.6 million in 1982/83 (when its allocation appeared separately from that of the ministry of defense) to K.D. 21.8 million in 1987/88, an increase of 53 percent.[83] Also, the guard has acquired 20 V-150 and 62 V-300 American-made commando armored personnel carriers.

Despite the sophisticated hardware acquired by Kuwait, its armed forces are not devoid of flaws. With regard to manpower, favoritism has over-

TABLE 4.4 Kuwaiti Major Arms on Order

Country	No.	Equipment	Description
France*	40	Mirage 2000	Fighter/Bombers
Netherlands	2	Akmaar Class	Minehunters
Soviet Union	245	BMB2	APC
United Kingdom	16	Short-Tucano	Jet/Trainer aircraft
United States	32	F/A-18 "Hornet"	Fighter/Bombers
	8	F/A-18 "Hornet"	Twin-Seat Trainers
	200	AIM-7F Sparrow	AAM
	120	AIM-9L Sidewinder	AAM
	40	AGM-84D-1 Harpoon	AShM
	300	AGM-65G Maverick	ASM heat-seeking missiles
	400	GBU-10/12	Laser-guided bombs
	200	MK-20 Rockeye	Cluster bombs
	**200	M1-A1 Abrams	MBT
	1,500	TOW	Antitank Missiles
	7	Rocket	Artillery Systems
Yugoslavia	200	M-84	MBT
	15	---	Command tanks
	15	---	Recovery vehicles

*In final negotiation stage.
**Awaits Congressional approval for the tanks, artillery, and TOW orders.

Sources: Adapted from *The Middle East Economic Digest* (December 23, 1988), p. 34, (February 17, 1989), p. 20, and (June 2, 1989), p. 34; U.S. Congress, *Proposed Arms Sales to Kuwait*, p. 56; *The Wall Street Journal* (February 3, 1989), p. A16; *Arab News* (June 1, 1989), p. 2; *Flight International* (February 18, 1989), p. 3; *International Defense Review* (April 1989), p. 516; and *Asharq Al-Awsat* (August 17, 1988), p. 3.

shadowed professionalism, there is too much reliance on foreign support personnel and "stateless" Bedouin ranks, the troops have no combat experience, and excessive equipment far exceeds the small infrastructure and manpower base of the state. Technically, Kuwait's flat geographical terrain creates tactical problems, and its bases are too centrally located and too vulnerable to air attack. The armed forces have difficulty absorbing the various weapons systems because of continued heating and maintenance problems; the naval force lacks serious air defense capability; and some purchases are made for symbolic reasons or as what one expert has called "showpiece" buys, such as the French Mirages.[84]

In order to run the weapons systems and train the low-ranking troops, Kuwait relies extensively on expatriate experts and advisers. Some are locally contracted, others are arranged through the military establishments (government and arms industries) of Kuwait and the other countries concerned.

As of the middle of 1988, some 20-30 Americans provided training for the Hawk missiles and A-4 aircraft; about 100 British officers assisted in the operation of British-built arms; 20 French advisers helped with Mirages; some 10 Egyptians provided training in operating Soviet arms, and 4 Egyptian teams estimated at 50 persons trained Kuwaitis in infantry tactics, coastal defense, and special forces; the navy had 20 Pakistani advisers; and there were 5–10 Soviet military advisers on sporadic, short-term assignments. Previously Kuwait relied, in addition to these advisers, on large contingents of experts from Jordan and Syria in a variety of functions.[85] It has been reported that Kuwait and Turkey have agreed on a military relationship that might include Turkish advisers to the Kuwaiti defense establishment.[86] Since the summer of 1987, after continuous Iranian attacks on Kuwait, a number of Egyptians have provided their air defense expertise to Kuwait, even serving as pilots.[87] It is expected that a large contingent of American military and technical advisers will be assigned to Kuwait by the early 1990s to facilitate the new Kuwaiti arms purchases from Washington.

A 1985 survey of military expenditures by 144 countries, carried out by the U.S. Arms Control and Disarmament Agency sheds some light on Kuwait's military preparedness. Kuwait ranked 46 in military expenditures ($1.5 billion); 38 in arms imports ($300 million); 99 in armed forces (16,000); 38 in military expenditures/GNP (6.28 percent); 9 in military expenditures per capita ($857); 44 in armed forces per 1,000 people (9.35); 38 in proportion of arms imports to total imports (5.06 percent). In military expenditures per soldier Kuwait ranked 6 out of 144 states ($91,670). An expert justified the high rate of army pay by saying that it was needed to make the military establishment "loyal to the ruling family."[88]

All in all, the general evaluation of Kuwait's military capabilities is not a gloomy one. Generally speaking, military experts claim that the potential of Kuwait's armed forces "is not inconsiderable." Against an actual external threat, they could resist two to three days, until help from outside arrived.[89] Of the three main branches of the Kuwaiti armed forces, the air force is considered the best, or in the words of an expert, "the closest force Kuwait has to a real deterrent."[90] On the negative side, a recent congressional study characterized GCC consensus as elusive and the defense capabilities of GCC members as ranging from moderately effective to weak. Kuwait was classified as a weak country.[91] Through militarization, Kuwait should be able to free itself from dependence on regional powers and enable itself to resist external pressures.

In the final analysis, as the threats to Kuwait in particular and the Gulf states in general climaxed, the initial Kuwaiti goal of cooperation on nonmilitary, nonsecurity issues was subordinated to security considerations. This development may call into question the viability of the GCC as an instrument of political and economic integration, rather than a means of setting security and military priorities. One wonders whether the organization will wither away with its immediate cause, the Gulf war, or whether it will take a different shape, emphasis, or even membership.[92]

Conclusion

In evaluating the major events of the late 1970s and the early 1980s, we recognize the discernible impact of the changes in Iran on the politics of Kuwait, both internally and externally. Kuwait's politics have undergone metamorphosis. The shah of Iran considered himself the regional guarantor of security for the smaller states, as well as a balancer and neutralizing element against both the Iraqi threats and Saudi designs against Kuwait. The Iranian revolution and the Iran-Iraq war created for the first time a real external threat to Kuwait coupled with a perceived potential domestic Shiite threat to the regime. In reality, most Kuwaiti Shiites are loyal citizens. Before Iran's revolution, the Shiites had not functioned as militant opposition to the regimes in power;[93] and, indeed, their earlier enthusiasm for Khomeini was shared by most of the Sunnis, since at its inception the Iranian revolution promised freedom, justice, and equality. When the actual absolutism of Iranian theocracy had been exposed, a good percentage of the Kuwaiti Shiites rejected it, and a delegation of Shiite notables expressed these feelings to the government.

But since some Shiites were involved in antistate terrorist activities, the Sunnis' fear was generalized. Unfortunately the entire Shiite community became viewed as trouble-makers or at least unreliable. Iran's moral and political support of the "fundamentalist" Shiites and its threats to Kuwait's economic lifeline put new pressures on decision-makers in Kuwait, forcing them to take action primarily viewed as self-defense. Ethnic and communal strife during the 1970s and 1980s was not a phenomenon peculiar to Kuwait. Division by ethnicity has long been part of the international political system, and has become more frequent in the last decade or so in the Indian subcontinent, Lebanon, Africa, and even Europe. Therefore the issue of Shiism-Sunnism should not be overdramatized or not be given more emphasis than it really deserves. Once we broaden the cleavage, it may take a life of its own and the stakes may become greater.

Kuwait's history of negative and fearful interactions with Iraq made it vulnerable to Iraqi pressures to tilt toward Iraq. It must be stated that Kuwait's relations with the shah of Iran were better than those with the Iraqi regime; however, after the war began, Iraq became the lesser of two evils. Kuwait's continuous bankrolling of Iraq and the regime's leniency toward the propaganda warfare against Teheran in the Kuwaiti media contributed to the latter's decision to instigate internal and external threats to the city-state and bring retribution against Kuwait. The combined internal instabilities and external threats forced Kuwait to align itself with the status quo regimes of the Gulf and seek collective protection in the form of the GCC.

Within the Gulf region, Kuwait was hardest hit next to the combatants of the Gulf war. Its social, political, security, and economic structures have been damaged, and will probably take a long time to recover. Its lively intellectual and "open" social style shifted to what has perhaps a little jokingly been called "a hodge-podge of concrete, blast-proof glass, tank traps, search lights, metal detectors, and armed guards."[94] The only comfort and short-term gain is that through subsidies to Iraq, Kuwait was able to neutralize the Iraqi threat on an ad hoc basis. In essence, the perennial threats have continued but have been "dwarfed," whereas a new threat from Iran has become "huskier," even though over the years Kuwaiti relations with Iraq have been characterized as "black," whereas its relations with Iran have been "brown." The Iraqi president, Saddam Hussein, acknowledged Kuwait's aid, in a variety of ways, to Iraqi war efforts, by calling the Kuwaitis "our few distinguished brethren."[95] Yet his statement is of a dubious nature, whether in appreciation for past generosities, or to mellow the Kuwaitis with an eye on future Iraqi gains.

Kuwait's GDP fell from K.D. 5.9 billion ($20 billion) in 1985 to K.D. 4.9 billion ($17 billion) in 1986, then rebounded to K.D. 5.44 ($18.9 billion) in 1987. The deficit for 1987/88 was approximately K.D. 779 million ($2.69 billion), but Kuwait's interest on its investments more than made up for this loss.[96] This general shortfall not only affected domestic economic policy, but also lessened Kuwait's international leverage, since it was less able to play an active financial role in inter-Arab politics. (Indeed, it began a domestic borrowing policy.)

Kuwait sought political and security protection and coordination through the GCC, thus coming indirectly under the sway of Saudi pressures and demands. Its previously centrist policy in external regional relations became identified more with Iraqi war efforts and Saudi military and security designs. One reason was that Iraq succeeded in convincing the Kuwaitis and other Arabs that the war with Iran essentially pitted all Arabs versus Persians, despite Iranian attempts to show it as a limited challenge and confrontation between two parties. The common denominator of the Gulf regimes was, in different degrees, fear of radical Islam. The issue between Kuwait and Iran, indeed between all the Arabs of the Gulf and Iran, is complicated by misunderstanding of each other's history, culture, sects, and ideology. The Iranian revolutionary regime and the Gulf traditional regimes tried to see each other through their own lenses, without finding an accommodation or a modus vivendi. The Iranians misread Kuwaiti politics and thought of Kuwait as a group of "mini-shaikhs," just like the rest of the Gulf states, not realizing that its unique political, cultural, and social life sets it apart from the rest of the Gulf states and legitimates its political system. The Iranians thought that the Gulf people would rise to topple their governments, just as the Iranians themselves had risen against the Shah. They never appreciated that their revolutionary model of Islamic fundamentalism is an Iranian one that might not be appropriate for Gulf Arabs. On the other hand, the Gulf states viewed the Iranians with fear as well as with ethnic and confessional prejudices. Some Gulf Arabs thought of the Iranian revolution as "less Islamic," a peculiar Shiite phenomenon brought about, as some say, by the CIA and designed to undermine the Gulf states' system. Others saw in Iran's export of theocratic revolution a mortal threat—a potential invasion of medieval fanatics similar to the Tartar invasion of the area during the Middle Ages, in essence, a giant step backward toward anarchy, destruction, and oblivion, all in the name of religion.

It should be stated, in all fairness, that Kuwait has not approved and would not approve an Iraqi attack against Iran; neither, for various reasons, did it wish to support either party against the other. Circumstances, Iranian pressure, and Iraqi leverage forced Kuwait into its current tilt towards Iraq, which seems in a sense to contravene Kuwait's own beliefs and national interests. Kuwait found itself caught in a quandary, politically, economically, and socially. Yet while Kuwait's regional balance became shaky indeed, it maintained a balanced, centrist orientation toward the superpowers in all fields, including military relations. Kuwait was qualified to become a bridge between the Soviet Union and the GCC, none of whose other members had a diplomatic relationship with Moscow or the rest of the Eastern bloc until the mid-1980s. Many factors affected Kuwait's decision to follow such a course, perhaps most of all a reluctance to put all its eggs in one basket. Kuwait has, after all, experienced the decline of one previously powerful sponsor.

Notes

1. *Al-Rai Al-Aam* (December 7, 1976), p. 2.

2. For the impact of Iran's revolution in Kuwait and the new forces of Islam, see Dilip Hiro, *Inside the Middle East* (New York: McGraw Hill Book Company, 1982), pp. 19–22 and 97–99; R. K. Ramazani, *Revolutionary Iran: Challenge and Response in the Middle East* (Baltimore and London: The Johns Hopkins University Press, 1986), pp. 32–35, and 42–48; Joseph Kostiner, "Shii Unrest in the Gulf," in Martin Kramer, ed., *Shiism, Resistance, and Revolution* (Boulder, CO: Westview Press, 1987), pp. 173–186; Majid Khadduri, *The Gulf War: The Origins and Implications of the Iraq-Iran Conflict* (New York: Oxford University Press, 1988), pp. 126–128; Rouhollah K. Ramazani, "Socio-Political Changes in the Gulf: A Climate for Terrorism," in H. Richard Sinclair, III and J. E. Peterson, eds., *Crosscurrents in the Gulf: Arab, Regional and Global Interests* (London; Routledge, for the Middle East Institute, Washington, 1988), pp. 133–137; U.S. Congress. House. Hearings. Subcommittee on Europe and the Middle East. The Committee on Foreign Affairs. *Islamic Fundamentalism and Islamic Radicalism*. June 24, July 15, and September 30, 1985 (Washington, D.C.: USGPO, 1985), 99th Cong., 1st Sess., pp. 1–279; Dilip Hiro, "Faces of Fundamentalism," *The Middle East* (May 1988), pp. 9–14; and Nazih N. M. Ayubi, "The Politics of Militant Islamic Movements in the Middle East," *Journal of International Affairs*, vol. 36, no. 2 (Fall/Winter 1982/83), pp. 271–285. For relations between the revolution and Arabism see Adeed Dawisha, "Iran's Mullahs and the Arab Masses," *The Washington Quarterly*, vol. 6, no. 3 (Summer 1983), pp. 162–168; and Shireen Hunter, "Arab-Iranian Relations and Stability in the Persian Gulf," *The Washington Quarterly*, vol. 7, no. 3 (Summer 1984), pp. 67–76.

3. Interview with the new Iranian Chief of Staff, General Mohammad Vali Gharaneh, *Al-Watan* (March 4, 1979), p. 8; and R. K. Ramazani, *Revolutionary Iran*, pp. 11–13, 19–27.

4. See James A. Bill, "Resurgent Islam in the Persian Gulf," pp. 108–127. For an understanding of the Shiite tenets of Iran's revolution see Said Amir Arjomand,

"History, Structure, and Revolution: The Shiite Tradition in Contemporary Iran," *International Political Science Review*, vol. 10, no. 2 (April 1989), pp. 111–119.

5. Analysis in this section is adapted from Marvin Zonis and Daniel Brumberg, *Khomeini, the Islamic Republic of Iran, and the Arab World* (Cambridge, MA.: Harvard Middle East Papers, Modern Series #5, 1987), pp. 17–30, and 42–46; also see Emmanuel Sivan, "Sunni Radicalism in the Middle East and the Iranian Revolution," *International Journal of Middle East Studies*, vol. 21, no. 1 (February 1989), pp. 1–30.

6. John K. Cooley, "Iran, the Palestinians, and the Gulf," *Foreign Affairs*, (Summer 1979), pp. 1017–1035; for threats to Kuwait from radicalism, see John Muttam, *Arms and Insecurity in the Persian Gulf* (New Delhi: Radiant Publishers, 1984), p. 69; and Lenore G. Martin, *The Unstable Gulf: Threats from Within* (Lexington, MA: Lexington Books, 1984), pp. 85–86, 95–96, and 114–115.

7. *Kuwait Times* (December 20, 1979), p. 1.

8. Kuwait's Mission to the UN, *Kuwaiti Foreign Minister Statement to the United Nations, General Assembly 36th Session*, New York (September 29, 1981), p. 6.

9. See Abdullah al-Nafisi, "The Mantikat Al-Khalij Bin Al-Bued Al-Araby Wal Islamy" (The Gulf Region in the Arabic and Islamic Dimension), unpublished paper, 1988, pp. 1–8; R. K. Ramazani, *Revolutionary Iran*, p. 121; *Al-Majala* (May 17, 1988), pp. 20–22; *The Christian Science Monitor* (May 12, 1988), pp. 7–8; *Kayhan International* (April 22, 1989), pp. 5, 15; and *The Middle East* (July 1989), p. 19.

10. See James A. Bill, "The Arab World and the Challenge of Iran," *Journal of Arab Affairs*, vol. 2, no. 2 (October 1982), pp. 40–42.

11. *The Middle East News Agency Bulletin* (April 29, 1980).

12. See *Al-Qabas* (September 29, 1979), p. 2; and R. K. Ramazani, *Revolutionary Iran*, p. 119.

13. *Al-Nahar* (September 26, 1979), p. 3; *Facts on File*, vol. 39, no. 2030 (October 5, 1979), p. 753. Freedom of political expression had been almost banned with the suspension of the National Assembly in August 1976, and again in July 1986; see *The Middle East Review 1988*, 14th ed. (London: World of Information, 1987), p. 95.

14. *Facts on File*, vol. 39, no. 2030 (October 5, 1979), p. 753.

15. *Majalat Al-Asbouh Al-Araby* (Beirut) (June 30, 1986), pp. 6–7; and Joseph Kostiner, "Shii Unrest in the Gulf," p. 180.

16. For the function of civil defense units, see Kuwait Oil Company, *The Kuwaiti Digest*, vol. 17, no. 1 (January/March 1989), pp. 15–18. It has been estimated that the number of volunteers in the Civil Defense Corps reaches 4700 persons, and it has 13 centers for training; see SWB, ME/0197-A18 (July 7, 1988).

17. *Keesing's Record of World Events*, vol. 33 (November 11, 1987), pp. 35545–35546. For freedom and human rights in Kuwait see Amnesty International, *Amnesty International Report 1988* (London: Amnesty International Publications, 1988), pp. 243–244; Arab Organization for Human Rights, Huqooq Al-Insan Fil Al-Alam Al-Araby *(Human Rights in the Arab World)* (Cairo: International Press, 1988), pp. 148–156; U.S. Department of State, *Country Report on Human Rights Practices for 1988*. Report submitted to the Committee on Foreign Relations, U.S. Senate, and Committee on Foreign Affairs, U.S. House of Representatives. 101 Cong., 1st Sess. (Washington, D.C.: USGPO, February 1989), pp. 1396–1407; and International Committee for the Defense of Human Rights in the Gulf and Arabian Peninsula, Report No. 9/89/22K (April 1, 1989) (London and Nashville, TN.: I.C.H.R.G. & A.P., April 1, 1989), pp. 1–3.

18. *Al-Watan* (July 22, 1979), p. 2.

19. *Al-Riyadh* (July 23, 1979), p. 1.

20. *The Sunday Times* (December 30, 1979), p. 3.

21. *Al-Watan* (February 23, 1980), p. 2; and *Al-Qabas* (February 13, 1980), p. 3.

22. *The Sunday Times* (December 30, 1979), p. 3; *Al-Nahar* (December 27, 1979), p. 2; and *Kuwait Times* (January 7, 1980), p. 1, and (April 27, 1980), p. 2.

23. For the effect of the war in Kuwait and its position toward the war see *The Financial Times* (February 22, 1988), p. 15; Richard Nyrop ed., *Persian Gulf States*, p. 116; Frederick W. Axelgard, *A New Iraq? The Gulf War and Implications for U.S. Policy* (New York: Praeger for the Center for Strategic and International Studies, Washington, D.C., 1988), pp. 72–76; R. K. Ramazani, *Revolutionary Iran*, pp. 76–77; Shahram Chubin and Charles Tripp, *Iran and Iraq at War* (Boulder, CO: Westview Press, 1988), pp. 154–156; *The Middle East Review*, pp. 25–28, and 95–96; Jonathan Earle, "The Gulf War and the Littoral States," *The World Today* (July 1984), p. 272; Trevor Mostyn and Albert Hourani, eds., *The Cambridge Encyclopedia of the Middle East and North Africa* (Cambridge: Cambridge University Press, 1988), pp. 367–368 and 492–494; John Laffin, "The Middle East: Old Game—With New Results," in *Rusi and Brassey's Defense Yearbook 1984*, ed. Royal United Services Institute for Defense Studies, London (Oxford: Brassey's Defense Publishers, 1984), pp. 127–130; Edgar O'Ballance, *The Gulf War* (London: Brassey's, 1988), pp. 42, 52, 72, 142, 155, 194, and 205; and Christopher S. Raj, "The Iraq-Iran War and Arab Response," *IDSA Journal* (New Delhi), vol. 16, no. 3 (January-March 1984), pp. 232–259.

24. Ralph King, *The Iran-Iraq War: The Political Implications* (London: IISS, Adelphi Papers 219, Spring 1987), p. 18; and statement of Iraqi oil minister Isam Chalabi, *Middle East Economic Survey* (February 13, 1989), p. A7.

25. Gerd Nonneman, *Iraq, the Gulf States and the War: A Changing Relationship 1980-1986 and Beyond* (London and Atlantic Highlands, 1986), p. 97. Private donations are not included here.

26. For the UN meeting see United Nations, *Security Council Official Records: Thirty-Ninth Year, 1984* (UN: New York, 1985), pp. 14–15; and for attack on vessels see Center for Defense Information, Washington, D.C., staff report provided to the author (August 1988).

27. See Shahram Chubin and Charles Tripp, *Iran and Iraq at War*, pp. 170–172.

28. *The Middle East and North Africa 1988*, 35th ed. (London: Europa Publications, 1987), p. 523.

29. *Al-Watan Al-Araby* (Paris) (August 1, 1986), p. 1.

30. See Godfrey Jansen, "Home to Roost," and James M. Dorsey, "Kuwait's Fault-Line," *The Middle East International*, no. 215 (December 23, 1983), pp. 7–8. For Arab and Islam in the war and effect of the war on domestic situation in Iraq see Bruce Maddy-Weitzman, "Islam and Arabism: The Iran-Iraq War," *The Washington Quarterly*, vol. 5, no. 4 (Autumn 1982), pp. 181-188; and Hanna Batatu, "Iraq's Underground Shia Movements: Characteristics, Causes and Prospects," *The Middle East Journal*, vol. 35, no. 4 (Autumn 1981), pp. 578 –594.

31. *Facts on File*, vol. 43, no. 2248 (December 16, 1983), p. 943.

32. See *The Christian Science Monitor* (April 6, 1988), p. 7, (April 7, 1988), pp. 1, 32, (April 19, 1988), pp. 1, 11, and (April 22, 1988), pp. 12, 15; KUNA, *The Hijacking of Al-Jabriyah* (Kuwait, KUNA, July 1988), pp. 11–101; *The Los Angeles Times* (April 14, 1988), p. 1; *The New York Times* (April 21, 1988), pp. A1, A9, and (April 23, 1988), pp. 1, 6; and "Hijack: What Were the Iranians Doing?" *The Middle East* (May 1988), pp. 5–8.

33. *Keesing's Record of World Events*, vol. 33 (November 11, 1987), p. 35546. For the role of Hezbollah, as Iranian surrogate, and the terrorist groups in the Middle East see Department of Defense, *Terrorist Group Profiles* (Washington, D.C.: USGPO,

1988), pp. 5–30. In May 1988 a new group, "Kuwaiti Hezbollah," was allegedly formed; see *The Middle East and North Africa 1989*, p. 564.

34. For the linkage between Iran and terrorism in Kuwait see R. K. Ramazani, *Revolutionary Iran*, pp. 40–48; and Marvin Zonis and Daniel Brumberg, *Khomeini, the Islamic Republic of Iran, and the Arab World*, pp. 31–36; Amir Taheri, *Holy Terror: Inside the World of Islamic Terrorism* (Bethesda, MD: Adler and Adler, Publishers, Inc., 1987), pp. 165–167; R. K. Ramazani, "Iran's Islamic Revolution and the Persian Gulf," *Current History* (January 1985), vol. 84, no. 498, pp. 5–8 and 40–41; and Robin Wright, "The Islamic Resurgence: A New Phase?" *Current History*, vol. 87, no. 525 (January 1988), pp. 53–56 and 85–86.

35. *Al-Ahram* (February 9, 1969), p. 2; *The Christian Science Monitor* (June 6, 1988), pp. 32, 44; Milton Viorst, "Out of the Desert: Kuwait," *The New Yorker* (May 16, 1988), pp. 68–72; and *The Middle East Report (MERIP)*, vol. 17, no. 5 (September-October 1987), p. 32.

36. See Milton Viorst, "Out of the Desert: Kuwait," pp. 68–72; and *The MERIP Reports*, vol. 17, no. 5 (September-October 1987), p. 32.

37. *Newsweek* (March 3, 1980), p. 36.

38. Permanent Mission of Kuwait to the UN, *Speech of the Kuwaiti Foreign Minister to the 40th Session of the General Assembly*, New York (September 26, 1985), pp. 12–13; and *Al-Qabas* (January 8, 1984), p. 2.

39. *The Christian Science Monitor* (December 7, 1987), p. 10; also see R. K. Ramazani, "Socio-Political Change in the Gulf: A Climate for Terrorism," pp. 139–141.

40. James A. Bill, "Islam, Politics and Shiism in the Gulf," *Middle East Insight*, no. 3 (January/February 1984), pp. 4–12.

41. *The Baghdad Observer* (October 24, 1984), p. 4.

42. Ralph King, *The Iran-Iraq War: The Political Implications*, p. 17; and *The Middle East and North Africa 1988*, p. 523.

43. *Shaheed* (July 1, 1981), pp. 2–3.

44. U.S. Congress, House, *National Security and Policy Implications of United States Operations in the Persian Gulf*, Report of the Defense Policy and Investigations Subcommittee of the Committee on Armed Services July 1987 (Washington, D.C.: USGPO, 1987), 100th Cong., 1st Sess., p. 31; and Chubin and Tripp, *Iran and Iraq at War*, p. 156. For the strategies and development of the war see David Segal, "The Iran-Iraq War: A Military Analysis," *Foreign Affairs*, vol. 66, no. 5 (Summer 1988), pp. 946–963.

45. *Al-Nahar* (July 30, 1987), p. 2.

46. Personal Interview, Washington, D.C. (November 10, 1987), and Kuwait (April 4, 1988).

47. Gary Sick, "Iran's Quest for Superpower Status," *Foreign Affairs* (Spring 1987), p. 712; and the Economic Intelligence Unit, *Iran and Iraq: The Next Five Years* (London: Economist Publications, 1987), p. 61. For Iran's position toward the Gulf states see Henry Precht, "Ayatollah Realpolitik," *Foreign Policy*, no. 70 (Spring 1988), pp. 118–120; and *The Middle East Journal*, vol. 41, no. 3 (Summer 1987), p. 429.

48. *Facts on File*, vol. 47, no. 2411 (February 26, 1987), p. 60.

49. For an analysis of the role of Kuwait and the Gulf states as small entities see Hassan Ali Al-Ebraheem, *Kuwait and the Gulf: Small States and the International System* (Washington, D.C.: Georgetown University Center for Contemporary Arab Studies, 1984), pp. 57–105; for the shah's visit to Kuwait see *The Middle East Journal*, vol. 24, no. 1 (Winter 1970), p. 59; and for the shah's attitude toward regional security see R. K. Ramazani, "Iran's Search for Regional Cooperation," *The Middle East Journal*, vol. 30, no. 2 (Spring 1976), pp. 173–186; and William D. Brewer, "Yesterday and

Tomorrow in the Persian Gulf," *The Middle East Journal*, vol. 23, no. 2 (Spring 1969), pp. 149–158.

50. Permanent Mission of the State of Kuwait to the UN, *Statement of the Kuwaiti Foreign Minister to the 36th Session of the General Assembly*, New York (September 29, 1981), p. 5.

51. Kuwait News Agency (KUNA), *Gulf Cooperation Council* (Kuwait: KUNA, January 23, 1983), p. 19.

52. See Fouad H. Bissisou, "Majlis Al-Taawun Wa Strateoiat Al-Arabiya" (GCC and Arab Strategy), *Al-Mustaqbil Al-Araby*, vol. 4, no. 31 (1981), p. 38; and R. K. Ramazani, *The Gulf Cooperation Council: Record and Analysis* (Charlottesville: University Press of Virginia, 1988), pp. 4–6.

53. For an analysis of the security threats to Kuwait see The Middle East Research Institute, University of Pennsylvania, MERI Report, *Kuwait* (Dover, NH: Croom Helm, 1985), pp. 21–45; and for GCC containment of regional subversion see R. K. Ramazani, *Revolutionary Iran*, pp. 128–143; and Shahram Chubin, "Soviet Policy toward Iran and the Gulf," in Charles Tripp, ed., *Regional Security in the Middle East* (New York: St. Martin's Press, for the International Institute for Strategic Studies, 1984), pp. 125–174.

54. *Journal of the Gulf and Arabian Peninsula Studies*, vol. 5, no. 18 (April 1979), pp. 11–12; and *Facts on File*, vol. 39, no. 2033 (October 26, 1979), p. 804.

55. KUNA, *Gulf Cooperation Council*, p. 6. For the genesis of the GCC see R. K. Ramazani, *Revolutionary Iran*, pp. 114–127; and for the GCC'S nature see Abdullah Bishara, *The Gulf Cooperation Council: Its Nature and Outlook* (Washington, D.C.: National Council on US-Arab Relations, 1986), pp. 1–8.

56. *The Washington Post* (September 17, 1974), p. 5; *The Middle East: U.S. Policy, Israel, Oil and the Arabs*, 2nd ed. (Washington, D.C.: Congressional Quarterly, Oct. 1975), p. 90; and James H. Noyes, *The Clouded Lens: Persian Gulf Security and U.S. Policy* (Stanford: Hoover Institution Press, 1974), p. 41.

57. For Kuwaitis' and other expectations and reactions to the GCC see Emile A. Nakhleh, *The Gulf Cooperation Council: Policies, Problems and Prospects* (New York: Praeger, 1986), pp. 81–97. For GCC security cooperation see The International Institute for Strategic Studies, *The Military Balance, 1986-1987* (London: IISS, 1986), p. 90; and R. K. Ramazani, *The Gulf Cooperation Council: Record and Analysis*, pp. 34–36.

58. *The Washington Post* (June 19, 1984), p. 3; and R. K. Ramazani, *Revolutionary Iran*, p. 136. For the military capabilities of all the Gulf states see Alvin J. Cottrell and Frank Bray, *Military Forces in the Persian Gulf* (Washington, D.C.: The Center for Strategic and International Studies, 1978, *The Washington Paper*, vol. 6, no. 6), pp. 15–60.

59. For an analysis of the GCC air forces, see Assad Al-Tahan, "The Gulf Cooperation Council's Airpower Build Up and the Failure of the U.S. FX Policy," *Strategic Studies* (Islamabad), vol. 9, no. 4 (Summer 1986), pp. 57–83; and Roland C. Smith, "Coalition Air Defense in the Persian Gulf," *Airpower Journal*, vol. 1, no. 2 (Fall 1987), pp. 28–39.

60. The figures are based on many sources: John Keegan, *World Armies* (New York: Facts on File, Inc., 1979), p. 417; International Institute for Strategic Studies, *The Military Balance*, various editions; U.S. Arms Control and Disarmament Agency, *World Military Expenditures and Arms Transfers*, various editions; Stockholm International Peace Research Institute, *World Armaments and Disarmaments SIPRI Yearbook*, various editions; Personal interview, Kuwait (March 30, 1988); CIA, *The World Factbook*, 1988; John Muttam, *Arms and Insecurity in the Persian Gulf*, pp. 121–123; and Lenore G. Martin, *The Unstable Gulf*, p. 169; IISS, The Military Balance, 1987–1988, p. 104;

Ruth Leger Sivard, *World Military and Social Expenditures 1987-1988*, 12th ed. (Washington, D.C.: World Priorities, 1987), pp. 12, 27, and 48–49. *The Middle East and North Africa 1989*, 35th ed. (London: Europa Publications, 1988) puts the paramilitary forces at 18,000 (p. 583). The latest figure is put at 20,300 active armed forces; see IISS, *The Military Balance 1988-1989* (London: IISS, 1988), p. 105.

61. Colin Legum, ed., *Middle East Contemporary Survey vol. 1, 1976–77* (New York and London: Holmes and Meier Publishers, 1978), p. 343; *Al-Qabas* (May 10, 1977), p. 2; and Anthony H. Cordesman, *The Gulf and the West: Strategic Relations and Military Realities* (Boulder, CO: Westview Press, 1988), p. 166.

62. Various sources, including John Keegan, *World Armies*, p. 417; *Al-Watan* (July 7, 1981), p. 4; *Middle East Economic Digest*, (December 18, 1981), p. 22; and *Al-Yaqza* (July 8–14, 1988), pp. 14–15.

63. See Robert O. Freedman, "Soviet Policy toward the Persian Gulf from the Outbreak of the Iran-Iraq War to the Death of Konstantin Chernenko," in William J. Olson, ed., *U.S. Strategic Interests in the Gulf Region* (Boulder, CO: Westview Press, 1987), pp. 43–80; and Dilip Hiro, *Inside the Middle East*, p. 294.

64. *Al-Qabas* (May 10, 1977), p. 2. For the 1989 Tucano deal see *Al-Majalla* (March 8–14, 1989), p. 43; *Middle East Economic Digest* (June 2, 1989), p. 36; *Flight International* (February 18, 1989), p. 3; *International Defense Review* (4/1989), p. 516.

65. Colin Legum, ed., *Middle East Contemporary Survey, Vol. 1*, p. 343; and John E. Peterson, *Defending Arabia* (New York: St. Martin's Press, 1986), p. 209. For a review of the Kuwaiti-Soviet relationship see V. Yuryev, "Kuwait Facing the Future," *International Affairs* (Moscow) (March 1984), pp. 141–147; Roger F. Pajak, "Soviet Designs and Dilemmas in the Gulf Region," in H. Richard Sinclair, III and John E. Peterson, *Crosscurrent in the Gulf*, pp. 75–78; and Mark N. Katz, "Soviet Policy in the Gulf States," *Current History*, vol. 84, no. 498 (January 1985), pp. 25–28, and 41.

66. It was reported that the $325 million arms deal was a bluff to provoke Washington, and that the deal was actually for $30 million; see *The Washington Post* (December 1, 1984), p. 3; *Arab News* (July 11, 1988), p. 1; *The Times* (July 25, 1988), p. 52; *Asharq Al-Awsat* (August 17, 1988), p. 3; *Al-Majalla* (August 31-September 6, 1988), p. 33; *Al-Yaqza* (July 22–28, 1988), p. 14; *The Middle East Journal*, vol. 43, no. 1 (Winter 1989), p. 92; and *Al-Watan* (December 25, 1988), p. 21. For the Kuwait-Yugoslavia deal see *Middle East Economic Digest* (June 2, 1989), p. 34, and (June 9, 1989), p. 34; and *Arab News* (June 1, 1989), p. 2.

67. Colin Legum, ed., *Middle East Contemporary Survey, Vol. 1*, p. 344.

68. John Keegan, *World Armies*, p. 417; and Lenore G. Martin, "Patterns of Regional Conflict and US Gulf Policy," in J. Olson, ed., *U.S. Strategic Interests in the Gulf Region*, pp. 9–25. For a review of Kuwaiti-Saudi relations and Saudi irritation over Kuwaiti-Soviet relations see Hafeez Malik, ed., *International Security in Southwest Asia* (New York: Praeger, 1984), pp. 85–91; Nadav Safran, *Saudi Arabia*, p. 269; and William B. Quandt, *Saudi Arabia in the 1980s: Foreign Policy, Security, and Oil* (Washington, D.C.: The Brookings Institution, 1981), p. 24.

69. Personal interview, Kuwait (April 5, 1988); for the issue of Kuwait's boundaries with its three neighbors see Lenore G. Martin, *The Unstable Gulf: Threats from Within*, Kuwait-Iraq, pp. 45–47, Kuwait-Saudi Arabia, pp. 53–54, and Kuwaiti-Iran continental shelf, p. 50.

70. *The Washington Post* (October 4, 1984), p. 5; and personal interview Kuwait (March 30, 1988).

71. *Al-Watan* (January 31, 1987), p. 2.

72. U.S. Congress, House, Subcommittee on International Political and Military Affairs, Committee on International Relations, Hearing, *Proposed Sales to Kuwait of*

Air-to-Air Missiles, 94th Cong., 1st Sess., October 24, 1975 (Washington, D.C.: USGPO, 1976), pp. 21, 48. For an example of the influence of Israeli lobbying efforts against a Kuwaiti arms purchase, see *Flight International* (August 6, 1988), p. 6, and (August 13, 1988), p. 5.

73. *The Washington Post* (June 19, 1984), p. 3.

74. *Al-Watan* (July 25, 1984), p. 3; and *The Washington Post* (December 1, 1984), p. 5. For the total Kuwaiti personnel training see U.S. Department of State, *Background Notes: Kuwait, 1988*, p. 3.

75. Saad Al-Abdullah, speech to the National Press Club, Washington, D.C. (July 13, 1988).

76. *Al-Majalla* (August 31-September 6, 1988), pp. 32–33; *The Christian Science Monitor* (July 12, 1988), pp. 1, 9, 28, and (August 5, 1988), p. 3; *Al-Watan* (December 25, 1988), p. 21; *FBIS* (August 29, 1988), p. 18; Congress, *Proposed Arms Sales to Kuwait* 2nd Session, July 7, 1988 (Washington, D.C.: USGPO, 1988), pp. 1–90; *Aviation Week and Space Technology* (July 11, 1988), p. 15. For an analysis of the Kuwaiti-U.S. relationship see Joseph Wright Twinam, "America and the Gulf Arabs," *American-Arab Affairs*, no. 25 (Summer 1988), pp. 138 –139; for the predicted 1989 deal see *Middle East Economic Digest* (February 17, 1989), p. 20; and Robert Greenberger, "Bush Administration Considers Selling Modern Tanks to Saudi Arabia, Kuwait," *The Wall Street Journal* (February 3, 1989), p. A16.

77. *Al-Watan* (September 24, 1984), p. 5; and see the statement of the French defense minister, Charles Hirnu, *Kuwait News Agency* (KUNA), File No. 8 (April 1984), pp. 16–19. For the 1988 deals see House, *Proposed Arms Sales to Kuwait*, p. 56; Geoffrey Kemp, "Middle East Opportunities," *Foreign Affairs* (1988/89), vol. 68, no. 1, p. 153; and *Middle East Economic Digest* (December 23, 1988), p. 34.

78. *U.S. News and World Report* (July 25, 1988), p. 36.

79. *Middle East Economic Digest*, vol. 28, no. 33 (August 17, 1984), p. 17.

80. The data and information on the armed forces and their structure are adapted from various sources including, but not limited to, IISS, *The Military Balance 1987-1988*, pp. 103–104; IISS, *The Military Balance 1988-1989*, p. 105; *SIPRI Yearbook*, various editions; Mark Heller, ed., *The Middle East Military Balance 1984* (Boulder, CO: Westview Press, 1984, for Tel Aviv University's Jaffee Center for Strategic Studies), p. 129–134; Richard F. Nyrop, ed., *Persian Gulf States*, pp. 389–397; and Richard F. Nyrop, ed., *Area Handbook for the Persian Gulf States* (Washington, D.C.: USGPO, 1977), pp. 194–199.

81. SIPRI, *SIPRI Yearbook 1987: World Armaments and Disarmament* (London: Oxford University Press, 1987), p. 255; for the strength of Kuwait's combat airpower see Michael J. H. Taylor, *Encyclopedia of the World's Air Forces* (New York: Facts On File Publications, 1988), pp. 81 and 92.

82. Anthony H. Cordesman, *The Gulf and the West*, pp. 166–167; and for the function of the coast guard and the most recently acquired Korean barges, see Kuwait Oil Company, *The Kuwait Digest*, vol. 17, no. 1 (January/March 1989), pp. 29–32.

83. Data are adapted from the Ministry of Planning, *Annual Statistical Abstract, 1987*, p. 272, *1982*, p. 242, *1970*, p. 148, *1974*, p. 144, *1977*, p. 218, and *1966*, pp. 99–100. Internal security forces are put at approximately 13,000; see "Kuwait: Deterrence and Instability," *Armed Forces Journal International* (November 1980), p. 59. For an analysis of Kuwait's national guard and public security forces see Richard F. Nyrop, ed., *Area Handbook for the Persian Gulf States*, pp. 196, and 199–200.

84. For the multiple problems that Kuwait forces face see Anthony H. Cordesman, *The Gulf and the West*, pp. 165–170; Anthony H. Cordesman, *The Gulf and the Search for Strategic Stability*, pp. 537, and 569–577; John E. Peterson, *Defending Arabia*, pp.

208–210; John Keegan, *World Armies*, pp. 416–420; and "Kuwait: Deterrence and Instability," *Armed Forces Journal International* (November 1980), pp. 59–60.

85. The estimates are adapted from John Keegan, *World Armies*, p. 415; personal interview, Kuwait (March 30, 1988); and *Middle East Economic Digest* (July 8, 1988), p. 17.

86. *Al-Mjtama* (November 18, 1986), p. 4.

87. *The Christian Science Monitor* (January 29, 1988), p. 9; and *The Economist* (October 31, 1987), p. 58.

88. ACDA, *World Military Expenditures and Arms Transfers, 1987* (Washington, D.C.: USGPO, March 1988), pp. 30, 31, 32, 34, 35, and 36; and Anthony H. Cordesman, *The Gulf and the Search for Strategic Stability*, p. 576.

89. John Keegan, *World Armies*, pp. 417 and 420.

90. Anthony H. Cordesman, *The Gulf and the Search for Strategic Stability*, p. 576; see also John Muttam, *Arms and Insecurity in the Persian Gulf*, pp. 121–123.

91. U.S. Congress, Senate, *War in the Persian Gulf: The U.S. Takes Sides*, a Staff Report to the Committee on Foreign Relations (October 1987), pp. 6 and 38.

92. For an objective and critical analysis of the GCC see Abdullah F. Al-Nafisi, *Majlis Al-Taawun Al-Khaliji: Al-Itar Al-Siyasi Wal-Istratigi* (The Gulf Cooperation Council: The Political and Strategic Dimension) (London: Ta-Ha Publishers, 1982), pp. 2–72; Majid Al-Majid, *Majlis Al-Taawun Al-Khaliji: Azmat Al-Siyasat Wal-Shariyat* (The Gulf Cooperation Council: The Crisis of Politics and Legitimacy) (London: Ta-Ha Publishers, 1986), pp. 23–95; Rex B. Wingarter, "The Rocky Road to GCC Integration," *Middle East International*, no. 276 (May 30, 1986), pp. 14–15; and John A. Sandwick, ed., *The Gulf Cooperation Council: Moderation and Stability in an Interdependent World* (Boulder, CO: Westview Press; Washington, D.C.: American-Arab Affairs Council, 1987), pp. 1–216.

93. Joseph Kostiner, "Shii Unrest in the Gulf," p. 177.

94. *The Christian Science Monitor* (December 7, 1987), p. 10.

95. Interview of President Saddam Hussein, see *Al-Yaqza* (March 4–10, 1988), p. 6.

96. The National Bank of Kuwait, *Kuwait Interim: Economic and Financial Report: Winter 1988* (Kuwait: NBK, 1988), p. 6; *Al-Watan* (January 9, 1988), p. 2; *Al-Kuwayt Al-Yoom* (Kuwait Gazette) (January 3, 1988), pp. 2–3; and *Al-Seyassah* (February 21, 1989), p. 8. For the impact of the oil recession on Kuwait see H.D.S. Greenway, "Kuwait: The Party's Over—the Hangover's Just Setting In," *The Boston Globe* (January 19, 1986), pp. 96, 99.

5

Anxiety and
Uncertainty (1987–1989)

By mid-1986, the low-intensity conflict between Iran and Iraq had broadened into a high-intensity confrontation involving more parties. Kuwait found itself coming under unrelenting attacks from Teheran, and dragged farther and farther into a quagmire. Kuwait was individually unable to influence the war's developments: to slow it down, let alone stop it; to halt Iranian direct and indirect attacks; or even to narrow its own commitments to Iraq. Its aid was an incitement for Iranian attack as well as a "credit" against future Iraqi threats. Kuwait's diplomatic and financial leverage with other Arab states did not help to modify Iran's behavior toward Kuwait, for it was linked to Kuwait's own behavior towards the war. All along, Kuwait's internal and external policies and thinking were dictated by the war and its spill-overs.

Since it had few choices, Kuwait began to play the old card game of "international responsibility" to stop the war. To revive the "forgotten" issue of the war, refocus world attention and internationalize it, Kuwait raised the theme of the world's responsibilities to protect international passageways through the Gulf, where Iran was attacking Kuwaiti-flagged ships and ships trading with Kuwait. This policy represented an about-face from Kuwait's earlier position that the security of the Gulf was the responsibility of the littoral states. Kuwait was perhaps the only Gulf state that shipped all of its oil through the Gulf, unlike Iraq and Saudi Arabia, which maintained pipelines bypassing the Gulf. Thus the so-called tanker war proved to be a bottleneck for Kuwait's oil trade.[1]

Kuwait's course of action, undertaken to protect the state's vital economic interests and to "globalize" the regional war, eventually dampened and shortened the war. In other words, Kuwait's reflagging and chartering actions were the seeds for an international operation to end the Iran-Iraq war. What began as Kuwaiti wishful thinking turned into actual and tangible policy achievements and credits. The Kuwaiti decision to "politicize" a commercial issue paid off. Once again, Kuwait took the lead as the regional innovator and initiator in international politics.

TABLE 5.1 Attacks on Commercial Vessels 1980–1988

	Iran	Iraq	Total
1980	5	--	5
1981	--	5	5
1982	--	22	22
1983	--	16	16
1984	18	53	71
1985	14	33	47
1986	45	66	111
1987	92	89	181
1988	52	38	90
Total	226	322	548
& Percentage	(41.3%)	(58.7%)	

<u>Source</u>: Center for Defense Information, Washington, D.C., Monitor Staff, August 1988.

Chartering and Reflagging of Kuwaiti Oil
Tankers (1987–1989)

In the spring of 1984, when the so-called tanker war flared up, Kuwaiti and Saudi oil tankers became a target of Iranian attacks. On May 13 and 14 Iranian aircraft and speed gunboats attacked the Kuwaiti oil tankers *Umm Qasbah* and *Bahrah* respectively. After an urgent GCC foreign ministers' meeting, the Gulf states lodged a complaint against Iran at the UN Security Council (Chapter 4). Kuwait's foreign minister, Sabah Al-Ahmad, explained to the council, "Since that war broke out, Kuwait has been involved in concerted efforts to stop the fighting between the two Moslem neighbors. These acts of aggression constitute an extension of the evils of that war and have grave and dangerous implications for the stability and security of the region." He added that Kuwait "while exercising the maximum degree of self-restraint, hopes to see a halt to these illegal practices against our tankers, and a guarantee of the freedom of navigation in the Gulf area, in the interest of all countries of the region and the entire world."[2] However, despite the council's call to cease attacking nonbelligerent vessels, Kuwaiti ships and ships trading with Kuwait became an easy prey to continuous, vicious Iranian harassment and grave attacks.

By 1980, five merchant ships had been attacked by both Iran and Iraq, and the figures jumped drastically in the mid-1980s (see Table 5.1). Examples are legion. By 1984, seventy-one vessels and by 1986, 111 vessels were attacked by both parties. By 1987, 181 vessels were attacked, among them eleven Kuwaiti-flagged, fourteen Saudi-flagged, three Qatari-flagged, and one UAE-flagged vessels, not to mention several neutral ships trading with the GCC countries, all apparently attacked by Iran. Out of thirty-two ships attacked by Iran between 1984–1985, twenty-six were bound to or from Kuwaiti ports. On the human side, in 1986, fifty-two merchant seamen were killed. In addition, in 1987, 108 more merchant seamen were killed. By the time of the cease-fire (August, 1988), more than 474 sailors had been killed. Insurance rates for ships calling on Kuwaiti ports had risen more than fifty percent.[3]

Kuwait's attempts to influence Iranian behavior were limited. Kuwait's direct leverage was minimal, if any; except for a low-level diplomatic mission, no channel of influence existed. And Kuwait had exhausted its margin of indirect influence through friendly states such as Algeria, Syria, Pakistan, Turkey, and the UAE.

Iran was determined to "retaliate" against Kuwait's support of Iraq, and was willing to stop attacking only if Kuwait ceased all forms of "war relief" subsidies to Baghdad—an act Kuwait could not afford. The Iranian intention was to break the backbone of the "weak" supporters of Iraq in order to beat Baghdad. In addition, Teheran was increasingly displeased about the alleged mistreatment of Shiites in Kuwait. And, finally, Iran was antagonized by the reflagging of Kuwaiti ships, not to mention the subsequent military escort plan. The Iranians perceived that the Kuwaitis had invited the Americans back to the Gulf, after the Iranian revolution had succeeded in expelling them from the area. Hussein Montazeri, formerly Khomeini's designated successor, castigated Kuwait as well as Saudi Arabia for that policy. Without these "Arab leaders . . . the Americans could not possibly do anything in the region." Holding that it enjoys a clearly powerful role in the Gulf area, Iran's newly announced policy combined a tough approach with flexibility.[4]

But by spring 1986, after the Iranian occupation of the Iraqi Faw peninsula, Kuwaiti decision-makers came to realize their inability to change Iran's retaliatory policies and its actual threats to the commercial interests and security of the state. Therefore, they began carefully entertaining a host of options, uppermost among which was the idea of collective security. In other words, they sought security elsewhere, primarily through the GCC states. Since the GCC theoretically functions as a "defense" mechanism for its member states, it should be able to provide some form of security umbrella, either actual or symbolic, in the form of a deterrent force to challenge any possible aggressor against the GCC states and their interests. Therefore, at the seventh GCC summit conference in Abu Dhabi, November 3–5, 1986, Kuwait confronted its GCC partners with the immediate threats to its survival and presented the Gulf leaders with three plain demands: (1) station a contingent of the GCC forces, preferably the Peninsula Shield, in Bubiyan Island, across the Iranian-occupied Faw peninsula; (2) provide a blanket of freedom of navigation, in any form, to the Kuwaiti oil and merchant fleets through the Gulf's international waterways; and (3) include Kuwait, on a permanent basis, within the AWAC's surveillance zones, thus giving Kuwait the advantage of early warnings against possible Iranian attacks. Furthermore, the Kuwaitis informed the meeting that should the

GCC summit turn down the Kuwaiti requests, then Kuwait would consider itself free to seek security elsewhere, in any form, even through the five permanent members of the UN Security Council.[5]

To Kuwait's astonishment, the GCC states turned down its requests and reluctantly left it up to Kuwait to decide on the feasibility of any alternative that might meet its requirements. After this GCC "snub," Kuwait found itself left out in the cold, in a state of helplessness and profound frustration. It therefore seriously sought a shield for its commercial interests and security elsewhere.

The GCC states' rationale was their unwillingness, for a variety of political, commercial, and military reasons, to confront Iran, the largest of the Gulf states. Also, some GCC states, particularly Oman and the UAE, had prospered from commercial trade with Iran during the war.[6] Furthermore, the GCC states did not want to abandon all means of contact with Iran; they wanted to have a long-term "insurance policy" with their large neighbors. The GCC's dismissiveness showed the GCC states' lack of interest in Kuwait and its concerns.

By the end of the GCC summit, the Iranian intimidation of Kuwait's oil shipping had become tantamount to a blockade of Kuwaiti commerce. The Iranian actions, in the words of Kuwait's foreign minister, Sabah Al-Ahmad, reached the point "that pumping our oil to the outside world was extremely threatened . . . [thus] damaging our main source of national income."[7] Inevitably, by December 1986 and early 1987, Kuwait was approaching the permanent members of the Security Council (the Soviet Union, the United States, Britain, France, and China, in that order), about chartering and reflagging Kuwait's twenty-two oil tankers. According to the minister of state for foreign affairs, Saud Mohammad Al-Osaimi, Kuwait's new strategy was to "facilitate the superpowers' task in keeping peace in the world." The minister emphasized that "after all, the Gulf is considered an international waterway, where the rights of free navigation are confirmed in international law. Part of the responsibility for keeping the peace is to keep the international waterways open."[8]

Kuwait's tactics were thus seemingly based on the assumption that the duty of the superpowers was to police the world for safety and security, and that the safety of Gulf commerce was part and parcel of their responsibilities. Not surprisingly, then, they thought that shipment of Kuwaiti oil could be achieved through "reliance" on larger and stronger powers. The political security and safety of the oil trade could be attained through commercial means; and the best means to deter Iranian attacks was to charter or reregister the ships under the flags of the most powerful nations, particularly the United States and the Soviet Union. Simply put, the Kuwaiti assumption was that Iran might be too "timid" to attack any ships that carried the superpowers' flags. Deductively, a diplomat reasoned, the Iranians had not disturbed any Soviet ships earlier.[9] Moreover, the Kuwaitis rationalized, should their reflagged ships be attacked, it would be natural and necessary for the governments involved to come to their rescue through whatever means those governments deemed necessary, including armed protection. In fact, hoisting the flag of a superpower was viewed as a deterrent by itself because it will increase the superpowers' stake in the conflict. Moreover, Kuwait had already reregistered or chartered some sixty-six ships carrying different flags,[10] so this approach was not a new experiment even though it reversed a long-established tradition of superpower noninvolvement in the Gulf. In short, Kuwait's request to the superpowers was not a naive action, but a well-calculated political decision with far-reaching political and security implications, though it used the relatively commercial means of the "flag of convenience."[11]

In fact, from a geostrategic perspective, the Gulf region is cumulatively an important passageway for international trade. Over 12,000 ships pass through the Gulf each year, and 100 are present in the Gulf at any given moment.[12] In 1986, some six million barrels of oil were shipped through the Gulf daily. Twelve percent of that oil, or 727,000 b/d, was Kuwaiti oil. The Gulf states are important commercial partners to the West, since that area possesses some two-thirds of the world's known oil reserves; about fifty percent of the world's reserves are in Kuwait, Qatar, Saudi Arabia, and the UAE. The Gulf is a passageway for one-eighth of the free world's oil imports. In 1986, it produced more than twenty-two percent of the fuel consumed in the world. Six percent of oil consumed in the U.S. was supplied by the Gulf, in contrast to twenty-five percent of Europe's and sixty percent of Japan's fuel requirements. Kuwait's former defense minister, Salem Al-Sabah, described the political economy of the Gulf and its significance to the world's economy this way: "protection of the Gulf is desired from the Europeans and others . . . who want 'oil' from this important and vital source to reach them. . . . Hence they can maintain . . . the continuation of their factories, etc."[13]

Because the Soviet Union has always sought to reduce Western involvement in the oil economy of the Gulf, because Kuwait had maintained a good working relationship with the Soviets, and because the Kuwaiti request presented a golden opportunity for them to make inroads into the Gulf, Moscow gladly approved Kuwait's request. Kuwait's oil minister, Ali Al-Khalifa, referred to the Soviets' response as "extremely positive." On April 19, 1987, Kuwait and the Soviet Union signed an agreement under which Kuwait was to lease three Soviet oil tankers, with an option of leasing two more. In addition, the Kuwaitis were allowed to lease tankers to the Soviet Union, and thus to raise the Soviet flag on Kuwaiti vessels. The three Soviet chartered vessels cost Kuwait between $15 and $18 million a year.[14] In early May 1987, the Soviet chartered vessels began their mission. Unluckily, on May 16, 1987, the charter tanker *Marshal Chuikov* struck a mine off Kuwait.[15]

In the meantime, Kuwaiti eyes were on Washington, whose response to the initial contacts was lethargic and indeed ambiguous, because the Americans did not want to commit themselves to such a large-scale, open-ended, and unpredictable venture. After all, Kuwait individually and in itself might present little geostrategic advantage to the United States, and Kuwait's general policies have been vocally anti-American (see Chapter 3); therefore Kuwait neither generated sympathy nor promised tangible gains.

In December 1986 the Kuwaiti government approached the U.S. Coast Guard about the procedure for reregistration, but the Coast Guard's response was that a decision might take up to six months.[16] In January 1987, Kuwait formally requested that the United States reflag up to eight Kuwaiti vessels.

Two major developments influenced the Americans to join the bandwagon before it was too late. First, the revelation of Iran's arms-for-hostages deal had ruined America's reputation in the Arab world, particularly among the Gulf states, whose "enemy" it was engaged in rearming. A congressional document linked reflagging to a broader goal: to "recover from that sorry aberration from a long-standing policy, and through credible and persuasive behavior, to rebuild confidence in the Middle East and elsewhere that the affair was indeed nothing more than a bizarre blunder that will not be repeated." Second, Kuwait's initial maneuver with the Soviet card, and the speedy Soviet acceptance of the Kuwaiti proposal, generated fears of the old czarist dream of reaching the warm waters of the Gulf. In the words of Michael H. Armacost, the former undersecretary of state for political affairs, the Americans hoped "to limit the efforts of both Iran and the Soviet Union to expand their influence in the area—to our detriment and that of the West."[17] In general, the American reflagging plan was "based first on inhibiting Soviet expansion into the Gulf and meddling in Gulf states politics, and perhaps only secondarily on improving relations with the Kuwaitis and other moderate Gulf states."[18]

A timely incident contributed to the final American decision. The May 17, 1987, Iraqi attack on the *USS Stark* and the high toll of casualties (37 dead) changed the issue's political dimensions in the United States and abroad, and reflagging became a controversial public policy. On May 19, the Reagan administration approved Kuwait's request to reflag half of its fleet, and announced that it would raise U.S. defense capabilities in the Gulf in order to escort the reflagged oil tankers. But did Kuwait, perhaps unknowingly, thus become a pawn in the international politics of superpower rivalry and competition? In essence, the American move was meant to counterbalance any Soviet involvement in the Gulf, and was primarily an anti-Iranian action rather than a pro-Kuwaiti or pro-Arab change of attitude or policy.

Kuwait Petroleum Corporation, which technically owned the shipping fleet, set up a subsidiary (the Chesapeake Shipping Corporation) in Delaware. Meanwhile, the United States waived some of its maritime law requirements in order to speed up the reregistration of the Kuwaiti ships. The eleven reflagged tankers (see Table 5.2) consisted of one crude oil carrier, four liquefied petroleum gas carriers, and six petroleum product carriers. They carried some thirty-five percent of Kuwait's oil exports, with another fifteen percent under the British flag.[19]

Despite the U.S. government's initial reservations and wariness toward the Kuwaiti request, a State Department document showed that reflagging

TABLE 5.2 Protected Tankers In Kuwaiti Oil Fleet

	Old Name	New Name	Tonnage	Type
U.S.	Ar-Rekkah	Bridgeton	401,000	ULCC
Reflagged	Al-Funtas	Middleton	290,000	VLPC
	Kazimah	Townsend	295,000	VLPC
	Umm Casbah	Ocean City	80,000	Product
	Umm Matrabah	Chesapeake City	80,000	Product
	Umm Al-Aish	Surf City	81,000	Product
	Umm Al-Maradem	Sea Island City	81,000	Product
	Gas Al-Kuwait	Gas Queen	47,000	LPG
	Gas Al-Ahmadi	Gas Princess	47,000	LPG
	Gas Al-Burgan	Gas King	47,000	LPG
	Gas Al-Minagish	Gas Prince	47,000	LPG
U.S.	Maryland*		265,000	VLCC
Chartered	New York*		265,000	VLCC
British	Chilham Castle	Ras Al-Jalayah	27,841	Product
Reflagged	Tonbridge	Al-Faihah	263,679	ULCC
	--------	Ras Al-Barshah	28,031	Product
British	B.T. Banker		315,000	ULCC
Chartered	B.T. Banker		340,000	ULCC
	Red Sea**		210,000	VLCC
USSR	Marshal Chulkov		39,000	Product
Chartered	Marshal Bagrasyan		58,000	Product
	Makop		25,000	Product

*Kuwait backed out of chartering these two supertankers; see *The Washington Post* (December 22, 1987), p. A20.
**Was under consideration

Source: U.S. Congress, House, *National Security Policy Implications of United States Operations in the Persian Gulf*, Report to the Defense Policy Panel and the Investigations Subcommittee, Committee on Armed Services, 100th Cong., 1st Sess. (Washington, D.C.: USGPO, July 1987), p. 88; *The New York Times* (October 27, 1987), p. A13; and *The Times* (London) (August 25, 1987), pp. 1, 18.

is not a new phenomenon in U.S. maritime history. Since 1981, more than fifty ships have been reflagged.[20]

Britain approved the chartering of three tankers to Kuwait, and the reflagging of another three tankers. Kuwait Petroleum Corporation purchased Kent Petroleum and transferred the ownership of the tankers to this British company. Meanwhile, two tankers (*Modhi* and the Brazilian *Marina*) were reregistered in Gibralter, thus entitling them to the protection of British warships. France was uncommitted, but replied that it would "look seriously" at Kuwait's request. The Chinese, in contrast, informed Kuwait that they were unaccustomed to such procedures, and faced technical difficulties because they had "neither tankers nor warships in the area." Six other tankers were reregistered in Liberia.[21]

The new Kuwaiti "realignment" with the superpowers brought little measurable political opposition at home. Indeed, opposition and protests were either muted or sedated, since the National Assembly was closed in July 1986 and the press was subsequently censored.[22] In general, there has been neither a whole-hearted public support for the Kuwaiti strategy nor an outright rejection of it—merely a sort of apathy. But it should be made clear, as well, that there is an almost unanimous consensus in matters relating to the survival of the state and maintenance of its "splendid" lifestyle, which of course depends on marketing its oil. After all, it should be recognized that the new strategy is not unprecedented in Kuwait's past and contemporary practices. Identification and even "alliance," in a variety of forms, with external power(s) is the last resort to safeguard the state. In the nineteenth century (see Chapter 1), Kuwait aligned itself through a protective treaty with Britain to preempt regional claims and international competition. And, as Chapter 2 explained, in 1961 it invited foreign troops (British and Arab League) to halt Iraqi aggression against the new independent entity. The new strategy was different only in scope and political context. Of course, Arab nationalist and Palestinian groups tend not to be identified with the United States in particular, and there is always "some apprehension that a superpower is intruding in the Arab world."[23] But in reality, Arab nationalists and other groups in Kuwait dare not disturb their "affluent" prosperity, well-being, and status quo, which depend in large part on the economy of oil.

Meanwhile, the Kuwaitis were viewing the reflagging procedure, at least in public, as a strictly commercial deal, and refused to offer the Americans any direct bases or access facilities for their escort forces. Kuwait's prime minister and crown prince, Saad Al-Abdullah, defended Kuwait's decision as "a purely commercial operation, aimed at insuring the continued transportation of Kuwaiti oil to its markets and Kuwait's fulfillment of its contractual commitments." Furthermore, the reflagging "measure was neither new nor novel. We have been hiring ships and tankers from various countries of the world." The Kuwaiti official downplayed any potential misinterpretations of the reflagging as a warning to other parties by saying that this step "was not intended as a provocation to anyone nor was it directed against anyone. It does not seek to involve or draw in anyone or to invite anyone to interfere in the region."[24] In fact, in order to preempt and placate any opposition to the new Kuwaiti initiative, and probably reflecting Kuwait's genuine intentions, Kuwait's oil minister, Ali Al-Khalifa, declared that "Kuwait is ready to give priority to hoisting the flags of any . . . Arab, Islamic, or friendly states on its tankers over the flags of the superpowers, if they are able to guarantee the safety of these tankers in the Gulf."[25]

Nevertheless, Kuwait began a diplomatic campaign to convince Arab and other nations that it had legitimate reasons for reflagging, and that this policy was "impermanent." Indeed, Kuwaiti officials interpreted reflagging as being not an expression of Kuwait's ongoing foreign policy, but merely a brief interlude between "self-reliance" and the bitter turmoil of the Iran-Iraq war. Thus, to bring wider public and official support to what seemed to be a controversial plan, Kuwaiti officials met with more than sixty foreign accredited representatives in Kuwait. Moreover, high-ranking official delegations toured a number of friendly capitals to explain the Kuwaiti perception of the new policy.[26]

At the time, Kuwait's then defense minister, Salem Al-Sabah, declared, "we would not allow U.S. bases to be erected in Kuwait no matter what they may be or in any form they may take and there is no way possible that pressure can be exerted on us from outside to erect such facilities." Another Kuwaiti official reiterated Kuwait's objection to becoming involved in convoy operations: "They are your vessels now, it is your responsibility to protect them."[27] However, it has since become clear that Kuwait provided logistical support to the American naval forces accompanying the escorted vessels. It provided free energy supplies and access for minesweeping helicopters.[28] In addition, Kuwait made available two tugboats fitted for minesweeping gear, as well as two large barges that provided offices and rooms for 150 servicemen and served as temporary bases. Before the reflagging date, Kuwait allowed a twenty-member U.S. mine disposal team to clear mines in waters near Kuwait. And Kuwait agreed to provide protection for the eleven reflagged tankers within fifty miles of Kuwaiti ports.[29] The side-effect of these arrangements was closer Kuwaiti-United States relations in a number of fields, in "an atmosphere of increasing candor and intimacy."[30]

Indeed, on July 10–16, 1988, the Kuwaiti crown prince and prime minister, Saad Al-Abdullah, paid an official working visit to Washington, the first such visit by a high-ranking Kuwaiti since 1968. This occasion reflected the new warmth in the two countries' relationship. In general, the credibility of the United States had increased in the area. By early 1988, Kuwaiti and American officials pronounced the reflagging policy "a strategic victory."[31]

→ But the decisions of the superpowers to reflag the Kuwaiti tankers infuriated and further isolated the Iranians. Direct attacks against Kuwait using Silkworm missiles continued unabated, and internal acts of subversion did not cease either. Moreover, the Iranians promptly used a new tactic of intimidation: mining the main shipping routes in the Gulf waterways. The Iranians began in July 1987 to mine Kuwait's main shipping channels. In the words of a Kuwaiti diplomat, the mining of the Gulf was an indirect Iranian challenge to America's prestige and power; hence the U.S. decided to augment its involvement in the Gulf.[32]

Meanwhile, seven Silkworm and other missile attacks (see Appendix C) were launched against Kuwait, beginning with a hit against the 400,000-ton American-registered tanker *Bridgeton* in Kuwait waters on July 24, 1987, in the first convoy of Kuwaiti ships. Other attacks took place on September 3, October 15, 16, and 22, December 7, 1987, and April 20, 1988, all against either Kuwaiti oil and industrial targets, or oil tankers in Kuwaiti territorial waters. Moreover, by January 1988 it was reported that sixteen merchant ships carrying oil or cargo to or from Kuwait had been attacked by Iranian gunboats at the entrance of the Gulf.[33] More than twenty-five incidents of sabotage were reported in Kuwait in 1987, involving both human and economic costs. Kuwait's options for direct action against Iran were limited to harmless diplomatic protests.

However, on September 21, 1987 the United States retaliated against Iranian attacks on its reflagged ships by attacking an Iranian naval vessel (the *Iran Ajr*), killing three crew members, and capturing twenty-six in the act of laying mines. In retaliation for the October attacks, the United States destroyed Iranian oil platforms in the offshore Rostam oil field. When an American frigate, the *Samuel B. Roberts*, hit a mine on April 14, 1988, the navy destroyed two Iranian platforms (Sassan and Sirri) and crippled six Iranian ships.[34] The tit-for-tat patterns led to increased American-Iranian confrontations, a warlike atmosphere of tension in the Gulf waterways, and an increased presence of naval powers. Hence it became appropriate to speak of the "internationalization" of the localized war. These actions undoubtedly made the war a larger international conflict involving stronger outside forces, thus by accident meeting a long-standing Iraqi demand to broaden the scope of the war and bring in more outside participants, in order to halt the Iranian advances through the moral presence and actual commitment of the powerful nations. Therefore, in a sense, the new Kuwaiti actions proved to be a back door to relieving the Iraqis from the Iranian pressures. And the international community, fearful, for the first time, of the high cost to its own interests in the region, increased the momentum of its search for a diplomatic and peaceful means to end the conflict. In other words, Kuwait's act was an exceptional occasion for all superpowers to work harmoniously toward a common goal.

On July 20, 1987, the United Nations Security Council unanimously passed a resolution (598) demanding an immediate cease-fire in the war, withdrawal of the troops to internationally recognized borders, exchange of prisoners of war, formation of an impartial committee to investigate the war, and talks to settle the conflict. This compromise resolution was meant to meet almost all of the legitimate Iranian and Iraqi demands, hoping to convince both parties, through various means, of the advantages of settling their differences and indeed their competition at the negotiating table. A congressional report emphasized the effectiveness of settlement through the international organization: "the best means to prevent Iraqi defeat and Iranian advances is to end the Iran-Iraq war . . . the United Nations . . . constitutes the best means to accomplish the task of bringing concerned world pressure to bear toward this objective."[35] And as part of the American containment of Iran, before the reflagging scheme the United States initiated "Operation Staunch" to halt arms supplies to Iran in order to lessen its capabilities to wage the war.

In sum, through this shrewd and far-sighted action Kuwait was able to draw worldwide attention to its plight and to ship its oil virtually unharmed, and more importantly to involve the superpowers in the resolution of the "forgotten" Gulf war and its potential spill-overs. A side-effect of the reflagging and the "internationalization" of the war was lowering the number of attacks on commercial vessels from 181 in 1987 to 90 in 1988. Furthermore, no Kuwaiti-owned vessels were involved except the reflagged *Bridgeton* and *Sea Isle City*.[36]

An American official explained the Kuwaiti attempt to identify with all the superpowers as an effort "to retain its . . . balance in its foreign policy and to engage the military presence of as many permanent members of the Security Council as possible." The Kuwaiti political coup was, according to this official, an "unusual step in an unusual situation."[37] Another observer described the Kuwaiti course as a balancing act that avoids dependence on either superpowers yet aligns both against the aggressive tendencies of Iran.[38] This policy in essence reflects Kuwait's traditional balanced, centrist orientation toward all superpowers. The new approach was not to supplant that centrist orientation, but rather to reinforce it. The involvement of all the superpowers represented a sort of all-or-nothing position. In brief, the chartering and reflagging course was a microcosm of Kuwait's centrist, nonideological, and nonpolitical commitments towards both superpowers.

By mid-1988, because of the foreign naval presence, international pressures and other factors, among them Teheran's failure to occupy Basra, Iran felt "besieged." And some analysts believe that Iran had to choose between continuing a stalemated war and the eventual internal decomposition of the revolution, as well as the consequent overthrow of the Islamic regime. It was becoming abundantly clear that the superpowers would not have allowed the Iraqis to lose or, for that matter, the Iranians to win. Realizing the futility of its challenge to and confrontation with the regional states, world powers, and world public opinion, Iran surprisingly agreed to accept Security Council resolution 598. In other words, it concluded that it could not afford to fight the world altogether,[39] thus paving the way, it is to be hoped, for an eventual peaceful settlement of this devastating war. Meanwhile, by late September 1988, as the threat to Gulf shipping was minimized, the United States agreed to drop its widely publicized "escort" system, thus removing a major incitement to violence or, conversely, an element of security in the area. Up to December 1987, the navy had carried out twenty-three convoy transits escorting a total of fifty-six tankers. By the time the military escort was dropped (September 1988), the navy had carried out eighty-nine convoy operations.[40] Meanwhile, in late September 1988, Kuwait announced its plan to send its first Kuwaiti-flagged oil tanker (the *al-Kuwaitiah*) through the Gulf since reflagging began in July 1987.[41] These acts undoubtedly reflect the initial return of normalcy in the Gulf waterways.

In retrospect, then, the Kuwaiti act was a political deal concealed in commercial practices, a tactic that achieved Kuwait's economic security. By the same token, the superpowers' reactions to the Kuwaiti demands were political in kind. The new arrangements were merely a means to larger and broader political goals. A congressional report succinctly illustrated that point: "reflagging and chartering the Kuwaiti tankers is an action of the most profound political, military, and diplomatic consequences that increasingly is attracting the attention of the people of the United States and the world."[42]

The Internationalization of the Iran-Iraq War (1987–1988)

Since Iran recaptured its own territories, expelled the Iraqis, and chased them into their territories in 1982, it has been the Iraqi goal to bring in the Americans to stop Iranian adventurism and expansionism.[43] However, the United States has been, all along, reluctant to alienate and confront Iran directly. Instead, it indirectly encouraged the Gulf states to increase their "subsidies" to Iraq's war efforts, and provided the latter with intelligence information, from which it benefited.[44]

Moreover, in light of Iranian occupation of the Faw peninsula, the threats to and actual attacks on neutral ships and nonbelligerent third party Kuwaiti commerce added new urgency to the conflict. The war went out of control, and confrontations between Iran and the various Gulf states, as well as the United States, reached a new level of brinkmanship. As a result of Kuwait's new policy, the superpowers gradually initiated a pattern of power concentration in the Gulf as a deterrent and a show of force. By mid-to-late 1987, the Gulf had been turned into an international turf occupied by different military "insignias," in numbers unprecedented in the region's history.

Traditionally, the United States had maintained a small, symbolic Middle East Force (MIDEASTFOR) flotilla since 1948. It consisted of a flagship (the *USS LaSalle*) and two combatants, and maintained an administrative support unit at the Jufair base in Bahrain.[45]

The Carter Doctrine of 1980, which set U.S. policies for the area in the postshah era, proclaimed that the U.S. would prevent any attempt "by [an] outside force" to control the region, and that any such attempt would be considered an act of war.[46] The doctrine set up the Rapid Deployment Force (RDF), later formalized into the U.S. Central Command (CENTCOM), and resulted in the expansion of the Middle East Force by two ships.

By the summer of 1987, the MIDEASTFOR had twelve ships: the *LaSalle*; the amphibious assault ship *Guadalcanal*, a landing ship dock used to carry the minesweeping boats and other craft; the guided missile destroyer *Kidd*, which serves as convoy leader; two guided missile cruisers; and six guided missile frigates. Another carrier group that normally functioned in the Gulf of Oman contained about fifteen ships, including the battleships *USS Ranger* and *USS Missouri*. Moreover, the United States had four Airborne Warning and Control System (AWACS) aircraft and two accompanying tanker planes operating out of an air base near Riyadh. In fact, the MIDEASTFOR has direct communication links with these AWACS, and with five other Saudi AWACS and eight accompanying tankers. By summer 1987, therefore, the total United States presence reached some thirty ships and at least 15,000 naval personnel.

By winter 1987, the U.S. military presence peaked at forty-eight ships, supported by an estimated 25,000 personnel and assigned on a 6-month rotation schedule. They included one aircraft carrier; one battleship; six minesweepers; four guided missile cruisers; two guided missile destroyers; two destroyers; five guided missile frigates; two frigates; two auxiliary landing ships; and five auxiliary support ships.[47] The new show of force represented "the greatest concentration of naval firepower in a region since the Vietnam war."[48]

In order to cement and solidify the new pattern of military relationships with the Gulf states, the then Secretary of Defense Frank Carlucci twice visited Kuwait and other Gulf states in January and December 1988 to discuss bilateral relations, and to define the new American responsibilities toward the security of Kuwait.[49] The Americans assured the Kuwaitis that they would help Kuwait if the war expands.[50] In essence, Kuwait and the United States discussed issues that had previously been tabled,[51] and the military relationship between the two countries has grown closer as a result.

By the time of the August 20, 1988 cease-fire, there were twenty-seven American ships in the Gulf region, sixteen of them inside the Gulf itself, in addition to two large barges that served as observation posts and bases for armed helicopters.[52]

Meanwhile, a plethora of unrivaled access facilities, developed to support the new American role, had engulfed the region in a wave of militarism. After 1980, in the aftermath of Iran's revolution, the United States made up for its lost position in Iran by augmenting a network of access facilities on the periphery of the Gulf, in Oman, Bahrain, Somalia, Kenya, Portugal, Morocco, and Diego Garcia. The United States spent over $1.1 billion on these projects. In Oman, the United States spent more than $256 million on runways, refueling areas, storage sheds in Masirah Island, Seeb Air Base in the north, and Thumrait Air Base in the south. Moreover, the United States had $121 million worth of equipment, such as food, trucks, electronics, artillery shells, and air-to-air missiles, cached in Oman. The United States is also allowed to use Masirah Island as a landing and refueling point for P-30 Orion maritime aircraft.[53] Bahrain provides port facilities for the MIDEASTFOR station, and the CENTCOM has a small headquarters there.[54]

In Somalia, the United States spent $54 million to reconstruct two air and port facilities in Berbera and Mogadishu. In Kenya, the United States puts more than $30 million into dredging the harbor of the port of Mombasa and into the Nanyuk airfield. The United States uses Portugal and Morocco as part of its supply and communication network, and has expended more than $100 million toward improving that network. Most of these facilities are not permanent American bases and do not have permanent American staff; but they are invaluable as places where American forces would use in a crisis.[55]

Since the increased American forces were restricted to deterring Iran from attacking the Kuwaiti ships, while other commercial vessels were left prey to Iranian and/or Iraqi attacks, by early 1988 Saudi Arabia requested that the United States extend its protection to all neutral ships calling at Arab ports of the Gulf.[56] In April 1988, the Reagan administration altered its escort policy to provide protection for some ships flying non-U.S. flags, provided that they not carry contraband, resist legitimate search requests, or serve the ports of the belligerents. On April 18, the United States attacked Iranian speedboats that had hit a British-flagged tanker and an oil platform operated by an American firm but owned by the UAE. And in July 1988, when an Iranian commercial aircraft was shot down, the American forces had been engaged to rescue a Danish freighter being attacked by the Iranians. Since 1984, the American forces had escorted four to ten U.S.-flagged merchant ships in and out of the Gulf each month.

The new escort assignments resulted in additional financial stress. The fiscal year 1987 incremental cost for the military operation in the Gulf was $69 million. The fiscal year 1988 incremental cost has been put at around $10 million to $15 million per month, or about $130 million to $150 million. By the end of the first six months of the reflagging, the U.S. Navy spent some $120 million for twenty-three successful convoys, or $5 million per escort.[57] Since eighty-nine convoy operations were carried out throughout the period July 1987–September 1988, we may assume that the escort policy had cost the Americans roughly $445 million. The financial cost of the escort missions to Kuwait is unclear. Former Kuwaiti defense and currently interior minister Salem Al-Sabah stated that "the United States has not yet furnished Kuwait with a bill."[58] However, the American administration did acknowledge that Kuwaiti support of reflagging operations totalled in excess of $5 million a month (in free gas, etc.).[59] We may thus estimate that Kuwait's contribution to the procedure was approximately $75 million.

The other NATO allies also committed themselves militarily, in different degrees, to safeguarding the Gulf and the interests of the West. By July 1987, France had dispatched the aircraft carrier *Clemenceau*, two frigates, and one support ship to the Middle East, just outside the Gulf waters. And by October it had one aircraft carrier, six combatants, three minesweepers, and four auxiliaries in the area.[60] The increased French activities followed an attack on July 13, 1987, on a container ship the *Ville d'Anvers*) carrying the French flag. In addition, the French maintained a base in Djibouti, with 4,000 men and several squadrons of Mirage fighter-bombers. In other words, the French had committed about one-half of their warships to the region.

Although the French had maintained a policy of "accompanying" French-flagged ships on a case-by-case basis, they agreed to come to the assistance of commercial ships in the area on humanitarian grounds. As a commander of the French task force in the Gulf stated, "it is a duty for any ship to answer any Mayday call." By late 1987 and early 1988, the French warships had stopped attacks on two Liberian-flagged ships.[61]

The British maintained three combatants (the frigate *Broadsword*, the guided missile destroyer *Cardiff*, and the support ship *Orangeleaf*) and an oiler in the area. And in August 1987, Britain sent four minesweepers to the Gulf. As of October 1987, Britain had three combatants, four minesweepers, and two auxiliaries in the area. The British have escorted British-flagged ships since December 1980. In fact, since 1987, British military ships have accompanied over 100 British-flagged vessels traveling south of Bahrain.[62]

Italy had sent three minesweepers, three guided missile frigates, and two auxiliaries (a supply ship and a salvage vessel) to the Gulf.[63] In early October 1987, Italy conducted its first convoy operations, when two Italian warships escorted an Italian-flagged ship. The cost for operation of the Italian naval units in the Gulf reached some $13.5 million per month. The Italian parliament authorized $80 million for the first six months of 1988.

Despite the Dutch on-and-off attitude toward engagement in the Gulf, on August 10, 1987, following an incident in which a Dutch vessel was damaged by a mine, the Dutch government announced that it would deploy two minesweepers to the Gulf. In the meantime, Belgium sent a force of two minesweepers and one support vessel to the Gulf.

The allied forces maintained some degree of coordination and cooperation in the Gulf waterways. After a NATO meeting of May 1987, informal arrangements and contacts developed between the various forces. While the French, British, and Italian forces took responsibility for minesweeping operations in the lower Gulf, the United States was assigned clearing responsibilities in the upper Gulf.[64] The various forces shared intelligence information on the Gulf, and their ships communicated with one another regularly, but "each nation's military presence is dedicated to its commercial shipping."[65]

Meanwhile, West Germany and Spain expressed a desire to use their ships to fill any NATO vacuum caused by the allied deployments to the Gulf. Japan expressed its willingness to make a financial contribution to the collective Western mission and to other projects in the area, including the purchase of a $10 million navigation system for the Gulf to enable the ships to avoid danger areas.[66]

In January 1988 the Western military forces consisted of one aircraft carrier, six destroyers, six frigates, fourteen minesweepers, and six auxiliaries. By winter 1988, then, the allied forces had thirty-three combat ships, minesweepers and support vessels, and there were a total of eighty-two western vessels in the Gulf and the adjacent areas.[67]

In the aftermath of the Gulf war cease-fire, there were an estimated sixteen Western minesweepers in the region: six Americans, three British, three French, two Italian, one Belgian, and one Dutch. Belgium and the Netherlands announced their intentions to withdraw. In spite of the respite in the fighting, American officials estimated that there were still some 150 to 175 mines deployed in the Gulf.[68]

The Gulf Arab states took both token and actual roles in the "internationalization" of the war. They provided in a variety of ways many "small, unreported things"[69] for the American missions. Besides the already mentioned roles of Kuwait, Bahrain, and Oman, the Saudis used their AWACS planes to patrol parts of the Gulf. Moreover, the Saudis allowed two of their four minesweepers to help clear Kuwaiti waters. The United Arab

Emirates allowed the Saudi AWACS to overfly its territories. The Gulf states permitted American minesweeping and other helicopters to use their bases for occasional "emergency" stops, although they refused to grant permanent bases. All in all, these states provided considerable maintenance support, port visits, etc., for the United States naval forces.[70]

Although the GCC states left Kuwait directly exposed to Iranian threats, they nevertheless extended diplomatic support to the "encircled" Kuwaiti regime. The GCC was successful in organizing an Arab summit conference in Amman in November 1987, devoted almost entirely to the single issue of the Iran-Iraq war. Through the conference, the GCC states were able to send signals to Iran, other regional states, and other states of their frustrated desire to end the war and to isolate Iran diplomatically.

The GCC was able to use its collective financial muscle to pressure Syria to support the GCC states and censure Iran. Likewise, the summit gave the "green light" for Egypt's rehabilitation into Arab politics as a counterweight to Iran. Moreover, the GCC was able to warn both Moscow and Beijing that arming Iran would result in no loans, aid, or investment.[71]

Other regional superpowers also played a role in "internationalizing" the war. Egypt, the largest Arab nation, helped the Gulf states in a number of ways. By November 1987, the Gulf states had restored their diplomatic relations with Cairo, which had been severed after the Camp David accord of the late 1970s. On October 2, 1987, President Hosni Mubarak declared that Egypt supported Kuwait "with all our feelings and our potentials."[72] And in January 1988 Mubarak visited the Gulf states, thus marking the re-emergence of Egypt as a major player in Arab politics. By summer 1988 Egypt had provided Kuwait with about 100 pilots, technicians, and air defense specialists, and had sold Kuwait some 100 "Fahd" and "other" armored personnel carriers and the Amoun defense system. Some observers even expected that Egyptian troops might replace the Pakistanis in Saudi Arabia.[73]

In return for Egypt's new role, the Gulf states have contributed $100 million toward Egypt's repayments for arms purchases, plus more than $45 million in direct aid in 1987. Moreover, it was reported that Kuwait was cooperating with other Gulf states to give Egypt a financial package of $20 billion in interest-free loans. It seems that Mubarak was interested in supporting the Gulf states, in part as these countries were a source of help to Egypt in dealing with its problem of debt burden.[74] Egypt, also, was eager to regain its central role in directing Arab politics after many years of boycott and isolation.

If these forceful actions by the United States, its allies, and Kuwait's friends in the region had not been enough to broaden the scope of the Iran-Iraq war, the Soviet Union was not altogether out of the scene. Yet its military involvement was miniscule compared with that of the West. By July 1987, the Soviet Union's naval forces in the Gulf included a Kara cruiser, a Kashin class destroyer, three minesweepers, and several support ships. By September 1987, nine Soviet naval vessels were in the region. And by

January 1988, the estimated Soviet presence reached twenty-three combat ships, minesweepers, and support ships. As the cease-fire approached, the Soviets had three minesweepers in the Gulf.[75]

The role of the Soviet forces in the Gulf was to escort the chartered Soviet tankers as well as those merchant ships traveling with military supplies destined for Iraq. In the period fall 1986 to fall 1987, the Soviets escorted more than forty transits of arms carriers to Kuwait.[76] The Soviets began this policy after Iran boarded a Soviet ship in September 1986.[77]

But unlike the U.S. Navy, the Soviet navy was not allowed regular access to the Gulf states' ports; it therefore relied on support from bases at Socotra or Aden, more than 1000 miles away from the Strait of Hormuz. Nevertheless, the Gulf crisis had presented the Soviet Union with one of its best opportunities in recent years to make notable diplomatic and economic inroads in that region.[78] The last stages of the Gulf war (reflagging) had elicited coordinated efforts on the part of the regional states, the Western allies and the Soviet Union, for the first time in contemporary history. Kuwait's interior minister, Salem Al-Sabah, summed up the collective endeavor as "a prime factor in the search for a way out of the long, dragging war of attrition between Iraq and Iran."[79] Richard Murphy, the then assistant secretary of state for Near Eastern and South Asian affairs, termed the joint activities "an extraordinary display of Western resolve."[80]

The "militarization" of the Gulf served simultaneously as deterrence and provocation, for it enhanced the scope of confrontation and widened the stakes of all parties. It deterred attacks against Kuwaiti oil shipping, but it provoked Iran to act at times erratically and irrationally. The Gulf has become in a real sense an international lake, with forces and powers representing all nations. As the *Wall Street Journal* reported, "for the first time in the modern history of this region, Arabs and Israelis are united in their support of an American initiative; and for the first time since the Korean War, almost all of America's European allies are providing direct military support for a U.S. military action outside of Europe."[81]

The "internationalization" of the Gulf may also have led to a détente between the East and the West in the waters of the Gulf through regular contacts, joint searches for mines, and early warning of mines. Meanwhile, the Soviet Union pushed for multinational forces as a means of legitimating and institutionalizing its naval presence, thereby limiting the American role in the Gulf.[82]

Kuwait's Deterrent Capabilities

Kuwait, being smaller, less populated, and less powerful than any of its three immediate neighbors and possible adversaries (Iran, Iraq, and Saudi Arabia), could not under any circumstances, except in an extreme case of self-defense, fight or even become a full-fledged participant in an all-out war or any conventional military engagement. Its military capabilities and potentials (Table 5.3) cannot match those of any of its three neighbors. Yet

TABLE 5.3 Military Capabilities of the Gulf States 1988

	Size (sq.km.)	Popu-lation	GDP 1987 $bil	Def.* Budget 1988 $bil	Total Armed Forces	Para-Military Reserves	Army	Navy	Air Force	Tanks	Aircraft	Combat Ships
Kuwait	17,818	1,951,000	18.84	1.55	20,300	7,000	16,000	2,100	2,200	275	70	8
Bahrain	676	613,000	3.97 (1986)	.16	2,850	2,500	2,300	350	200	60	12	6
Oman	212,380	1,430,000	6.24	1.38	25,500	6,000	20,000	2,500	3,000	75	51	4
Qatar	11,000	385,000	4.80	.165 (1984)	7,000	—	6,000	700	300	24	23	3
Saudi Arabia	2,149,690	13,096,000	74.25	13.57	72,300[a]	56,000[b]	38,000	7,800	16,500	550	182	26
UAE	83,600	1,589,000	23.15	1.59	43,000	—	40,000	1,500	1,500	216	44	6
Iran	1,648,000	52,800,000 (1986)	174.46 (1986)	8.69	604,500[c]	350,000	305,000	14,500	35,000	1,040	50	21
Iraq	434,924	16,278,000 (1985)	36.50 (1985)	13.99 (1987)	1,000,000	650,000	955,000	5,000	40,000	4,800	500	16

*Estimates

[a]Includes 10,000 National Guard.

[b]The paramilitary forces include 26,000 tribal levies, and the ministry of Interior's forces.

[c]Includes 250,000 revolutionary guard corps (Pasdaran Inqilab).

Sources: The International Institute for Strategic Studies, The Military Balance 1987-1988 (London: IISS, 1987), pp. 95-116; IISS, The Military Balance 1988-1989, pp. 97-118, and other sources.

it should be capable of deterring aggression through a number of other kinds of indirect but effective power. Kuwait's greatest and probably most lasting asset is its moral power, a power that flows from its unique legitimacy and constitutionality, and a great degree of political tolerance and "freedom" unrivaled in the region. This moral authority, in conjunction with its contemporary role of donor/mediator, has perhaps offset its fragility and its "siege mentality." These combined forces may serve preventively to reduce or eliminate altogether the possibilities of conventional war. Indeed Kuwait has become in a sense "an untarnished gem" that everyone in the region wants to maintain as a model.

But in real terms, Kuwait lags behind its neighbors in almost all conventional measures of power. Kuwait's size, 17,818 square kilometers, is insignificant compared with those of Saudi Arabia (over 2 million sq. km); Iran (over 1.5 million sq. km); and Iraq (about half a million sq. km).[83] The ratios are 1:120, 1:92, and 1:24, respectively. Kuwait's population is currently over 1.9 million, Saudi Arabia's over 13 million, Iran's around 52 million, and Iraq's around 16 million, for ratios of 1:6.7, 1:27, and 1:8, respectively. Kuwait's GDP is $18.84 billion, Saudi Arabia's $74.25 billion, Iran's $174.46 billion, and Iraq's $36.50 billion. Here the ratios are much smaller: 1:3.9, 1:9.2, and 1:1.9. Still, Kuwait is outspent in defense allocations. Its 1988 defense budget was $1.55 billion; Saudi Arabia's was $13.57; Iran's was $8.69 billion, and Iraq's was $13.99 billion; for spending in the ratios of 1:8.7, 1:5.6, and 1:9. Kuwait's military forces, especially, are outmatched by those of its neighbors. Kuwait has armed forces numbering 20,300; Saudi Arabia, 72,300; Iran, over 600,000, and Iraq, 1 million; or disadvantages of 1:3.5, 1:29.5, and 1:49.3. Even in terms of paramilitary capabilities Kuwait is behind. Kuwait's paramilitary/reserve sector has some 15,000 to 17,000 troops; Saudi Arabia's 56,000; Iran's 350,000; and Iraq's 650,000.

On the other hand, Kuwait maintains an asymmetrical imbalance in terms of major armament and weapon systems in relation to its neighbors. Kuwait has 275 tanks, Saudi Arabia 550, Iran 1040, and Iraq 4600. (The ratios are 1:2, 1:3.7, and 1:16). Kuwait possesses 70 fighting aircraft, Saudi Arabia 182, Iran 50, and Iraq 500, for ratios of 1:2.6, 1:0.7, and 1:6. Kuwait has acquired 8 combat ships, Saudi Arabia 26, Iran 21, and Iraq 16.

Even if one compares the collective powers of all the GCC states combined to those of Iran and Iraq, some startling results emerge. The GCC's combined population is estimated at 19 million people, as compared to some 52 million in Iran and 16 million in Iraq, for ratios of 1:2.7 and 1:0.8. The GCC's military budgets total $18.42 billion; that of Iran is $8.69 billion and that of Iraq is $13.99 billion, for ratios of 2.1:1 and 1.3:1. The GCC states have armed forces totaling 170,950; Iran's reach 604,500 and Iraq's 1 million, for ratios of 1:3.5 and 1:5.8. In paramilitary forces, the GCC states maintain 71,500 troops, Iran 350,000, and Iraq 650,000, for ratios of 1:4.8 and 1:9. The arsenals of the GCC countries contain 1200 tanks, 382 fighting aircraft, and 53 combat ships. Iran has 1040 tanks, 50 aircraft, and 21 combat ships. Iraq has 4600 tanks, 500 aircraft, and 16 combat ships. The ratios are as follows: tanks, 1:0.8 (GCC-Iran) and 1:3.8 (GCC-Iraq); aircraft, 7.6:1 (GCC-Iran) and 0.7:1 (GCC-Iraq); and combat ships, 2.5:1 (GCC-Iran) and 3.3:1 (GCC-Iraq).

In the period 1979–1986, the Gulf states together imported weapon systems costing over $85 billion (in 1984 dollars). The small Gulf states imported $5.04 billion worth of arms (Bahrain $256 million, the UAE $1.09 billion, Oman $1.15 billion, Qatar $1.16 billion, and Kuwait $1.39 billion). Among the larger states, Iran imported $12.14 billion in arms, Saudi Arabia $24.15 billion, and Iraq $44.08 billion. The ratio of the GCC small states' arms imports to those of Iran was 1:2.4; to those of Iraq 1:8.8; to those of Saudi Arabia 1:4.8. The ratios of Kuwait's arms imports to those of its larger neighbors are 1:17 (Kuwait/Saudi Arabia); 1:8.7 (Kuwait/Iran); and 1:31.8 (Kuwait/Iraq). Kuwait's total arms imports are mediocre in relation to the huge stockpiles of Saudi Arabia, Iran, and Iraq. Although this comparison might not be conclusive and does not give definite indications as to current and future trends, it should nevertheless offer the reader as well as the specialist a better picture of the combined military might of the Gulf states. It should not be construed as the only and major source of power of the regional states.

But despite the Gulf states' near parity with Iran and Iraq in some aspects of military supplies, it remains highly questionable whether the GCC states could take combined action against possible threats form their neighbors. A case in point was the reluctance of the GCC states, despite public expectation, to come to the aid of Kuwait against Iranian attacks. Kuwait's ex-defense minister, Salem Al-Sabah, explained that the GCC states "agree on . . . general outlook toward the defense, but differ on the mode of defense."[84]

For the present, the most militarized Gulf state, in terms of manpower, arms acquisitions, and probably battlefield experience, is Iraq; whereas in the long run the most potentially powerful, in terms of population, geographical area, natural resources, and experience, will be Iran. Threats to the Gulf states may continue to come from both sources, but in different eras and in different fashions. However, since both nations need a long period of postwar reconstruction and rebuilding of their devastated states, they may pose minimal direct threats to the Gulf states in the short and medium terms. As a result, no hegemonic power may appear in the Gulf in the immediate future.

In sum, it seems that Kuwait has lesser military capabilities than its neighbors, although its gross domestic product equals that of Iraq ($17.56 billion and $17.69 billion, respectively). Fortunately, because of Iran's mechanical and technical problems with its aging aircraft (over 500 during the shah's reign), Kuwait surpassed Iran by a ratio of 1.4:1 in operable military aircraft. In general, however, in strict military and other terms (see Chapter 4), Kuwait has neither the geographic depth, the population backup, the military forces, nor the military supplies to confront either of its potential aggressors. Of course Kuwait and its neighbors recognize this indisputable fact. The best Kuwait could achieve is a limited deterrence capability and perhaps the political will not to acquiesce to external demands.

Nevertheless, because of its astute political leadership and pragmatism, Kuwait has been able, throughout its not-so-long history, to maintain its integrity and keep from being absorbed by either of its neighbors. Kuwait's centrist orientation has paid off in the readiness of other powers to salvage the state from the two actual threats to its existence that have occurred since independence in 1961, the Iraqi and Iranian threats. In the first incident, in 1961, Kuwait was saved by British and Arab League troops, under the legal pretexts of the 1961 treaty of friendship with Britain and the Arab League Defense pact. Faced by the 1980s threats from Iran, Kuwait dealt by itself with internal subversion and called upon the superpowers to salvage its "economic" security, using the commercial mechanism of chartering and reflagging.

One may therefore conclude that Kuwait neither can afford nor desires to be involved in any crisis or military conflict since it has little political aspirations beyond its borders. In fact, stability and security in the region enhance Kuwait's role. During times of instability, the economic achievement, prosperity, and financial power that have been the cornerstone of Kuwait's foreign policy could be ruined. Security and stability in its immediate vicinity expand Kuwait's role and prestige, whereas insecurity and conflict semi-isolate Kuwait and constrain its activist policy.

Indeed, the three immediate neighbors themselves may in one way or another seek to keep Kuwait as neutral as possible, in their own political, social, and economic interests. Each state may see Kuwait as a little model of itself, and each has its own "constituencies" in the country. There are some, however, who contend that Kuwait's shining sociopolitical example poses a real threat and challenge to the other neighboring regimes. Hence, they attempt to reshape and influence Kuwait's system to parallel theirs.

Conclusion

By 1987, it was becoming clear that Kuwait individually would not be able to resist the Iranian direct and indirect attacks on its internal security and external commerce. Therefore, it set in motion a policy that proved to be both effective in the medium term and a harbinger of things to come. Kuwait skillfully employed the commercial methods of reregistering and chartering oil vessels to achieve the broader goal of internationalizing a regional conflict. Since Kuwait's primary foreign policy goal of state stability and military security was endangered, its underlying values of Arab ideology, Islamic tendencies, and a sense of mission were deemed subordinate. Kuwait realized that it could not implement these values without achieving the major objectives of economic security. Through closer identification and "alliance" with the superpowers, Kuwait gave up in the short term its projected image of a centrist, noncommitted state, its Pan-Arabism, and its anti-Western stance, in exchange for a political stage to settle the conflict peacefully despite a year of rising tensions in the Gulf. Realizing that it could neither challenge Iran individually nor become a full-fledged party to a regional conflict, Kuwait, assisted to some degree by the GCC states, laboriously employed its diplomatic and financial might to influence Iran's supporters to change their behavior, and thus to isolate Iran. In fact, Kuwait had to act, and act quickly, for its very survival was at stake.

Kuwait's new course of chartering and reregistering its shipping fleet provided opportunities for both superpowers. After some hesitancy, the United States saw a chance to reassert its dominance and reclaim the Gulf as a Western lake after its humiliating banishment following the fall of the shah of Iran. Moreover, the United States sought to prevent or minimize the Soviet gains and rebuild the region's tarnished confidence in Washington. True, the reaction of the American decision-makers and the media was theatrical and overdramatized, and perhaps influenced, in the words of a Kuwaiti official, by the "Hollywood mentality."[85]

The Soviet Union viewed the Kuwait call as the opportune time to support its ally Iraq by supporting the centrist and friendly regime of Kuwait and thus to limit possible American gains. Meanwhile, the Soviets hoped that through the gateway of tangible support to an Arab and GCC state, they might gain influence in the region. As a matter of fact, the Soviets' diplomatic and political presences have increased greatly in the area. At the start of the war, Kuwait was the only GCC state that maintained diplomatic and other relations with Moscow. By the summer of 1988, the Soviet Union had established diplomatic relationships with all the GCC states except Bahrain and Saudi Arabia.

The other GCC states were indecisive about Kuwait's invitation to the superpowers to protect its oil ships, yet they realized that Kuwait had limited choices at that stage, and they acknowledged their own inabilities to extend military help to it. The Iranians saw the Kuwaiti actions and subsequent "militarization" of the Gulf as further steps to strangle Iran's morale and will to fight. The Iraqis, on the other hand, perceived the Kuwaiti actions as the keys that would unlock the door out of their encirclement.

Unfortunately, despite their claim to be the defenders of the powerless and disadvantaged (*Mustaza'fin*), the Iranians neglected to realize the unique geopolitical situation Kuwait is in. The Kuwaiti-Iraqi relationship has never been an equal one, for Iraq maintains disproportionate leverages over Kuwait, and past interactions have created a fear syndrome on the part of the Kuwaitis. The Iranians never understood this complex phenomenon.

In general, however, despite Kuwait's increased hostilities with Iran and its new "realignment" with the superpowers, Kuwait and the other GCC states never closed the diplomatic doors with Teheran. By early 1988, the Gulf states began to explore the possibilities of GCC-Iran dialogue, and the president of the UAE was assigned to this task. Kuwait's foreign minister, Sabah Al-Ahmad, acknowledged the new approach, stating that the GCC's precondition for talks was that there be neither attacks against the Gulf states nor interferences in their internal affairs. Moreover, the Kuwaiti official categorically denied that Kuwait was in a state of war with Iran.[86]

Despite military and diplomatic defeats and pressures, the Iranians intractably continued fighting Iraq and other states for a long year after the reflagging and militarization of the Gulf and the internationalization of the conflict. The unfortunate downing of an Iranian civilian aircraft (Iran Air Flight #655) on July 3, 1988, by the American naval forces in the Gulf, with the loss of 290 civilians,[87] proved to be opportune as well as tragic. It set in motion a chain of events that culminated in Iran's acceptance of Security Council resolution 598, and thus in essence its acceptance of a peaceful formula to end this "monstrous" war, the bloodiest since World War II between Third-World states. Iran's rational reaction after the aircraft attack, and its acceptance of the will of the world community, was a light of hope in the dark and gloomy tunnel of despair.

By late July 1988, a United Nations team visited both Baghdad and Teheran to arrange the details of a cease-fire. As the cease-fire arrangements were announced for August 20, a United Nations Iran-Iraq Military Observer Group (UNIIMOG) was formed, made up of 350 observers from 12 countries and a 300-person communication and technical unit. The cost of the group for a six-month period was estimated at about $84 million. As part of the necessary worldwide support for this group, Japan contributed $10 million, and Kuwait gave an additional $1 million, in addition to its assessed contribution. On August 25, 1988, negotiations between Iran and Iraq were opened in Geneva in the presence of the UN Secretary-General, Perez de Cuellar.[88] This development relieved Kuwaiti decision-makers and the state itself, and indeed the whole region, of a painful hemorrhage that had sapped their strength for almost eight years. Indeed, the Kuwaitis, overjoyed, declared the Iranian acceptance of the cease-fire as a national holiday. Kuwait sent messages of congratulations to the leaders of both Iran and Iraq. Kuwait's foreign minister, Sabah Al-Ahmad, called the cease-fire a celebration for the world and the Iranian and Iraqi nations, and Kuwait began to take steps to reopen its embassy in Teheran.[89] Thus Kuwait was trying to open up a new channel of communication with Iran and restore its damaged credibility with its larger neighbor.

In general, the effects of the reflagging policy itself remain amorphous. But it forced Kuwait into the limelight; normally, Kuwaiti decision-makers tend to operate in a low-profile style, with little fanfare. And while the policy proved to be a successful short-term achievement, its long-term cost may be high if Kuwait continues to identify with the superpowers. Besides creating problems with Iran, some Arab states, and some national movements, which may not be fully supportive of this approach, it could have domestic repercussions. It will take a long while to assuage the domestic friction caused by Kuwait's position toward the war. Furthermore, reflagging might eventually lead to a closer military relationship between Kuwait and the United States, as was seen in the almost $2 billion arms deal of 1988. In the short term, reflagging froze the status quo in the Gulf, but it might, if the process continued, or if the Iran-Iraq negotiations reached a stalemate, boil the Gulf again.

Extraordinary circumstances forced Kuwait into actions and policies that seemed an aberration from its tradition of pan-Arabism, anti-Americanism, and noninvolvement with the superpowers. These circumstances clearly demonstrated that despite new armaments and the regional military "coalition" of the GCC, Kuwait would never be able to defend itself and its interests individually, without some form of external help, for Kuwait is "a small fish in a sea of sharks." The developments in the Gulf in recent years have led to increased militarization of all the Gulf states. They have acquired better, more lethal and sophisticated arms, spent more money on arms, and maintained increased armed forces.

In the final analysis, Kuwait should be credited with having the foresight to initiate the painful and controversial process of aligning with the superpowers and internationalizing the war in order to achieve its national goals. In point of fact, Kuwait had very little other choice. This process led eventually to the cease-fire and will perhaps lead to a peaceful settlement of the conflict. In fact, Kuwait was able to achieve in one year what the combatants and other powers failed to achieve in eight horrendous years. The war and subsequent actions have created a new and different balance of power, new alliances, and a new dynamism in the area. The Gulf war created a new triangle of regional forces, although not linked together: Iran, Iraq and the GCC. Iraq came closer to sharing the GCC's perception of Islamic threats, and much closer to the West. The Soviet Union was able through the Kuwaiti door to penetrate throughout the traditional GCC states, and once the communist-phobia of Saudi Arabia evaporates, it will reestablish its presence in the peninsula. The issue of security has overtaken the constitutional and liberal "permissive" characters of certain GCC states. Shiism has become a political issue arousing deep distrust. The United States was able to rebuild its damaged reputation in the area by reflagging and escorting the Kuwaiti oil tankers. But on balance, Kuwait did not receive a free ride; it contributed, logistically, militarily, and otherwise, to the American undertakings. Kuwait may seem to have strayed into a position of alignment with the superpowers; but one implication of this experience (like the 1961 crisis) is that Kuwait cannot rely on its neighbors to keep its own independent foreign policy. Its centrist orientation is linked with the external behavior of its neighbors. The goodwill of its neighbors is not the best deterrent. A strong military capability combined with domestic support broaden the role of the state as a donor/mediator.

Notes

1. The Iraqi and Saudi pipelines carried some 2.5 m b/d of Iraqi and Saudi oil in 1980. By 1987, that capacity had reached 4.5 m b/d, and it was estimated that by 1990, it would reach 9 to 10 m b/d, see *The Wall Street Journal* (June 19, 1987), p. 3; and Congressional Research Services, *Disruption of Oil Supply from the Persian Gulf: Near-Term U.S. Vulnerability (Winter 1987/88)* (November 1, 1987), pp. 5–8. For more understanding of the impact of the war on oil supplies see Thomas D. Mullins, "The Security of Oil Supplies," *Survival* (November/December 1986), pp. 509–523.

2. United Nations, *Security Council*, (May 1984) (S/PV.2541), pp. 5, 11.

3. Center for Defense Information, Washington, D.C., *Military Information* (October 2, 1987), p. 3 and (January 6, 1987), p. 1; Center for Defense Information monitor staff, information given to the author, (August 1988), U.S. Congress, Senate, *War in the Persian Gulf: The U.S. Takes Sides*, p. 48; *The Washington Post* (January 11, 1988), p. A18; *The Christian Science Monitor* (August 12, 1988), p. 9; Sheldon L. Richman, "Where Angels Fear to Tread: The United States and the Persian Gulf Conflict" (CATO Institute, Policy Analysis #90, September 9, 1987), p. 7; and "Insurance Foundering in the Gulf," *South* (October 1987), p. 75.

4. Montazeri, quoted in George Nader, ". . . and Iran's Sense of Religious Mission," *The Wall Street Journal* (January 13, 1988), p. 24. For the new Iranian policy see Gary Sick, "Iran's Quest for Superpower Status," p. 712; and Alex von Dornoch (pseudonym), "Iran's Violent Diplomacy," *Survival* (May/June 1988), pp. 252–266.

5. Personal Interview, Kuwait (April 5, 1988). For Kuwait's dissatisfaction with Iraq and the GCC's failure to support Kuwait during the tanker war see "No Change for the Paymaster," *South* (November 1985), p. 28.

6. Milton Viorst, "Out of the Desert: Kuwait," p. 49; Rosemarie Said Zahlan, *The Making of the Modern Gulf State*, pp. 154–155; and Chris Kutschera, "Oman: Skillfully Playing Both Sides," *The Middle East* (May 1989), p. 24.

7. *Al-Watan* (September 16, 1987), p. 19.

8. U.S. Congress, House, Report, Policy Panel and the Investigations Committee, *National Security Policy Implications of United States Operations in the Persian Gulf,* pp. 10–11. The Kuwaiti minister was interviewed by Milton Viorst; see "Out of Desert: Kuwait," p. 49.

9. Personal Interview, Washington, D.C. (November 12, 1987).

10. Statement by Kuwait's foreign minister; see *Al-Watan* (September 16, 1987), p. 19.

11. U.S. Congress, Senate, Report to the Committee on Appropriations, *U.S. Presence in the Persian Gulf: Cost and Policy Implications* (Washington, D.C.: USGPO, January 1988), pp. 12–13.

12. The analysis is based on Senate, *U.S. Presence in the Persian Gulf: Cost and Policy Implications*, pp. 12, 14, 15; and Senate, *War in the Persian Gulf: The U.S. Takes Sides*, p. 9. For the GCC states' oil reserves, see Kevin R. Taecker, *U.S.-GCC Relations: Economic and Financial Issues* (Washington, D.C.: National Council on U.S.-Arab Relations, 1987), pp. 6–8; John F. Cooley, "Kuwait and West Share Interests Far Beyond Free Navigation in the Gulf: Oil-Rich State Invests Billions in Foreign Economies," *The Christian Science Monitor* (July 10, 1987), pp. 9–10; Edward B. Atkeson, "The Persian Gulf: Still a Vital US Interest?" *Armed Forces International Journal* (April 1987), pp. 46–56.

13. Statement by the minister, *Al-Yaqza* (October 23–29, 1987), p. 11.

14. See *FBIS* (January 23, 1987), p. J1; Senate, *War in the Persian Gulf: The U.S. Takes Sides*, p. 58; and further information in Personal Interview, Kuwait (April 12, 1988).

15. *The Christian Science Monitor* (February 11, 1988), p. 11.

16. For Kuwaiti-U.S. reflagging approach see U.S. House, Democratic Study Group, *The Persian Gulf Controversy*, Special Report #100-9 (June 9, 1987), p. 6.

17. House, *National Security Policy Implications of the United States Operations in the Persian Gulf,* p. 27; and Statement presented before the Senate Foreign Relations Committee on June 16, 1987; see Department of State, *U.S. Policy in the Persian Gulf and Kuwaiti Reflagging*, Current Policy #97 (June 1987), p. 4. For a review of Iran's arms deal and the U.S. reflagging of Kuwaiti tankers see Nikki R. Keddie, "Iranian

Imbroglios: Who's Irrational?" *World Policy Journal*, vol. 5, no. 1 (Winter 1987/88), pp. 29–54.

18. House, *National Security Policy Implications of United State Operations in the Persian Gulf*, p. 30.

19. House, *The Persian Gulf Controversy*, p. 21; House, hearings, Committee on Merchant Marine and Fisheries, *Kuwaiti Tankers*, 100th Cong., 1st Sess., June and August 1987 (Washington, D.C.: USGPO, 1987), p. 104; Congress, Congressional Research Service, *The Persian Gulf and the U.S. Naval Presence: Issues for Congress*, No. IB87145 (August 3, 1987), p. 4; and House, *National Security Policy Implications of United States Operations in the Persian Gulf*, p. 13. For reasons for reflagging see the testimony of Admiral William J. Crowe, Jr., Chairman, Joint Chiefs of Staff; Michael H. Armacost, Undersecretary of State for Political Affairs; and Richard L. Armitage, Assistant Secretary of Defense for International Security Affairs, in U.S. Congress, Senate, Hearings, Committee on Armed Services. *U.S. Military Forces to Protect "Re-flagged" Kuwaiti Oil Tankers*. June 5, 11, 16, 1987. 100th Cong., 1st Session (Washington, D.C.: USGPO, 1987), pp. 36–37, 47–48, 56–57, and 90.

20. U.S. Department of State, *U.S. Policy in the Persian Gulf*, Special Report #166 (July 1987), p. 7.

21. The details of the arrangements were revealed to the author in a personal interview, Kuwait (April 12, 1988). See also *The New York Times* (October 27, 1987), p. A13; *The Times* (London) (August 26, 1987), pp. 1, 18; and *Middle East Economic Survey* (February 13, 1989), p. A9. For an opposing view see R. W. Scott, "Ship of Fools," *World Oil* (July 1987), pp. 5–7.

22. *The Financial Times* (February 22, 1988), p. 16.

23. House, *National Security Policy Implications of United States Operations in the Persian Gulf*, p. 64.

24. For details of the prime minister's press conference, see *Al-Qabas* (July 21, 1987), pp. 1, 2, and 6–8.

25. *FBIS* (July 16, 1987), p. J1.

26. See *Al-Yaqzah* (September 11–17, 1987), p. 7, and (September 18–24, 1987), pp. 10–11.

27. For the ex-defense minister's interview see *Al-Yaqza* (October 23–29, 1987), p. 13; and *The Washington Post*, (October 21, 1987), p. A27. For the Kuwaiti official statement see Senate, *War in the Persian Gulf: The U.S. Takes Sides*, p. 50. For Kuwait's indecisiveness towards the new U.S. role see Robert Fisk, "US Kept at Arm's Length in the Gulf," *The Times* (November 5, 1987), p. 8.

28. Senate, *War in the Persian Gulf: The U.S. Takes Sides*, p. 50; Congressional Research Service (CRS), *The Persian Gulf and the U.S. Naval Presence: Issues for Congress*, p. 11; and Caspar W. Weinberger, *Security Arrangements in the Gulf* (Washington, D.C.: National Council on US-Arab Relations, 1988), pp. 22–23.

29. For detailed information on Kuwait's help to the U.S., see Senate, *War in the Persian Gulf: The U.S. Takes Sides*, pp. 51–52; and Senate, *U.S. Presence in the Persian Gulf: Cost and Policy Implications*, p. 6.

30. Statement of an American diplomatic official; see Milton Viorst, "Out of Desert: Kuwait," p. 52.

31. *The Washington Post* (January 11, 1988), p. A18; *The New Yorker* (May 16, 1988), p. 52; and Richard W. Murphy, *Protecting U.S. Interests in the Gulf* (Washington, D.C.: National Council on US-Arab Relations, 1988), pp. 1–8. For new challenges for the U.S. see James A. Bill, "Populist Islam and U.S. Foreign Policy," *SAIS Review*, vol. 9. no. 1 (Winter-Spring, 1989), pp. 125–139. For exchange of remarks between President Reagan and Shaikh Saad Al-Abdullah, see *Department of State Bulletin*,

(October 1988), pp. 60–61. For the new U.S. roles see Leonard Binder, "The Changing American Role in the Middle East," *Current History*, vol. 88, no. 535 (February 1989), pp. 65–68 and 96–97.

32. Senate, *War in the Persian Gulf: The U.S. Takes Sides*, p. 12; and Personal Interview, Washington, D.C. (November 10, 1987). For an assessment of Kuwait's tanker deal and Iranian reaction to American reflagging see R. K. Ramazani, "The Iran-Iraq War and the Persian Gulf Crisis," *Current History*, vol. 87, no. 525 (January 1988), pp. 61–64 and 86–88; Rupert Pengelley, "Gulf War Intensifies: Shipping and Oil Rigs Face Increasing Threat," *International Defense Review* (3/1987), pp. 279–280.

33. *The Washington Post* (January 15, 1988), p. A25.

34. *The Christian Science Monitor* (April 25, 1988), p. 7; *The New York Times* (October 20, 1987), pp. A1, A26; *Aviation Week and Space Technology* (August 17, 1987), pp. 22–23; and *Time* (August 3, 1987), pp. 24–27.

35. Senate, *War in the Persian Gulf: The U.S. Takes Sides*, p. 8. For an understanding of the United Nations role in the Gulf War, see Brian Urquhart and Gary Sick, eds., *The United Nations and the Iran-Iraq War* (New York: Ford Foundation Conference Report, August 1987), pp. 4–39.

36. *The Christian Science Monitor* (September 28, 1988), pp. 1, 32.

37. Statement of Michael H. Armacost, State Department, *U.S. Policy in the Persian Gulf and Kuwaiti Reflagging*, p. 2.

38. Barry Rubin, "Drowning in the Gulf," *Foreign Policy* (Winter 1987-88), p. 125. For Kuwait's strategy to deal with Iranian threats see Wayne E. White, "The Iran-Iraq War: A Challenge to the Arab Gulf States," in *Crosscurrents in the Gulf*, pp. 97, 103–104; and "Kuwait's Balancing Act," Special Survey, *South* (January 1983), pp. 33–47.

39. For assessments of Iran's reasons for accepting the UN resolution, see James A. Bill, "Why Teheran Finally Wants a Gulf Peace," *The Washington Post* (August 28, 1988), pp. B1 and B4; *Middle East International*, no. 330 (July 22, 1988), pp. 2–6; *The Economist* (July 23, 1988), pp. 11–12 and 35–38; *U.S. News and World Report* (August 1, 1988), pp. 28–30; Paul Cooper, "Peace Breaks Out in the Gulf," *The Spectator* (July 23, 1988), pp. 12–13; *Aviation Week and Space Technology* (July 11, 1988), pp. 16–22; and Shahram Chubin, "The Last Phase of the Iran-Iraq War: From Stalemate to Cease-Fire," *Third World Quarterly*, vol. 2, no. 2 (April 1989), pp. 1–14.

40. Senate, *U.S. Presence in the Persian Gulf: Cost and Policy Implications*, p. 6; *The Christian Science Monitor* (September 28, 1988), pp. 1, 32; and *Middle East Monitor* (September 1988), p. 8.

41. *Al-Qabas* (September 27, 1988), pp. 1, 29.

42. Senate, *National Security and Policy Implications of United States Operations in the Persian Gulf*, p. 65.

43. *The Christian Science Monitor* (May 16, 1988), p. 11.

44. Senate, *War in the Persian Gulf: The U.S. Takes Sides*, p. 28; and Joe Stork and Martha Wenger, "US Ready to Intervene in Gulf War," *MERIP Reports*, vol. 14, no. 6/7 (July-September 1984), p. 46.

45. Congressional Research Service, *The Persian Gulf and the U.S. Naval Presence: Issue for Congress*, p. 5; and Caspar W. Weinberger, *Security Arrangements in the Gulf*, pp. 18–22.

46. The analysis is adapted from Senate, *War in the Persian Gulf: The U.S. Takes Sides*, pp. 47, 53, 54; and Congressional Research Service, *The Persian Gulf and the U.S. Naval Presence: Issues for Congress*, p. 11.

47. *The Washington Post* (January 11, 1988), p. A18; Senate, *U.S. Presence in the Persian Gulf: Cost and Policy Implications*, p. 7.

48. Senate, *War in the Persian Gulf: The U.S. Takes Sides*, p. 53. For United States naval capabilities to counter mining operations in the Gulf, see Congress, House, Hearing, Seapower and Strategic and Critical Materials Subcommittee, Committee on Armed Services, *Mine Warfare*, 100th Cong., 1st Session, September 19, 1987 (Washington, D.C.: USGPO, 1988), pp. 1–50. For the new U.S. Navy role in the Gulf see the speech by the Secretary of the Navy to the Los Angeles World Affairs Council on October 9, 1987, James H. Webb, Jr., "National Strategy, the Navy, and the Persian Gulf," *World Affairs Journal*, vol. 6, no. 2 (Fall 1987), pp. 38–47; for the new U.S. show of force see Ambrose Evans-Pritchard, "Our Goal in the Gulf," *The Spectator* (August 15, 1987), pp. 8–10; "Reagan's Tilt to Iraq," *The Spectator* (October 3, 1987), p. 12; "U.S. Will Stay in the Gulf," *Intelligence Digest* (July 1, 1987), pp. 2–3. American ambassadors in the GCC expressed their views about security in the area; see U.S. Department of Commerce, *Business America* (February 2, 1987), pp. 12–13.

49. *Al-Watan* (January 6, 1988), p. 2; *The Wall Street Journal* (January 13, 1988), p. 24; and *Al-Watan* (December 25, 1988), p. 21.

50. *The Washington Post* (January 15, 1988), p. A25.

51. *The Christian Science Monitor* (January 19, 1988), p. 36, and (January 5, 1988), pp. 7–8.

52. *The Christian Science Monitor* (September 28, 1988), pp. 1, 32.

53. *The Christian Science Monitor* (January 19, 1988), pp. 1, 36; and Congressional Research Service, *The Persian Gulf and the U.S. Naval Presence: Issues for Congress*, p. 10.

54. Secretary of Defense Caspar W. Weinberger, *A Report to the Congress on Security Arrangements in the Persian Gulf* (June 15, 1987), p. 20; and *The Christian Science Monitor* (January 19, 1988), p. 36.

55. *The Christian Science Monitor* (January 19, 1988), p. 1.

56. *The Christian Science Monitor* (January 5, 1988), p. 7, and (May 11, 1988), p. 15; Congress, House, Hearings and Markup, Committee on Foreign Affairs, *Overview of the Situation in the Persian Gulf*, 100th Cong., 1st Session (May and June 1987) (Washington, D.C.: USGPO, 1987), p. 133; and Congressional Research Service, *The Persian Gulf and the U.S. Naval Presence: Issues for Congress*, p. 5. For the statement of former Secretary of Defense Frank Carlucci on April 29, 1988, to extend U.S. protection to neutral ships see *Department of State Bulletin* (July 1988), p. 61; and *Middle East and African Economist*, vol. 42, no. 4 (April 1988), p. 27.

57. Congressional Research Service, *The Persian Gulf Crisis: U.S. Military Operations* (October 7, 1987), p. 5; and *The Washington Post* (January 11, 1988), p. A18.

58. For the interview with the minister see *Al-Yaqza* (October 23–29, 1987), p. 12.

59. See the testimony of Edward W. Gnehm, Jr., Deputy Assistant Secretary for Near Eastern and South Asian Affairs, Department of State, before the House. Hearing. *Proposed Arms Sales to Kuwait* (July 7, 1988), p. 26.

60. Congressional Research Service, *The Persian Gulf Crisis: U.S. Military Operations*, pp. 9, 10; Senate, *War in the Persian Gulf: The U.S. Takes Sides*, p. 54; and *Armed Forces Journal International* (November 1988), p. 40.

61. Congressional Research Service, *The Persian Gulf Crisis: U.S. Military Operations*, pp. 10, 2; and *The Christian Science Monitor* (January 21, 1988), pp. 7–8.

62. See Senate, *War in the Persian Gulf: The U.S. Takes Sides*, p. 54; Senate, *National Security Policy Implications of United States Operations in the Persian Gulf*, p. 36; and

Congressional Research Service, *The Persian Gulf Crisis: U.S. Military Operations,* p. 9.

63. Congressional Research Service, *The Persian Gulf and the U.S. Naval Presence: Issues for Congress,* p. 10; CRS, *The Persian Gulf Crisis: U.S. Military Operations,* p. 9; Senate, *War in the Persian Gulf: The U.S. Takes Sides,* p. 54; and *Jane's Defense Weekly* (December 19, 1987), p. 1412.

64. Senate, *War in the Persian Gulf: The U.S. Takes Sides,* pp. 54–55.

65. Senate, *U.S. Presence in the Persian Gulf: Cost and Policy Implications,* p. 7; and CRS, *The Persian Gulf and the U.S. Naval Presence: Issues for Congress,* p. 10.

66. CRS, *The Persian Gulf Crisis: U.S. Military Operations,* pp. 9–10.

67. Senate, *U.S. Presence in the Persian Gulf: Cost and Policy Implications,* p. 8; and *The Washington Post* (January 11, 1988), p. A18.

68. *The Christian Science Monitor* (October 4, 1988), pp. 9, 10; and *Kuwait Times* (September 28, 1988), p. 2. It was estimated that clearing the debris will take 12–15 months and will cost $1.75 million, see *Kayhan International* (July 6, 1989), p. 7; and *Platt's Oilgram News* (July 7, 1989), p. 1.

69. CRS, *The Persian Gulf Crisis: Cost and Policy Implications,* p. 10.

70. CRS, *The Persian Gulf Crisis: Cost and Policy Implications,* p. 10; and Caspar W. Weinberger, *A Report to the Congress on Security Arrangements in the Persian Gulf,* p. 20.

71. For the Arab summit see *The Middle East Economic Digest* (November 14, 1987), p. 18, and (November 21, 1987), p. 69; *The Christian Science Monitor* (January 4, 1988), pp. 1, 36; *The Times* (November 5, 1987), p. 8; and *South* (December 1987), p. 6.

72. For the new role of Egypt see *The Economist* (October 31, 1987), p. 58, and (May 20, 1989), pp. 15–16; and Joseph P. Lorenz, *Egypt and the New Arab Coalition* (Washington, D.C.: The Institute for National Strategic Studies, National Defense University, February 1989), pp. 1–26.

73. *The Christian Science Monitor* (January 8, 1988), p. 10; *The Economist* (October 31, 1987), p. 58; International Institute for Strategic Studies, *The Military Balance 1988-1989* (London: IISS, 1988), p. 99; *The Middle East Journal* (Autumn 1988), p. 663; *Al-Watan Al-Araby* (October 7, 1988), p. 29; *FBIS* (July 29, 1988), p. 17–18; *The Christian Science Monitor* (January 8, 1988), p. 10; Ahmed Rashid, "Pakistan, Afghanistan, and the Gulf," *MERIP Reports* (September-October, 1987), pp. 35–39; and *The Times* (June 27, 1988), p. 9.

74. *The Economist* (October 31, 1987), p. 58; *The Sunday Times* (October 25, 1987), pp. 1–2; and Mohamed Sid Ahmed, "Egypt: The Islamic Issue," *Foreign Policy* (Winter 1987-88), p. 33.

75. State Department, *U.S. Policy in the Persian Gulf,* p. 5; and *The Christian Science Monitor* (October 4, 1988), p. 10.

76. Senate, *War in the Persian Gulf: The U.S. Takes Sides,* p. 40.

77. Department of State, *U.S. Policy in the Persian Gulf,* p. 5. For the Western and Soviet arms buildup in the Gulf see Robert Van Tol and Paul Beaver, "Naval Line-up in the Persian Gulf," *Jane's Defense Weekly* (September 26, 1987), pp. 671–673.

78. Senate, *National Security Policy Implications of United States Operations in the Persian Gulf,* p. 21; *The Christian Science Monitor* (December 4, 1987), p. 7; and "Moscow's Aims in the Gulf," *Intelligence Digest* (February 3, 1988), p. 6; and Galia Golan, "Gorbachev's Middle East Strategy," *Foreign Affairs,* vol. 66, no. 1 (Fall 1987), pp. 48–49 and 52–54.

79. For the Kuwaiti minister's interview see *Al-Yaqza* (October 23–29, 1987), p. 16.

80. Voice of America, "Symposium on Gulf Security and the Iran-Iraq War," Washington, D.C. (May 6, 1988), p. 3. For an Iranian reaction to military concentration in the Gulf see Nader Entessar, "Superpowers and Persian Gulf Security: The Iranian Perspective," *Third World Quarterly*, vol. 10, no. 4 (October 1988), pp. 1427–1451.

81. *The Wall Street Journal* (January 13, 1988), p. 24.

82. *The Christian Science Monitor* (February 11, 1988), p. 9. For the evolution of Soviet policies toward the war see Dennis Ross, "Soviet Views toward the Gulf War," *Orbis*, vol. 28, no. 3 (Fall 1984), pp. 437–447.

83. The data and figures are adapted from the International Institute for Strategic Studies, *The Military Balance, 1987–1988* (London: IISS, 1987), pp. 95–116; *The Military Balance 1988–1989*, pp. 97–118; Arms Control and Disarmament Agency, *World Military Expenditures and Arms Transfers 1987* (Washington, D.C.: ACDA, 1988), pp. 91, 105, 108, 114, 116–117, and 123; ACDA, *World Military Expenditures and Arms Transfers 1988*, pp. 33, 47, 50, 56, 58, 59 and 65. For an analysis of the domestic stability and external activities of the three main Gulf states see Adeed I. Dawisha, "Saudi Arabia," pp. 89–100, Christine Moss Helms, "Iraq," pp. 101–115, and Robert S. Litwak, "Iran," pp. 116–135, in Samuel F. Wells, Jr., and Mark Bruzonsky, eds., *Security in the Middle East: Regional Change and Great Power Strategies* (Boulder and London: Westview Press, 1987); on the shah's military spending and Saudi Arabia's military expenditures see Robert E. Looney, *Third World Military Expenditure and Arms Production* (New York: St. Martin's Press, 1988), Chapters 7 and 8 respectively; and for the military powers of Iran, Iraq, and Saudi Arabia see Morris Mehdad Mottale, *The Arms Buildup in the Persian Gulf* (Lentham, MD: University Press of America, 1986), pp. 124–142.

84. For the security challenges and role of the GCC see Ursula Braun, "The Gulf Cooperation Council's Security Role," in B. R. Pridham, *The Arab Gulf and the Arab World*, pp. 252–267. For the Kuwaiti minister's interview see *Al-Yaqza* (October 23–29, 1987), p. 12. For GCC military cooperation see Laura Guazzone, "Gulf Cooperation Council: The Security Policies," *Survival* (March/April 1988), pp. 134–148. For a review of the GCC naval powers see "Latest Arab Force Levels Operating in the Gulf," *Jane's Defense Weekly* (December 12, 1987), pp. 1360–1361.

85. Interview with Sulaiman Majid Al-Shaheen, undersecretary of the ministry of foreign affairs, *Al-Majallah* (June 24–30, 1987), p. 11.

86. *The Christian Science Monitor* (January 6, 1988), p. 9; and the minister's statement in *Al-Qabas* (March 23, 1988), p. 2. For the new realignment in the region see Dankwart A. Rustow, "Realignments in the Middle East," *Foreign Affairs*, vol. 63, no. 3 (1985), pp. 581–601.

87. For details of the incident see *Newsweek* (July 18, 1988), pp. 16–31; *Time* (July 18, 1988), pp. 14–18; *The Middle East* (August 1988), pp. 5–7; and *The Spectator* (July 9, 1988), p. 12. For the official American statements on the incident see *Department of State Bulletin*, (September 1988), pp. 39–43.

88. *The Christian Science Monitor* (August 9, 1988), p. 13, (August 11, 1988), p. 7, (August 22, 1988), p. 10, and (August 29, 1988), p. 8; and *FBIS* (November 29, 1988), p. 30.

89. For cease-fire developments in Kuwait see *Al-Yaqza* (August 19–25, 1988), pp. 14–15, and (July 29-August 4, 1988), p. 14; for the reopening of Kuwait's Embassy in Teheran, see *The Middle East Journal*, vol. 43, no. 1 (Winter 1989), p. 90.

6

Conclusion and Prospects: Domestic Stability and International Outlook

In relative terms, Kuwait has had no historical "glory," no "legacy," no major contribution to the development of world civilization, no renaissance; yet in the last forty years it has made remarkable achievements in politics, economics, and social development. This hard work and application have generated worldwide respect for the relatively new political entity. In fact, the founders of the state, particularly the members of the ruling house of Al-Sabah, have become synonymous with the survival of the nation. The have been, and still are, the leading factor contributing to the country's continuity, stability, and security. Indeed, the Al-Sabah were able, by building internal stability and strength and external goodwill, to maintain the integrity of Kuwait. The Kuwaitis have historically felt a sense of encirclement or "siege mentality" because the state's immediate environment frequently has been politically inhospitable to its existence and survival. Kuwaitis tend to follow a policy more "independent" and less "subservient" to outside dominance. And in comparison with their trditional often larger, and more puritanical neighbors to the south, the Kuwaitis' daily conduct and easy-going practices are "permissive" to the point of laid-back Islam. Their external outlook serves to deter foreign aggression, while the variety of internal outlets and communications with the outside world provides a source of psychological comfort.

Kuwait's "alliance" with Britain at the end of the nineteenth century, and its external trade and interaction with faraway lands and people, became a source of both security and survival. The new set of factors and motives introduced into Kuwaiti life since 1961 are not totally unrelated to the country's past. In the last four decades, however, Kuwait has undergone changes in all spheres of life that have drastically undermined its socio-economic foundations. Such abrupt and virtually total transformation, according to a seasoned Kuwaiti observer, "usually takes other states 400 years to reach."[1] These changes, together with the influx of oil revenues, have made the Kuwaitis somewhat lax and less disciplined. Kuwait became the only Gulf state with an articulate and consciously loyal opposition; it also developed a lively cultural life stemming from these changes and from the mixture of so many nationalities. Indeed, the Arab world and regional countries began to regard Kuwait as the "miracle" of the Gulf, an "island of hope" for its economic prosperity and its political uniqueness.[2]

Despite discontinuity in the domestic norms, the external relations of the new independent State of Kuwait have shown certain degrees of continuity. Kuwait's foreign policy has been driven by a trio of goals and motives: the need to maintain state security and military stability; Arab ideology and Islamic tendencies; and a sense of human responsibility, together with a "mercantile" mentality. Building state security and military stability entailed creating both a different political structure at home and a balanced, "centrist" policy towards the outside world. Kuwait began in the early 1960s to move toward an elected national body, a constitution, and a "free" press, thus establishing itself as a model for participatory government in the region. Likewise, as threats to the state increased, Kuwait gradually began a military buildup typical of small, less powerful states. In essence, Kuwait's defense doctrine has been "Never initiate offensive war; do not get involved in regional fighting; and do create short-term military deterrence capabilities." But these policies proved inadequate in two different eras: in 1961 against the Iraqi threats, and in the 1980s against Iranian attacks. However, in both cases, Kuwait was able to withstand external pressures and internal sabotage while a combination of regional and external forces safeguarded it against the outside threats.

During the climax of Pan-Arabic politics in the 1950s, 1960s, and 1970s, Kuwait's Arab credentials made it a source of mediation and support for different Arab political camps, enhancing its respectability and stature among the Arab states and peoples. Kuwait has been a consistent champion of the Palestinian cause. In a September 22, 1988, address to the U.N. General Assembly, Kuwait's Amir, Jaber al-Ahmad, defended the Palestinians' case this way: "All that the Palestinian people are demanding is to have their independent state over their land, with their capital Jerusalem, under the leadership of the Palestine Liberation Organization, their sole legitimate representative." Moreover, on November 15, 1988, Kuwait immediately recognized the PLO-proclaimed state of Palestine, out of its genuine belief and commitment to the Palestinians' legitimate rights,[3] and donated land and construction costs for a Palestinian embassy in Kuwait.

In the 1970s and 1980s, Kuwait broadened its Islamic identification by becoming a major supporter of Islamic issues and states, occasionally even to the overshadowing of its Arab identity. Kuwait's Amir, Jaber Al-Ahmad, as the chairman of the fifth session (1987–1990) of the Islamic Conference, told the United Nations, "I . . . convey to all of you the greetings of peace from one thousand million moslems [sic] living in all corners of the globe. . . . We came here in order to cooperate with you in addressing our common problems and in seeking a fulfillment of our common aspirations."[4] It seems, though, that what has made Kuwait flexible in both its Arabic and its Islamic tendencies is its nonideological commitment and persuasion; it preached no ideological dogmas, but rather practiced flexibility and pragmatism.

Kuwait's Arab and Islamic identification affected its sense of missionary responsibility. Located in a relatively poor environment, Kuwait felt a sense of duty to share its wealth with its less fortunate, even destitute neighbors. Since the 1950s, Kuwait has set up a number of economic infrastructures geared toward human and social development in the Gulf, the Arab world, and the Third World countries. The General Board of the South and Arabian Gulf and Kuwait's Fund for Arabic Economic Development proved to be agents of economic and social change in a large number of states. The total contributions of these two agencies have exceeded $6.6 billion.

Kuwait's human inclination towards helping poorer states was evident when Kuwait's Amir, Jaber Al-Ahmad, backed the demands of the developing nations in the debt issue. Kuwait's ruler called for a conference of the creditor nations to write off the interest due on their loans to debtor countries: "Kuwait, for its part as a creditor country, stands ready to such a parley and is willing to comply with whatever resolutions might be adopted."[5] Yet Kuwait was not a nonpolitical donor state. "Dinar diplomacy," which took shape in the aftermath of the Kuwaiti-Iraqi crisis of 1961, remained a highly important tool for Kuwaiti policy. It is estimated that Kuwait's "politicized" financial assistance to the Arab states and in support of specific issues in the period 1961–1989 may have totaled over $30.00 billion.

The Kuwaitis' history of and natural inclination toward adventuresome trading, and their resultant profit-oriented mentalities, induced them to play either privately or jointly with the government, the role of global investors. Our estimate is that Kuwait's official foreign investment has reached over $120 billion. Moreover, some $40 billion are privately invested outside the country.

Kuwait's new role, then, has three tiers: economic loans, which are based strictly on human responsibilities and economic measures; politicized financial subsidies, which are based largely on Arab identity and the need for internal security; and investment schemes, which are based strictly on a mercantile mentality and profitability. As a city-state in world politics, Kuwait has surpassed the power of many small and medium-sized states. Its comprehensive activities in financial, political, and other spheres, directed toward positive actions and accomplishments, could be termed a "neodynamism." In essence, the capacity to respond to challenges with a sense of moral responsibility, intertwined with financial and political capabilities exceeding those of like-powered states.

When one analyzes Kuwait's foreign policy over its history of almost three decades (1961–1989), a number of themes emerge. First, Kuwait's foreign policy is not an inward-directed process, but a more outer-directed one; or, better, it consists more of reactions to events than of assertiveness or initiatives. In other words, the external environment may have a greater impact on Kuwait's foreign-policy behavior than do internal dynamics. The short-term and long-term planning and execution of the state's goals are vulnerable to changing policies of its neighbors. One expert noted that for the last two generations, external factors have acted as stimuli for the mobilization and crystallization of domestic tensions.[6]

Second, Kuwait's foreign policy is the exclusive domain of the executive branch. The role of the legislature (the National Assembly or Majlis Al-Ummah) is residual and secondary; it functions to control and constrain government actions. The assembly may be successful, when acting in conjunction with the press and other groups, in mobilizing public pressure, but for the most part the influence of the legislative branch is limited to domestic affairs, with little impact on the government's general external behavior. However, this does not mean that the Majlis has played an insignificant role. For example, it was successful in blocking the government from signing an internal security treaty with the rest of the GCC states in the 1980s. In the 1970s, it succeeded in forcing the government to renegotiate oil-sharing agreements with foreign oil companies.

Third, despite the marginal role of the Majlis, there are certain elements in the country that have maintained leverage and pressure over the government's foreign-policy orientation. The merchant elites and Arab nationalists were instrumental in eliciting government support for Pan-Arab issues, such as closer relations with Egypt under Nasser and with the Palestinians, and in strengthening aid and investment patterns in the Arab world. The merchant bloc was influential in the Kuwaiti government's decision to support Iraqi war efforts against Iran in the 1980s. The Sunni fundamentalists were able to secure some "latitude" from the regime for their own campaigns to provide financial and other aid to Islamic causes, e.g., the Afghan Mujahedeen. The only non-Kuwaiti group with access to and pressure on the government is the Palestinians. But because the government has been responsive to their influence, it is to be expected that in the longer term other emerging interest groups might demand more position and power.[7]

Fourth, Kuwait's internal stability and external "neodynamism" are manifested in the vitality of its domestic structure and its social accord. As long as this margin is maintained, the government will be able to make decisions strengthened by popular support and therefore may be able to resist external pressures. To use the words of the Amir Jaber Al-Ahmad, social resilience could prevent any activity aimed at "disrupting our national unity by implanting the seeds of grudges, envy, and hatred" in the country. Thus, by containing today's problem, Kuwait can avoid tomorrow's catastrophe.

Fifth, except in extreme situations, Kuwait would never be capable of defending itself individually against external and conventional threats, no matter what type of sophisticated weapon systems it acquired. Kuwait's power bases and military arsenals are simply inconsequential to its potential aggressors. However, the Kuwaiti people's determination and the regime's political will to resist pressures and to maintain the integrity of the state have been strong since its foundation. During a meeting with officials from the army, police, and national guards in early 1989, the Amir reiterated Kuwait's will: "though this country is small, it will not fall an easy prey."[8]

Sixth, Kuwait's resources for survival depend on a combination of domestic support and its external role as donor/mediator. Kuwait's political support for a wide variety of Arab causes, its political structure, its financial capabilities, and its sense of mission make it a candidate to mediate interregional disputes, simultaneously neutralizing foes and acquiring friends. In general, the bargaining power small nations have is the capacity to appeal to world opinion. To maximize this power, Kuwait has maintained a broad international political base by establishing diplomatic relationships with 101 nations—more than two-thirds of the world's countries.[9]

Seventh, the most threatening external challenges to Kuwait's security have emanated from Iraq in 1961 and 1973, and from Iran in the 1980s. The Iraqi threats left their imprints on the Kuwaiti political scene and radicalized Kuwait's previously evolutionary and traditional character, both internally and externally. In short, the Iraqi threats, actually continuous since the 1920s and 1930s and still unabated today, have generated an Iraqi complex among the Kuwaitis. The Iranian threat of the 1980s, on the other hand, radicalized, on an ad hoc basis, the centrist and uncommitted dimension of Kuwait's foreign politics. It forced Kuwait to align again, in less than 30 years, with the major superpowers. Although that policy was viewed by some experts as irrational, unwise, and even suicidal, it achieved the short-term goal of neutralizing Iranian attacks against Kuwait and was a factor in ending the Iran-Iraq war. If, however, as a side effect, Kuwait's new bilteral military and political relations with the United States are maximized and so long as the United States does not undertake serious efforts to resolve the Arab-Israeli conflict, then the realignment policy may create minor but irritating domestic and regional repercussions.[10]

Kuwait, as a small state, could not withstand external and internal stresses, and its political choices were limited; therefore it risked its cardinal policy of independence from superpower "alliances." This turnaround implied the view that small states, while they defend themselves in a variety of ways, must still rely primarily on superior force. Kuwait's new policy put on the shelf its rhetorical opposition to outside interference in the Gulf waterways. It means that no matter what regional, Arabic, and Islamic tendencies and value it preaches, its ultimate safeguard from direct external threat is the superpowers.

However, by late 1988, signs were growing that Kuwait was considering deflagging its oil tankers. Kuwait's information minister, Jaber Mubarak Al-Sabah, said, "the reflagging was strictly a commercial deal, and I see no reason why we should not return the Kuwaiti flag to the masts now that the reasons for reflagging are no longer there."[11] By early 1989, officials of the Kuwait Oil Tanker Company revealed plans to raise the Kuwaiti flag over six tankers as soon as the procedure with the United States was completed. By early May 1989, Kuwait restored its flag to six Kuwaiti tankers registered in the United States. Five more will continue their American registry until next year.[12] The Gulf governments were content with the presence of the 14 American naval ships in the Gulf. In May 1989, Kuwait oil minister Ali Al-Khalifa visited Washington to discuss issues relating to defense, energy and diplomacy, and other mutual concerns.[13]

Eighth, in pursuing capitalist and "mercantile" endeavors, the Kuwaitis have enmeshed themselves in a few controversial major operations that are beyond the capabilities of a small state to control. Their acquisitions of shares in companies important to national security, such as energy-related enterprises, have generated barrages of protests and opposition in Britain, Spain, and the United States. In October 1988, as a result of public pressures, the British government decided on the recommendation of the British Monopolies and Merger Commission to ask Kuwait to divest its share in British Petroleum (BP) by more than half. The British government requested that the Kuwait Investment Office in London cut its share from 21.68 percent to 9.9 percent in one year.[14] It was estimated that Kuwait might lose as much as £350 million ($593.6 million) from this forced sale. In the end, BP agreed to buy back the shares at cost plus 50 p., for a total amount of £2.4 billion, with a net profit of more than £380 million ($684 million). It might be prudent to limit Kuwaiti financial inroads into such ventures to a very modest, reasonable and noncontroversial scale. Because of the external and internal responses to the activities of the KIO, Kuwait set up an executive committee to oversee its major acquisitions. It may be that the shifts in oil and financial power during the 1970s have affected Kuwait's psyche, leading it on to pursue policies that are disproportionate to its constraints of real size, and perhaps more commensurate with that of major regional power or even of the superpowers. If this is the case, Kuwait may have become scarcely able to distinguish between its own actual power and illusionary or imaginary power. Its transient financial power and adventurism may have produced an aura or an illusion of permanence, thus damaging its own foreign policy. Likwise, the negative Western reaction to Kuwaiti investment may be motivated in part by ethnocentrism and mistrust of Arab character and image.

As to the future direction of Kuwait's international behavior, any prediction must be based on Kuwait's actual experience, over more than a generation, in contemporary world affairs. In addition, one must look at the 1990s and beyond with some imagination and dynamism as well as realism, realizing that politics is fluid and unpredictable.

To begin with, as a relatively small city-state Kuwait can be neither isolated nor super-active on a global scale. Its future is linked to a greater or lesser degree with those of other small entities in world affairs. At present, Kuwait's diverse foreign policy roles have reached a new level of activism. Its role should be proportional with its actual power, and it must be on good terms with its immediate neighbors. Kuwait should sustain its long-pursued basic policy of "non-interference in the affairs of other states, and ... good neighborhood"[15] in order to enhance its respectability and credibility, and its parameters of maneuverability.

The political regime needs to promote a strong and effective internal structure that will both undergird the political system and deter external pressures. It should emphasize social consensus and unity, aiming to create a Kuwaiti consciousness that will predominate over all other allegiances and thus avoid the social havoc of the 1980s. What is most needed is a kind of understanding or coexistence among the various social, tribal, and sectarian elements.[16] An elected national body can contribute to the achievement of national consensus and supplement the regime's capabilities to govern. However, the members of any such forum should realize the nature of the traditional system and the geopolitical situation in which Kuwait is caught. Moderation and a middle-of-the-road approach could supplant the polemical attacks and extremism that characterized both previous occasions (in 1976 and 1986) when the Majlis was disbanded.

Also, Kuwait's success in the role of mediator and donor may be further buttressed to build goodwill and friendship. The Kuwait Fund for Arab Economic Development and the regional Board for the South and Arabian Gulf could serve as exemplary cases. In combination, a participatory mode of internal governance and the support of foreign public opinion could function as a dual shield at home and abroad. In pursuing its centrist, uncommitted role, Kuwait should avoid being dragged into intraregional conflicts and disputes; such embroilments endanger its respected position and could create domestic backlashes. Moreover, Kuwait would benefit from continuing its successful tradition of balanced, centrist, and impartial policies towards the major powers.

Immediate external threats to Kuwait may emanate from three potential sources: Iran, Iraq, and Saudi Arabia. As for Iran, it would appear that most differences which plague the improvement of relations are reconcilable. Indeed, relations over the years had been smooth until Iran's attempt at exporting revolution, Kuwait's pro-Iraqi position vis-à-vis the Iran-Iraq war, and escalating Iranian propaganda warfare and attacks endangered that tradition. Kuwaiti-Iranian relations, then, can probably be normalized as the war calms down and the process of reconstruction begins in Iran. Kuwait could play a positive role in helping rebuild Iran, and might function, with the GCC states, to build bridges between Iran and Iraq, perhaps even undertaking a mini-regional "Marshall Plan." In fact, a high-ranking Kuwaiti delegation, visiting Baghdad in February 1989, discussed the potential role of the GCC states in reviving the deadlocked negotiations between Iran and Iraq, and in postwar reconstruction schemes.[17] Perhaps a coordinated multilateral package of financial and economic aid could stimulate regional political and military understanding. Even if Iran continues its revolutionary rhetoric, Kuwait should be able to contain such threats by building a strong national consensus, while preserving its normal tradition of healthy internal liberty along with fair and firm treatment of all its citizens, and continuing its centrist external posture. In fact, Kuwait and its Gulf neighbors seem for the most part impregnable to Iranian-like insurrection or revolution.[18] The key to improving Kuwaiti-Iranian relations is Teheran's realization that it is not the ordained guardian of Shiites in Kuwait, and that it cannot replicate its model of change either in Kuwait or the other Gulf states. As this book goes to press (late June 1989), the Ayatollah Khomeini has passed away from the political scene, thus removing a symbol of rebellion against the Gulf states. As Iran begins to assert itself and perhaps pursue power politics, Kuwait may gradually be able to rebuild its shattered relations with Teheran to balance the other two neighbors. A new framework of mutual respect, noninterference in each other's domestic affairs, and safe passage for Kuwaiti trade should govern their relationships. Naturally, after years of distrust, the reintegration of Iran into Gulf politics will be slow. A long period of conventional relations and conduct must lapse before mutual trust can exist between both sides of the Gulf.

By late 1988, there were growing indications of improved relations between Kuwait and Iran. On November 8, 1988, the Iranian deputy foreign minister Muhammad Ali Besharati delivered a message from the Iranian president, Ali Khameini, to Kuwait's Amir, Jaber Al-Ahmad. The Iranian official declared Iran's wish for a "normal relationship with its neighbors" and termed his Gulf states tour a "positive outcome." Another Iranian official, Ayatollah Jannati, the chairman of the Islamic information organization, visiting Kuwait in March 1989, expressed his hope to enhance Iran's relations with Kuwait beyond neighborly ties to a level of "full brotherhood in one body." Kuwaiti minister of state for foreign affairs, Saud Mohammad Al-Osaimi, stated, "We want to forget the past. There is no reason to keep the tension going."[19]

As to Saudi Arabia, comparatively no major issue separates the two countries, since both operate within a conceptual framework premised upon stability and security of the traditional Gulf regimes. Kuwaiti-Saudi Arabian relations entail political, economic, military, and other broader facets. The main irritant to the Saudis has been Kuwait's socially and politically "unrestrained" domestic system and its impact on Kuwait's external behavior.[20] But this pressure should not deter the Kuwaitis from reinvigorating their parliamentary experiment and trying to reintroduce it as a model for political participation and reforms in the Gulf states. Indeed, a strengthening of relations with Saudi Arabia should counterweigh any possible Iranian and/or Iraqi pressures. In the aftermath of the cease-fire in the Iran-Iraq war, evidence was growing of a closer Kuwaiti-Saudi rapprochement. On November 5–12, 1988, Kuwait's crown prince and prime minister, Saad Al-Abdullah, paid an official visit to Riyadh—a visit that he explained as "necessitated by current situations in the region." Kuwait and Saudi Arabia agreed to set up a committee of foreign, interior, and oil ministers to coordinate their activities.[21] This committee may be tantamount to a new security arrangement, which Kuwait has long resisted.

Kuwait's aid to Iraq in this past decade has neutralized any Iraqi threats in the short term. Moreover, Kuwait has accumulated large financial and other credits with the Iraqis, credits that should be converted in due time into political dividends. Yet despite some perceived Iraqi changes in attitude toward regional issues, little tangible change has taken place toward Kuwait. The boundary issue still seems pivotal. As Iraq begins to rebuild its economy and assume a larger role in Gulf politics and because it is a virtually landlocked country with very limited options for better naval and maritime access, and as it decides to dredge a new canal to replace the Shatt Al-Arab,[22] Iraq may eventually try to pressure Kuwait to "lease" or "relinquish" Warba and Bubiyan islands. It is this author's conviction that Kuwait must painstakingly seek to find a reasonable modus vivendi with Iraq. Between February 6 and 12, 1989, Kuwaiti crown prince and prime minister Saad Al-Abdullah visited Iraq. A number of issues were discussed, but the border dispute was left for later negotiations. Iraq agreed to supply Kuwait with 500 million gallons of water daily (350 million gallons of drinking water and 150 million gallons of brackish water), while Kuwait agreed to provide southern Iraq with electricity. Despite a Kuwaiti officials' declaration that the trip "opened the gateway for comprehensive political and economic coordination," some speculated that it "failed to resolve the question of border delineation."[23]

Overall, the issue of Warba is relatively easy to resolve because the island is small, its waters are shallow, and it has relatively little strategic and political importance. Bubiyan might be converted into a regional entrepôt used by both Kuwait and Iraq and even—one day—by Iran. Or perhaps—to speculate a bit—since Bubiyan is not more than an hour's drive from Kuwait, and the University of Kuwait still lacks a campus, Bubiyan could serve as an educational and research center. This could dampen Kuwait from possible Iraqi military threats, which are less likely against a populated area; a secondary benefit would be to move the university student population some distance away in the event of any future student agitation. It has been reported that the Kuwaiti government has undertaken to build a new town of Subiya, across from the island, that would accommodate 250,000 people by early next century. Iraq should realize that it will not be able to improve its relations with the Gulf states without resolving the boundary issue with Kuwait. Moreover, Kuwait's support to Iraq during the war should be translated into actual policy gains.

In the interim, serious thought should be given to including Iran and Iraq in a regional security understanding. Despite some calls for the inclusion of Iran and Iraq in the GCC,[24] the GCC remains a rather exclusive club of like-minded monarchical and traditional states. Such an expansion in membership could be self-defeating. However, the Gulf states need to develop a new concept of collective cooperation, either through existing non-GCC channels, or by means of new formal and/or informal structures. Coordinated multilateral projects would consolidate domestic support for the Gulf regimes and help the smaller littoral states to deradicalize their larger neighbors' designs. Moreover, under such circumstances, and in the long term, there would be no need for a military presence on the part of the superpowers to fill the so-called power vacuum in the Gulf. Any common accord can function as a strong stabilizing force for the region. Iraq has already shown its interest in and orientation toward the other Arab states by joining with Egypt, Jordan, and North Yemen in forming the Arab Cooperation Council, a move that may have relieved GCC policy-makers of Iraqi pressures.

By the end of the ninth GCC summit in Bahrain (December 19–22, 1988), the Gulf leaders put forward a general perspective on Gulf relations, based on neighborly cooperation and noninterference in domestic affairs. They privately expressed their willingness to improve relations with Iran. In fact, some officials expressed hopes that they would eventually be able to talk about a joint Gulf force to defend the area.[25] Furthermore, in October 1988, as the cease-fire was holding between them, Iran and Iraq joined the GCC states in a meeting in Kuwait under the auspices of ROPME to find ways of clearing the Gulf of mines, oil slicks, sunken ships and other debris. In fact, the current state of "no war, no peace," is worrisome to all the region, particularly Kuwait. Kuwaiti defense minister Nawaf Al-Ahmad stated that stalemate is "not reassuring, as it keeps alive fears and vigilance and hinders peace plans." The Kuwaiti officials viewed the GCC states as "partners in peace" with both Iran and Iraq. Although financially Kuwait was predicted to reap some $2.75 to $3.0 billion annually from reexport trade with both Iran and Iraq, the fear of new hostilities overwhelmed virtually everyone and dampened the financial gains.[26]

As the Gulf states acquired more sophisticated and lethal weapons systems, Kuwait could not afford to lag behind. But since Iran and Iraq already have acquired and even used chemical warfare capabilities, and are building their own arms industries,[27] the conventional arms race in the Gulf now seems less urgent. Kuwait might work, therefore, within a general regional and international strategy to limit the proliferation of sophisticated and chemical arms (or their components) in the region. Such an agreement would stabilize the region in the long run and divert resources to social and economic sectors. It is unfortunate that the Gulf countries and the larger Middle Eastern states are undertaking drives to build local military industries and to possess lethal arms. What is needed most in these states is human, social, economic, and political development, which would sustain their societies and systems beyond the mere superficial show of force.

Kuwait's external behavior is linked to its financial power and internal stability. Currently, its oil revenue is decreasing, its budget is in deficit, and it faces some complicated regional and domestic problems.[28] Furthermore, the Kuwaitis are continuing their expenditure streak, assuming a role larger than their long-term capabilities. Popular participation in government has been rescinded, the "pie" of economic and social benefits and opportunity is getting smaller, and so far there is no break in sight. One would hope that Kuwait moves toward a more rational spending pattern, works diligently toward national consensus and participation, avoids regional entanglements, and assumes a role proportional to its size and power matrices; otherwise it may in the long term be relegated to the less viable states in the developing group, becoming in effect a negligible state.

Notes

1. Personal Interview, Kuwait (April 9, 1988).
2. For a comparison of Kuwait's internal structure with those of other Arab states, see "Tribes with Flags," *The Economist* (February 6, 1988), pp. 14–28. For Kuwait's

parliamentary experiment see John E. Peterson, *The Arab Gulf States: Steps toward Political Participation* (New York: Praeger Publishers for the Center for Strategic and International Studies, Washington, D.C., 1988), pp. 27–61; Nicolas Gavrielides, "Tribal Democracy: The Anatomy of Parliamentary Elections in Kuwait," in Linda L. Layne, ed., *Elections in the Middle East: Implications of Recent Trends* (Boulder and London: Westview Press, 1987), pp. 153–213. For the effects of parliament closures see "Kuwait: When Democracy Runs Afoul of Privilege," *South*, (November 1987), pp. 16–17; and "Democracy Becomes a Dangerous Game in the Gulf," *South* (August 1986), p. 13.

3. The Amir's speech is in Permanent Mission of the State of Kuwait to the United Nations, *Statement by His Highness Sheikh Jaber Al-Ahmad Al-Sabah*, 43rd Session, UN General Assembly, New York (September 28, 1988), p. 16. For Kuwait's support to Palestine see *Asharq Al-Awsat* (November 16, 1988), p. 1; *Al-Watan* (November 16, 1988), p. 1; *Al-Ahram* (November 16, 1988), p. 1; and *The Washington Post* (November 16, 1988), p. A21.

4. *Statement by His Highness Sheikh Jaber Al-Ahmad Al-Sabah*, p. 21.

5. *Statement by His Highness Sheikh Jaber Al-Ahmad Al-Sabah*, p. 10; and Marvine Howe, "Kuwait Offers Plan to Ease Debts of Poor Nations," *The New York Times* (September 29, 1989), p. A8.

6. Rosemarie Said Zahlan, *The Making of the Modern Gulf States*, p. 77.

7. Barry Rubin, "Drowning in the Gulf," *Foreign Policy* (Winter 1987/88), p. 134.

8. For the Amir's statements see *Arab Report and Record* (May 1–16, 1966), p. 100; and SWB, ME/0399/A/9 (March 3, 1989).

9. Annette Barker Fox, *The Power of Small States*, p. 2; Kuwait maintains diplomatic relationship with 101 states; there are 67 foreign missions in Kuwait; Kuwait maintains 44 missions abroad, and 29 non-resident representations in other countries. See Ministry of Foreign Affairs, *Diplomatic and Consular Corps in Kuwait* (Kuwait: January 1989), pp. 1–4; and Ministry of Foreign Affairs, *Diplomasion Fi Wizarat Al-Kharijiah Wa Mumathily Al-Kuwayt Fil Al-Kharij* (Foreign Service of Kuwait and its Representatives Abroad) (Kuwait: April 1989), pp. 25–26.

10. See *The Christian Science Monitor* (February 9, 1989), p. 8, and (February 7, 1989), pp. 1, 2; and Joseph Wright Twinam, "America and the Gulf Arabs," pp. 107–124.

11. *Arab News* (December 7, 1988), p. 4. For Kuwait's position vis-à-vis recent developments in the area see Ambassador Saud Nasir Al-Sabah, "Developments in the Arabian Gulf: A View from Kuwait," *American-Arab Affairs* (Fall 1988), pp. 92–95. For the warmth of relations with the U.S. see the statement of Ambassador Al-Sabah, "A World of Nations: Kuwait," *The Washington Post* (April 9, 1989), p. v.

12. Interview with Abdul-Fatah Al-Bader, Executive Director of Kuwait Oil Tanker Company; see *Al-Watan* (February 4, 1989), pp. 1, 3. See also *Middle East Economic Survey* (May 8, 1989), pp. A7, A8; *Arab News* (April 30, 1989), pp. 1–2. The deflagged ships are the *Gas King*, the *Gas Queen*, the *Gas Princess*, the *Gas Prince*, the *Townsend*, and the *Middleton*; see *Middle East Economic Survey* (February 13, 1989), p. A9.

13. *The Christian Science Monitor* (January 10, 1989), pp. 1–2, and (December 6, 1988), p. 14. For the Kuwaiti official visit see *Platt's Oilgram News* (May 16, 1989), p. 3, and (May 11, 1989), p. 3; *Middle East Economic Digest* (March 31, 1989), p. 7; for the future U.S. role in the Gulf see Foreign Policy Association, *Great Decisions 1989* (New York: Foreign Policy Association, Inc., 1989), pp. 16–25; and Lynn Teo Simarski, "U.S. and the Middle East: Washington's New Opportunity in the Middle East," *The Middle East* (January 1989), pp. 5–9.

14. *Asharq Al-Awsat* (October 6, 1988), pp. 1, 2; *The Times* (October 6, 1988), p. 1, and (October 5, 1988), pp. 1, 24; *The Financial Times* (January 4, 1989), pp. 1 and

14–15; *Business Week* (October 17, 1988), p. 48; *The Oil and Gas Journal* (January 9, 1989), p. 20; *Middle East Economic Digest* (July 8, 1988), p. 16; and *Middle East Monitor* (October 1988), p. 5.

15. Speech of Kuwaiti crown prince and prime minister Saad Al-Abdullah, The National Press Club, Washington, D.C. (July 13, 1988).

16. Personal Interview, Kuwait (March 29, 1988). A secret petition signed by 30,000 to 40,000 male Kuwaitis reportedly called for a return to parliamentary life; see SWB, ME 10399/A/9 (March 3, 1989); *The New York Times* (March 25, 1989), p. 3; and *FBIS* (March 2, 1989), pp. 22–23.

17. *Al-Anba* (February 8, 1989), p. 7.

18. For an analysis of the future direction of Iran's revolution and its impact on the Gulf states, see Fouad Ajami, "Iran: The Impossible Revolution," *The Foreign Affairs* (Winter 1988/89), pp. 135–155; and Graham E. Fuller, "War and Revolution in Iran," *Current History*, vol. 88, no. 535 (February 1989), pp. 81–84 and 99–100. For an assessment of Iran's revolution after its first decade see Richard Cottam, "Inside Revolutionary Iran," *The Middle East Journal*, vol. 43, no. 2 (Spring 1989), pp. 168–185. For the orientation of Iran's foreign policy see R. K. Ramazani, "Iran's Foreign Policy: Contending Orientations," *The Middle East Journal*, vol. 43, no. 2 (Spring 1989), pp. 202–217. For the new post-Khomeini era see *Al-Majalla* (June 7, 1989), pp. 15–23; *The Economist* (June 10, 1989), pp. 14–15 and 35–36; and *Middle East Economic Digest* (June 16, 1989), pp. 4–5.

19. *Asharq Al-Awsat* (November 9, 1988), pp. 1, 2; *Al-Yaqza* (November 18–24, 1988), p. 15; *Kayhan International* (November 13, 1988), p. 2. For Jannati's visit see SWB, ME/0408/A/10 (March 14, 1989); for the Kuwaiti official statement see *The Times* (September 30, 1988), p. 9.

20. For the impact of Saudi Arabia on domestic affairs in Kuwait see Anthony H. Cordesman, *The Gulf and the Search for Strategic Stability*, pp. 570–571; Hermann Frederick Eilts, "Foreign Policy Perspectives of the Gulf States," in *Crosscurrents in the Gulf*, p. 25; and Adeed Dawisha, "Saudi Arabia's Search for Security," in *Regional Security in the Middle East*, p. 20.

21. *Asharq Al-Awsat* (November 5, 1988), p. 1; *Al-Mjtama* (November 15, 1988), p. 11; *Al-Yaqza* (November 18–24, 1988), pp. 2–9; and *FBIS* (November 9, 1988), pp. 18–19.

22. *Asharq Al-Awsat* (September 21, 1988), p. 1; *Time* (December 5, 1988), p. 46; and *The Christian Science Monitor* (April 25, 1989), p. 4. For a review of the future policies of Iraq in the Middle East, see Laurie A. Mylroie, "After the Guns Fell Silent: Iraq in the Middle East," *The Middle East Journal*, vol. 43, no. 1 (Winter 1989), pp. 51–67.

23. See *Asharq Al-Awsat* (February 17, 1989), p. 1, (February 13, 1989), p. 1, (February 4, 1989), pp. 1–2, and (January 30, 1989), pp. 1–2; *Al-Qabas* (January 30, 1989), pp. 1–2; *Al-Anba* (February 8, 1989), pp. 1, 7; and *Al-Majalla* (February 28, 1989), p. 21.

24. See Shahram Chubin and Charles Tripp, *Iran and Iraq at War*, p. 179; and Majid Khadduri, *The Gulf War*, p. 165. As to the future of the GCC, see J. E. Peterson, "The GCC States after the Iran-Iraq War," *American-Arab Affairs* (Fall 1988), pp. 96–106.

25. *The Christian Science Monitor* (December 22, 1988), pp. 7–8; *Middle East Economic Survey* (December 26, 1988/ January 2, 1989), p. C3. For the GCC summit communiqué and other developments, see *Al-Anba* (December 23, 1988), pp. 1, 28, 30–31; *Al-Yaqza* (December 23–29, 1988), pp. 16–17; *Al-Nahda* (December 24, 1988), pp. 4–5; *Al-Majaless* (December 24, 1988), pp. 12–17; *Al-Qabas* (December 23, 1988),

pp. 1, 20, and (December 24, 1988), pp. 1, 3; *Al-Watan* (December 23, 1988), pp. 1, 1–19, and (December 25, 1988), pp. 1, 3; *Kuwait Times* (December 24, 1988), pp. 1, 5; and *Arab Times* (December 24, 1988), pp. 1–4. A Bahraini official, Ibrahim Abd Al-Karim, minister of finance and national economy, asserted that "The GCC . . . was always a sort of lubricant between Iraq and Iran;" see "Diplomacy of Accommodation: Changes in the Middle East," *The Fletcher Forum of World Affairs*, vol. 13, no. 1 (Winter 1989), pp. 43–48. For the post-cease-fire impacts on Iran and Iraq see *The Middle East* (July 1989), pp. 6–10.

26. *Kayhan International* (November 1, 1988), pp. 1, 2; and *The Middle East* (June 1989), pp. 24–25. For the Kuwaiti statement see Alan Cowell, "Sluggish Iran-Iraq Talks Worry Kuwait," *The New York Times* (March 25, 1989), p. 3; and *FBIS* (January 10, 1989), p. 17. For the trade forecast see U.S. Department of Commerce, *Business America* (April 10, 1989), p. 46. For assessment of the war see Gary Sick, "Trial by Error: Reflections on the Iran-Iraq War," *The Middle East Journal*, vol. 43, no. 2 (Spring 1989), pp. 230–245; and Efraim Karsh, "Lessons of the Iran-Iraq War," *Orbis*, vol. 33, no. 2 (Spring 1989), pp. 209–223.

27. *The Christian Science Monitor* (November 22, 1988), pp. 1, 12, and (December 13, 1988), pp. B1–B12; see also International Institute for Strategic Studies, *The Military Balance 1988-1989* (London: IISS, 1988), pp. 94, 247; *The Washington Post* (May 25, 1989), p. A50; "Third World Missiles: Look What I found in My Backyard," *The Economist* (May 27, 1989), pp. 44, 46; *The Middle East* (September 1988), pp. 23–24; *Intelligence Digest* (March 2, 1988), pp. 6–7; *Flight International* (May 13, 1989), pp. 20–21; *International Defense Review* (6/1989), pp. 835–838, 841, 845–846, and 857; Martin S. Navias, "Ballistic Missile Proliferation in the Middle East," *Survival* (May/June 1989), pp. 225–239; ACDA, *World Military Expenditures and Arms Transfers 1988*, pp. 17–20. It was assumed that the Middle East was the world's principal market for arms in 1987. It imported some $17.9 billion in arms, or about 38% of the world market, see Ibid., p. 6. For the impact of arms transfers on the recipient states see Christian Catrina, *Arms Transfers and Dependence* (New York: Taylor and Francis, for the United Nations Institute for Disarmament Research in Geneva, 1988), pp. 145–362.

28. Because of financial deficits in Fiscal Year 1986/87 of about K.D. 1.31 billion ($4.7 billion) (see *Al-Kuwayt Al-Youm*, January 3, 1988, p. 1), the government began a policy of local borrowing through issuing public bonds totaling K.D. 1.4 billion ($5.4 billion). See Law No. 50/1987, *Al-Kuwayt Al-Youm* (October 4, 1987), p. 4. The ceiling on government borrowing has been raised to K.D. 3 billion ($10.36 billion) in early 1989; see *Middle East Economic Digest* (March 24, 1989), p. 21. After the 1982 collapse of the unofficial stock market (*Souq Al-Manakh*), the government paid the equivalent of $7 billion in compensation to investors; see "Kuwait: Economy Adjusts to Sharp Drop in Oil Revenues," *IMF Survey* (March 23, 1987), p. 3. For the political economy of the crisis see Fida Darwiche, *The Gulf Exchange Crash: The Rise and Fall of the Souq Al-Manakh* (London: Croom Helm, 1986), pp. 90–114. For the effect of the oil slump on the economy see Roger Owen, "The Arab States under Stress: The Impact of Falling Oil Prices," *World Policy Journal*, vol. 3, no. 4 (Fall 1986), pp. 643–665; and on the relation between oil and politics see Essa Al-Sadi and Richard U. Moench, "Oil, Prices, State Policies and Politics in Kuwait," *Arab Studies Quarterly*, vol. 10, no. 2 (Spring 1988), pp. 214–224.

Appendix A

Kuwait: Basic Facts

Official Name: Dawlat Al-Kuwait (State of Kuwait)

Type of Government: Nominal constitutional monarchy (the National Assembly was dissolved on July 3, 1986, certain articles of the Constitution were suspended, and the press was censored).

Head of State (Amir): Jaber Al-Ahmad Al-Sabah (since December 31, 1977).

Crown Prince and Prime Minister: Saad Al-Abdullah Al-Sabah (crown prince since January 31, 1978, and prime minister since February 8, 1978).

Deputy Prime Minister and Minister of Foreign Affairs: Sabah Al-Ahmad Al-Sabah (foreign minister since January 28, 1963).

Parliamentary Experiences:

1. A 20-member Constituent Assembly (Majlis Al-Tasisi) was elected in December 31, 1961 to draw up a constitution.

2. A 183-article constitution was promulgated on November 11, 1962.

3. A National Assembly (Majlis Al-Ummah) of 50 members holding four-year terms was elected on January 23, 1963.

4. The National Assembly was dissolved on August 26, 1976, and again on July 3, 1986, and remains dissolved.

Population:

1,958,477 (estimate mid-1988)
annual growth rate 3.71%

767,295 Kuwaitis 39.1%
1,191,182 non-Kuwaitis 60.8%

Area:

17,818 km^2 (6960 m^2), of which 0.1% is arable, including 9 offshore islands.
240 km boundary with Iraq
255 km boundary with Saudi Arabia
290 km coast on the Gulf
Rainfall ranges from 25 to 75 mm (1 to 7 inches) annually.

National Account:

Gross National Product: 6,453.5 million Kuwaiti Dinars* (1987)

---

*rate of exchange, 1 K.D. = $0.280 (1988).

Appendix A
(Continued)

Per Capita National Income: 3,446 K.D.
Growth Rate: 3% (1987)
Inflation Rate (consumer prices): 1.0% (1986)
Gross Domestic Product: 5,444.5 million K.D. (1987)

Petroleum Production (1987):

1,215,000 million barrels per day (b/d) of oil
6,956 million cubic feet of natural gas
Local consumption: 88.4 thousand barrels per days
Proven crude oil reserves: 94.5 billion barrels (about 10.3% of world's reserves)
Proven reserves of natural gas: 1,205 billion cubic feet

Government Finance:

Estimated Revenues
    K.D. 2,230,500 million (1989/90)
    K.D. 2,054,000 million (1988/89)
    K.D. 1,979,390 million (1987/88) Actual

Estimated Expenditures:
    K.D. 3,326,000 million (1989/90)
    K.D. 3,194,800 million (1988/89)
    K.D. 3,158,000 million (1987/88) Actual

Estimated Oil Revenues:
    K.D. 1,942,000 million (1989/90)
    K.D. 1,788,500 million (1988/89)
    K.D. 1,726,380 million (1987/88) Actual

Estimated Deficits:
    K.D. 1,318,600 million (1989/90)
    K.D. 1,346,200 million (1988/89)
    K.D. 1,431,620 million (1987/88) Actual

Allocation (in millions in 1987/88):
    K.D. 838.5 (42.4%) for salaries
    K.D. 266.0 (13.4%) for purchases of goods and services
    K.D. 24.5 (1.2%) for transport and equipment
    K.D. 650.0 (32.8%) for construction projects
    K.D. 100.0 (5.1%) for public properties
    K.D. 197.9 (10.0%) for Future Generations Fund

Fiscal Year: July 1 - June 30

Total Assets of the Central Bank: K.D. 1458.7 million

**Appendix A
(Continued)**

Total Assets and Liability of the Commercial Banks: K.D. 9,894.1 million

Total Exports: $7.4 billion. Crude oil accounted for 81% (1987).

Total Imports: $5.8 billion

Labor Force: 566,000 (1986); 70% non-Kuwaitis
    25.0% service
    20.0% construction
    12.0% trade
    8.6% manufacturing
    2.6% finance and real estate
    1.9% agriculture
    1.7% power and water
    1.4% mining and quarrying

The Kuwaiti labor movement has 27,000 members (4.77% of the labor force) organized into 13 unions.

Education (1987/88): Literacy rate about 71%

Public Schools
    No. of public schools: 636
    No. of public classrooms: 11,700
    No. of public school students: 370,301
        (190,290 male; 180,011 female)
    No. of public school teachers: 27,673
        (12,519 male; 15,154 female)
    Teacher/Student ratio: 1:13.4

Public Kindergartens
    No. of schools: 112
    No. of classrooms: 1,167
    No. of teachers: 2,225 (all female)
    No. of students: 33,357
     (16,872 male; 16,485 female)
    Teacher/student ratio: 1:14.9

Private Schools
    No. of private schools: 115
    No. of private classrooms: 3,622
    No. of private school students: 64,269 male; 55,152 female
    No. of private school teachers: 5,885 (1,286 male; 4,599 female)
    Teacher/student ratio: 1:10.9

Appendix A
(Continued)

Higher Education
    University of Kuwait students: 14,458 (10,355 Kuwaitis)
    No. of Faculty: 863 (288 Kuwaitis)
    Faculty/student ratio: 1:16.7

Health: Life expectancy: men 69, women 74
    No. of hospitals: 16
    No. of physicians: 2,535 (678 Kuwaitis)
    Beds in public hospitals: 5,503
    Population per bed: 340
    Population per doctor (private and public): 598

Social Indicators:
    No. of public cinemas: 14
    No. of daily newspapers: 7
    No. of magazines:
        Weekly 14
        Bimonthly 1
        Monthly 20
        Quarterly 15
    Other specialized publications: 54
    No. of public libraries: 23

Sources: Ministry of Planning, *Annual Statistical Abstract 1988*, pp. XL, 27, 203, 282, 292, 374, 402, 411, 412, 427, 428, 429, and 449; Central Bank of Kuwait, *Quarterly Statistical Bulletin* (October-December 1987), p. 5; *The Middle East and North Africa 1989*, 35th ed., p. 565; *Middle East Economic Survey* (November 28, 1988), p. D4 and (July 3, 1989), pp. B1-B2; CIA, *The World Factbook 1988*, pp. 132-133; Ministry of Information, *Kuwait: Facts and Figures 1988*, pp. 31-33, 38-39, 105-110, 112-113, 125-128, and 214-217; D. I. Milton, *Geology of the Arabian Peninsula; Kuwait*, pp. F1-F7; Hassan S. Haddad and Basheer K. Nijim, eds., *The Arab World: A Handbook*, pp. 81-88; and Department of State, *Country Reports on Human Rights Practices for 1988*, p. 1405; *Al-Watan* (July 4, 1989), p. 6; *Al-Qabas* (June 28, 1989), pp. 1, 26; and *Middle East Economic Digest* (July 21, 1989), p. 22.

Appendix B

**Kuwait's Political–Financial Cash Grants
to Arab States and Causes
1963–June 1989***

	Egypt	Jordan	Syria	PLO	Iraq	Lebanon	Others
1963							$80 m[a]
1964	$70 m $70 m[b]			$3 m[c]			
1965	$98 m $13 m[d]			$14 m[d]			
1966	$42 m[d]						$39 m[d]
1967							K.D. 55m ($154 m) + K.D. 25 m ($75m)[e]
1968				$10 m[e]			K.D. 55 m ($154 m)[e]
1969							K.D. 55m ($154m)[e]

Appendix B
(Continued)

	Egypt	Jordan	Syria	PLO	Iraq	Lebanon	Others
1970	$28 m^f			$14 m$^+$ $3 m^f			$154 m^e
1971							$154 m^e
1972			$30 m^g				$154 m^e
1973	$8.5 m^g		$30 m$^+$ $5 m^g		K.D.11.6 m ($30 m^g)		$154 m^e^+ $400 m^g
1974	$1.3 b^h		$25 m^h				$400 m^g
1975							$400 m^g
1976							$400 m^g

**Appendix B
(Continued)**

	Egypt	Jordan	Syria	PLO	Iraq	Lebanon	Others
1977							$400 m[g]
1978		$196 m[l]	$290 m[l]	$47 m, + $15 m[l]			$400 m[g]
1979	$5.5 b[i]	$196 m $30 m[l]	$290 m[l]	$47 m+ $15 m+ $20 m[l]		$62 m[j]	
1980		$196 m+ $30 m[l]	$290 m[l]	$47 m+ $15 m+ $20 m[l]	$2,000m[k]		
1981		$196 m+ $30 m[l]	$290 m[l]	$47 m+ $15 m+ $20 m[l]	$2,000m[k]		$1 m[m]+ $300,000
1982		$196m+ $30 m[l]	$290 m[l]	$47 m+ $15 m+ $20 m[l]	$2,000m[l]		$500,000[m]
1983		$196m+ $30 m[l]	$290 m[l]	$47 m+ $15 m+ $20 m[l]	$1,200m[n]		

**Appendix B
(Continued)**

	Egypt	Jordan	Syria	PLO	Iraq	Lebanon	Others
1984		$136.0m[o]	K.D.53m[o] ($177 m)	$49.8m[o] +$100m[p]	$1,200m[n]		
1985		$136.0m[o]	K.D.53m[o] ($177 m)	$49.8m[o]	$1,200m[n]		
1986		$136.0m[o]	K.D.53m[o] ($177 m)	$49.8m[o]	$1,200m[n]		
1987		$136.0m[o]	K.D.53m[o] ($177 m)	$49.8m[o]	$1,200m[n]		
1988		$136.0m[o]	K.D.53m[o] ($177 m)	$49.8m[o] + $5 m+ $2.0 m[q]	$1,200m[n]	$5 m[r]	$128m[s]
June 1989		$68.0m + $80m[o]	K.D.26.5m ($88.5m)	$24.9m+ $5 m[o]			
Totals	$7,129.5 m	$2,154 m	$2,813.5 m	$891.9 m	$13,310.0 m	$67 m	$3,594.1 m
Grand Total	$29,960 m						

Appendix B

Notes

a. $80 million ostensibly an aid in return for Iraqi recognition of Kuwait, *The New York Times* (October 19, 1963), p. 34.

b. $70 million was given to Egypt to build houses for army officers, see The Planning Board, *Statistical Abstract 1965* (Kuwait: Government Printing Press, 1965), p. 87. Another $70 million went for Suez Canal purposes, see *The Middle East and North Africa 1964-1965*, 11th ed., p. 328.

c. $3 million for the establishment of the Palestine Liberation Army, the PLO's conventional military wing, see *Kuwait News Agency* (KUNA), *Twenty-Five Years of Modern Kuwait* (Kuwait: KUNA, February 1986), p. 195.

d. $98 million to alleviate Egypt's financial crisis, see *The Middle East Journal*, vol. 19, no. 2 (Spring 1965), p. 202; $13 million for civil projects of Egypt's War Ministry, see *The Middle East Journal*, vol. 19, no. 3 (Summer 1965), p. 343; $14 million was Kuwait's commitment to the PLO, see *Arab Report and Record* (March 16-31, 1969), p. 119; $42 million credit to Egypt in 1966, see *The Middle East Journal*, vol. 20, no. 3 (Summer 1966), p. 370; $39 million was Kuwait's commitment to Arab states excluding Egypt, see *Arab Report and Record* (July 16-31, 1966), p. 160.

e. Khartoum Arab Summit decision of 1967, Kuwait's annual share to the frontline states of $154 million, plus a K.D. 25 million ($75 million) extra donation in 1967, see *The Middle East and North Africa 1972-1973*, pp. 72-73; $10 million aid to Syria in 1968, see interview with Rashed Al-Rashed, undersecretary of the ministry of foreign affairs at the time, *Al-Majallis* (June 19, 1973), pp. 10-11.

f. In February 24, 1970, the National Assembly approved $28 million and $14 million in aid to Egypt and the PLO, respectively, see *The Middle East Journal*, vol. 25, no. 2 (Spring 1971), p. 237; $3 million for PLO war victims of fighting in Jordan in 1970, see *The Middle East Journal*, vol. 25, no. 2 (Spring 1971), p. 237.

g. $30 million aid to Syria for military spending in 1972, see *The Middle East Journal*, vol. 26, no. 4 (Autumn 1972), p. 438; $8.5 million to purchase 20 Mirage F-2 fighters for Egypt in 1973, see *World Armaments and Disarmament: SIPRI Yearbook 1975*, p. 227; $30 million in aid to Syria for use in confronting Israel in 1973, see *The Middle East Journal*, vol. 2, no. 4 (Autumn 1973), p. 492; in 1973, after the nationalization of the Iraqi petroleum company and the closing of its pipelines through Syria, Kuwait gave $5 million to Syria and $30 million to Iraq; $400 war fund to support the military and political capabilities of the confrontation states in the aftermath of the October war in 1973, see *Al-Qabas* (November 3, 1974), p. 1; and *The Middle East and North Africa 1974-75*, p. 466.

h. $1.3 billion reportedly to finance housing, industrial projects, tourism, and transportation in Egypt in 1974, see *Arab Report and Record* (December 1-5, 1974), p. 547; *Middle East Journal*, vol. 28, no. 4 (Autumn 1974), p. 430.

i. Since 1978, Kuwait's contribution of $196 million to Jordan, $290 million to Syria, $47 million for the PLO, and $15 million for the occupied territories has been based on the Baghdad Summit. Kuwait gave an additional $30 million to Jordan and $20 million to the PLO to make up for Algeria's and Libya's shares after they refused to make payments in 1979; see *Al-Rai Al-Aam* (May 17, 1979), p. 2; *Al-Qabas* (August 20, 1982), p. 2; *Al-Hadaf* (Kuwait) (June 10, 1982), p. 12; $5.5 billion is the total Kuwaiti cash aid to Egypt from 1974 to 1979, see *Aramco World Magazine*, vol. 36, no. 6 (November-December 1979), p. 3.

j. $62 million aid to Lebanon in 1979 implemented the Tunis Summit decision of 1979 to rebuild Lebanon, *Al-Qabas* (August 20, 1982), p. 2.

k. $4.00 billion for Iraqi war efforts against Iran, see Gerd Nonneman, *Iraq, The Gulf States and the War*, p. 85.

l. $2.00 billion aid in 1982 for Iraqi war efforts, see *Al-Rai Al-Aam* (April 16, 1982), p. 1. Kuwaiti officials admitted that they had given Iraq more than $6 billion during the war, see *Al-Majalla* (February 28, 1989), p. 20; and *Asharq Al-Awsat* (January 30, 1989), pp. 1-2; U.S. Department of State, *Background Notes: Kuwait*, p. 7; some sources claim that Kuwaiti aid reached some $8 billion; see Christine Moss Helms, *Iraq: Eastern Flank of the Arab World* (Washington, D.C.: The Brookings Institution, 1984), p. 184; and *Al-Majalla* (May 9, 1989), p. 15.

m. $1 million donation to the Palestinians in Lebanon in 1981; $300,000 for the Arab Institute in Jerusalem in 1981; and $500,000 to UNRWA, see *Al-Qabas* (December 26, 1982), p. 1, and (February 6, 1983), p. 13.

n. The estimates are for annual revenue from Kuwait's shared neutral zone oil, sold on behalf of Iraq; see Gerd Nonneman, *Iraq, The Gulf States and the War*, pp. 103-104. His estimates are for 1983-85. The author made his own estimate up to 1988. The Iraqi oil minister admitted that "war relief" crude oil supplied had ceased with the beginning of 1989, see *Middle East Economic Survey* (February 13, 1989), p. A7. Another Iraqi official, Nizar Hamdoun, deputy foreign minister, acknowledged that the aids were nonpayable grants, see *The Middle East* (July 1989), p. 9. Moreover, Kuwait made large down payments to Kuwaiti companies and British contractors doing business in Iraq, see Gerd Nonneman, *Iraq, the Gulf States and the War*, p. 97.

o. Because of budgetary deficits, Kuwait lowered its aid to these states by some 39 percent, Jordan's share became $136.0 m, and the PLO's $49.8 m, whereas the contribution to Syria was adjusted to $177 million, see *Al-Rai* (Jordan) (May 21, 1984), p. 1. In early 1989, as a result of civil disturbances in Jordan, Kuwait committed $80 million ($40 million in cash and $40 million in oil delivery) to Jordan, see *Al-Anba* (June 1, 1989), p. 9, *Al-Watan* (June 1, 1989), p. 1, and *Asharq Al-Awsat* (May 31, 1989), pp. 1-2; and $5 million to revive the PLO-Jordanian Fund, see *The New York Times* (February 18, 1989), p. A5.

p. $100 million contribution for Palestinian refugees through UNWRA in 1984, see *Sout Al-Shaab* (Jordan) (November 19, 1984), p. 15.

q. $5 million contribution for the Intifadah in 1988, plus one day government staff's salary (the amount is unknown), see *Al-Watan* (January 4, 1988), p. 2 and (January 19, 1988), pp. 1, 2; $2.0 million was the total cinema "stamp tax" from 1965-1980; adapted from the Ministry of Planning, *Annual Statistical Abstract 1973*, p. 156, and *Annual Statistical Abstract 1987*, p. 49.

r. $5 million contribution for medicine, food, and school buses to Lebanon in 1988, see *Al-Watan* (January 20, 1988), p. 2.

s. The $128 million per year to the PLO and a contribution to the Intifadah implemented the Algeria Summit decision of June 1988; because Kuwait's share of this amount is yet unknown, the figures were not included in the total of Kuwaiti aid, see *Al-Rai Al-Aam* (June 11, 1988), p. 1; it was also claimed that the annual payment to the PLO was $100 million, see *The Christian Science Monitor* (June 10, 1988), p. 9.

---

*1.   Cash contributions to regional and international agencies are not included. For example, in 1987, Kuwait gave $25 million to the World Bank; see *The World Bank Annual Report*, 1987, p. 29.

2.   The table does not include private donations, which in 1987-1988 amounted to about $9 million; see *The Christian Science Monitor* (March 28, 1988), p. 12.

3.   Contributions made to other Palestinian factions and causes have not been documented; therefore they are not included in the table.

4. Many large private contributions are made by the members of the ruling family, and not considered within the figures.

5. The Amir contributed $10 million for the reconstruction of Faw, not included in this table.

6. The Palestinian workers' 5 percent salary deduction (1965-1989) amounted to an estimated $122.5 million but is not included within the total figure; information provided to the author (November 3, 1988).

Appendix C

Political Protests and Violence in Kuwait
1968-June 1989

1968-69	1972-75

<table>
<tr><td>1.</td><td>November 14-16, 1968
Several bombs explode at
different public places
during the shah of Iran's
visit to Kuwait.</td><td>1.</td><td>March 31, 1972
Assassination of Hardan   Al-
Tukriti, former vice president
and defense minister of Iraq, in
Kuwait; Iraqi secret agents are
charged.</td></tr>
<tr><td>2.</td><td>January 25, 1969
Bombs explode at the National
Assembly, the residence of
the minister of defense and
interior, and the Ministry of
the Interior. 21 persons, all
Kuwaitis except one
Palestinian, and all members
of the Gulf Liberation Front,
an offshoot of Arab
nationalism, are charged and
sentenced.</td><td>2.</td><td>April 7, 1972
Explosion near the Jordanian
embassy, with material damage.</td></tr>
<tr><td></td><td></td><td>3.</td><td>July 8, 1972
Explosion near the Prime
Minister's residence; little
damage.</td></tr>
<tr><td></td><td></td><td>4.</td><td>March 20, 1973
Iraqi troops attack a Kuwait
border post; two Kuwaiti soldiers
die.</td></tr>
<tr><td></td><td></td><td>5.</td><td>September 8, 1973
Five Arab hijackers fly to Kuwait,
free hostages taken from the
Saudi embassy in Paris, and
surrender to police.</td></tr>
<tr><td></td><td></td><td>6.</td><td>November 11, 1973
Explosion near the British
Council.</td></tr>
<tr><td></td><td></td><td>7.</td><td>February 6, 1974
Occupation of the Japanese
embassy in Kuwait by
Palestinians and Japan's Red
Army; no casualties.</td></tr>
<tr><td></td><td></td><td>8.</td><td>April 11, 1975
Explosion near the office of the
American Insurance Company. A
cell of Arab communists arrested
and charged; no casualties.</td></tr>
</table>

Appendix C
(Continued)

1976	1977
1. **May 25, 1976** Explosion in the Shuwaikh industrial area destroys 40 cars; bombs exploded in an oxygen factory kill 3 persons; and a bomb threat in the National Assembly cancels the meeting.	1. **June 5, 1977** A Lebanese hijacks a Kuwaiti airliner.
2. **May 31, 1976** Bomb threat at Kuwait University.	2. **June 20, 1977** Bombs explode at a car parked near the Iranian ambassador's residence in Kuwait; material damage.
3. **June 10, 1976** Bomb threat at Kuwait's Telecommunication Center.	3. **July 8, 1977** Kuwaiti Airways plane is hijacked from Beirut; the passengers are released in Kuwait.
4. **June 17, 1976** Explosion at *Al-Anba* newspaper; 5 persons injured including its editor.	4. **July 12, 1977** Bomb threat at Kuwait airport.
5. **July 1, 1976** Bomb threat at Kuwait Airport.	5. **October 2, 1977** Hijacked Lufthansa plane makes refueling stop in Kuwait.
6. **July 2, 1976** Bombs exploded at Syrian Airlines office in Kuwait; no casualties.	6. **October 3, 1977** Hijacked Japan Airlines plane refuels in Kuwait and departs for Damascus after releasing 7 hostages.
7. **July 6, 1976** Bomb threat at Fahaheel.	7. **October 18, 1977** Hijack attempt against a Czechoslovakian airplane in Kuwait.
8. **August 25, 1976** Bomb threat at *Al-Watan* newspaper.	8. **December 5, 1977** Demonstration against Sadat's visit to Israel; 30 students arrested.
	9. **December 25, 1977** Bomb discovered at the office of Egypt Air in Kuwait.

**Appendix C
(Continued)**

1978	1979
1. May 23, 1978 Fire at Al-Manaqish oil facility destroys 3 oil storage tanks and damages oil pipeline.	1. March 25, 1979 Demonstrators storm the Egyptian embassy in Kuwait after Sadat's peace treaty with Israel; no casualties.
2. June 15, 1978 Assassination of Ali Yassen, chief of PLO office in Kuwait; Abu Nidal charged.	2. September 26, 1979 Sayed Abbas Mohri, Khomeini's special envoy in Kuwait, and 18 members of his family have their citizenship rescinded and are deported to Iran.
	3. November 21, 1979 Bomb threat at Al-Hamra movie theater.
	4. November 30, 1979 U.S. embassy is the target of several thousand anti-U.S. Shiite demonstrators.

Appendix C
(Continued)

1980

---

1.   April 29, 1980
     Assassination attempt on
     Iranian foreign minister,
     Sadeq Qotbzadeh in Kuwait.

2.   May 2, 1980
     Kuwaiti diplomat shot and
     wounded in Teheran.

3.   May 21, 1980
     Two bombs exploded in front
     of Iran Air Office in Kuwait;
     no casualties.

4.   May 24-25, 1980
     Kuwait Airways plane hijacked
     en route from Beirut; no
     casualties.

5.   June 1, 1980
     Bomb explodes at the London
     office of Kuwait Oil Co.; no
     injuries.

6.   June 4, 1980
     Iranian embassy in Kuwait
     is damaged by explosions; no
     injuries.

7.   June 11, 1980
     Three Iranian aircraft violate
     Kuwaiti air space.

8.   June 21, 1980
     Assassination attempt on the
     chief of the PLO office in
     Kuwait, Awni Batash.

9.   June 26, 1980
     Attack at Kuwaiti embassy in
     Beirut; material damage.

10. July 24, 1980
     Two Jordanians hijack Kuwaiti
     airliner en route from Beirut;
     no injuries.

11. September 12, 1980
     Explosion at *Al-Rai Al-Aam*
     newspaper building; 1
     person dies and 6 are
     injured. Damages
     estimated at K.D. 4
     million.

12. September 20, 1980
     Kuwaiti freighter *Al-Farwaniah*
     is attacked by Iranian machine
     guns en route from Basra to
     Kuwait.

13. September 21, 1980
     Kuwaiti freighter *Ibn Abdoun* is
     attacked by Iranian guns en route
     from Basra to Qatar.

Appendix C
(Continued)

1981

---

1. February 8, 1981
   Man carrying Syrian diplomatic
   passport, but thought to be an
   exiled Iraqi opposition member,
   is killed in Kuwait.

2. February 9, 1981
   Kuwait University students
   strike to protest the
   cancellation of an Islamic
   culture course.

3. February 12, 1981
   Bomb threat at Syrian embassy
   in Kuwait.

4. March 28, 1981
   Explosions in 5 different
   places in Kuwait; no
   casualties.

5. March 28, 1981
   Explosions at the office
   of the Iranian Shipping Co.;
   1 person dies.

6. April 30, 1981
   Kuwaiti seismic research ship
   Western Sea is confiscated by
   Iranian authorities; released
   May 19, 1981.

7. April 30, 1981
   Three thousand non-Kuwaiti
   Arab oil workers strike for 5
   days, demanding improved
   working conditions.

8. June 13, 1981
   Three Iranian aircraft attack
   the Abdali border post.

9. June 25, 1981
   Explosions in oil storage facilities
   in Shuaiba; damages estimated at
   $50 million. Fire put out
   after 2 weeks.

10. June 26, 1981
    An attack against Kuwait
    Embassy in Beirut; material
    damage.

11. August 25, 1981
    Bomb threat at Kuwait airport.

12. August 30, 1981
    Bomb threat at Kuwait's
    Telecommunication Center.

13. September 1, 1981
    Bomb threat at Kifan
    Cooperative Society
    (supermarket).

14. October 19, 1981
    Iranian aircraft attack
    a petroleum complex at Um Al-
    Eish.

15. December 19, 1981
    Bomb threat at Kuwait's
    Central Bank.

**Appendix C
(Continued)**

1982

1. February 26, 1982
    Kuwaiti airliner hijacked
    at Beirut airport; no
    casualties.

2. March 8, 1982
    Bomb threat at the Hilton
    Hotel.

3. March 28, 1982
    Palestinian student
    demonstrators clash with
    police; dozens injured.

4. May 1, 1982
    Bomb threat at a high school.

5. May 9, 1982
    Bomb threat at Mubarak Al-
    Kabir hospital.

6. May 10, 1982
    Bomb threat at the Ministry
    of Foreign Affairs.

7. May 17, 1982
    Bomb threat at Kuwait T.V.
    station.

8. June 4, 1982
    Kuwaiti diplomat assassinated in
    New Delhi by the Abu Nidal
    group.

9. August 23, 1982
    UAE diplomat shot and wounded
    in Kuwait by a Palestinian
    gunman.

10. September 16, 1982
    Assassination attempt on Kuwaiti
    diplomat in Karachi.

11. September 16, 1982
    Kuwaiti diplomat assassinated
    in Madrid by the Abu Nidal
    group.

12. October 28, 1982
    Shiite demonstration after an
    Ashura celebration in Kuwait.
    One Iranian and others arrested.
    Exchange of protests between
    Kuwait and Iran.

13. October 30, 1982
    Bomb explodes in a public park
    in a residential area; little
    damage.

14. December 9, 1982
    Explosions at Kuwait Airways
    office in Athens; little damage.

**Appendix C
(Continued)**

1983

1. August 22, 1983
   Iran confiscates 6 private
   Kuwaiti fishing boats.

2. December 12, 1983
   Explosions in seven places,
   including the American and
   French embassies in Kuwait,
   the airport control tower,
   and an oil refinery. Five
   persons die; 63 are wounded.
   Pro-Iran Islamic Jihad claims
   responsibility. Seventeen
   people arrested and charged.

3. December 24, 1983
   Anti-Kuwait demonstration in
   front of the Kuwaiti embassy in
   Teheran.

1984

1. January 6, 1984
   Bomb threat at a Saudi
   airliner in Kuwait airport.

2. February 12, 1984
   Bomb threat at Kuwait's
   Teacher Association buildings.

3. May 13, 1984
   Iran attacks the Kuwaiti
   commercial oil tanker
   Um Qasbah.

4. May 14, 1984
   Iran attacks the Kuwaiti oil
   tanker *Bahrah.*

5. May 16, 1984
   Bomb threat at Rikka
   Cooperative Society.

6. June 6, 1984
   4 Iranians arrested on charges
   of attempted explosions at the
   Ministry of Information.

7. June 23, 1984
   Bomb threat at Kuwait
   Investment Corporation.

7. June 23, 1984
   Bomb threat at Kuwait
   Investment Corporation.

8. July 13, 1984
   Iran attacks the Kuwaiti
   commercial freighter *Ibn
   Rashed.*

9. September 12, 1984
   Assassination attempt on the
   editor of *Anba* newspaper.

10. November 17, 1984
    Attack on the Kuwaiti embassy
    in Beirut; no casualties.

11. December 4, 1984
    Kuwaiti airliner hijacked to
    Teheran. Two die, several
    wounded. Plane is returned
    to Kuwait May 5, 1986.

Appendix C
(Continued)

1985

1. February 13, 1985
    Assassination attempt on a
    candidate to the National
    Assembly.

2. March 1, 1985
    Assassination of an Iraqi
    diplomat and his son in
    Kuwait.

3. April 23, 1985
    Editor of *Al-Siyassah*
    Palestinian charged.

4. May 25, 1985
    Assassination attempt on
    the Amir; 3 dead, 15
    wounded. Islamic Jihad
    claims responsibility.
    Twenty people arrested, 5
    Iraqis charged.

5. May 27, 1985
    Bomb threat at the Colleges
    of Law and Art in Kuwait
    University.

6. June 10, 1985
    Anti-Kuwait demonstration
    against the Kuwaiti embassy
    in Damascus.

7. June 20, 1985
    Iran confiscates the Kuwaiti
    freighter *Al-Muharaq*.

8. July 11, 1985
    Bombs exploded in two popular
    seafront cafes. Ten people
    killed, 56 injured.

9. July 11, 1985
    Kidnapping of a Kuwaiti
    diplomat in Beirut.

10. August 30, 1985
    Bomb threat at the
    Entertainment City.

11. September 4, 1985
    Iran confiscates the
    Kuwaiti freighter
    Al-Watiah in the Gulf of
    Oman.

12. September 9, 1985
    Iran confiscates the Kuwaiti
    freighter *Al-Musailah*.

13. November 25, 1985
    Iran confiscates the Kuwaiti
    freighter *Ibn Bittar*.

14. December 25, 1985
    Iranian aircraft attack the
    Kuwaiti ship *Kazmah* near
    Qatar.

15. December 30, 1985
    Three Lebanese and a Syrian
    are arrested for allegedly
    plotting to blow up power
    and water desalinization
    plants in Doha, Kuwait.

Appendix C
(Continued)

1986

---

1.   February 22, 1986
     Iranian helicopters
     intercept Kuwaiti fishing
     boats.

2.   March 11, 1986
     Anti-Kuwait demonstration
     in Teheran.

3.   June 17, 1986
     Five explosions at 4 sites
     in the Mina Al-Ahmadi and Al-
     Muqwah fields; no casualties.

4.   September 18, 1986
     Kuwaiti oil tanker *Al-Fintas*
     intercepted by Iranian navy.

Appendix C
(Continued)

1987

1. January 19, 1987
   Three bombs explode in Kuwait
   city; material damage.

2. January 21, 1987
   Iran launches Silkworm missile
   into Failaka island;
   casualties.

3. January 24, 1987
   Parcel bomb explodes under a
   car in Salihiyah. A new
   "Revolutionary Organization
   forces of the Prophet Mohammed
   in Kuwait" claims
   responsibility.

4. January 31, 1987
   Security forces arrest 12
   persons and charge them,
   plus 4 others who have
   escaped, with June 1986
   explosions. All are
   Kuwaiti Shiite citizens.

5. April 26, 1987
   A car explodes in front of
   Kuwait Oil Co.; damage to
   cars parked nearby.

6. May 11, 1987
   Bomb explodes in TWA office
   in Kuwait before the arrival
   of U.S. envoy Richard Murphy.
   One dies.

7. May 22, 1987
   Explosion in Mina Al-Ahmadi
   kills Kuwaiti Shiite who
   planted the device.

8. June 1, 1987
   Iran confiscates 7 private
   Kuwaiti fishing boats.

9. July 15, 1987
   Car bomb explodes in Al-
   Salhia business district,
   near the Air France office,
   killing the 2 Kuwaiti
   Shiites who planted the
   bomb.

10. July 24, 1987
    An Iranian Silkworm hits the
    Bridgeton (an American-
    registered ship) in Kuwait;
    no casualties.

11. August 1, 1987
    Iranian demonstrators,
    reacting to the Hajj killings
    in Mecca, ransack the Kuwaiti
    and Saudi embassies in Teheran.

12. September 1, 1987
    Iran confiscates the Kuwaiti
    freighter *Jabel Ali*.

13. September 3, 1987
    Iran launches a Silkworm missile
    into Kuwait's southern industrial
    territories; no casualties.

14. September 4, 1987
    Fire bombs in the College of
    Science, Kuwait University;
    material damage.

15. September 7, 1987
    Kuwait declared 6 Iranian
    diplomats *persona non grata*.

16. September 9, 1987
    Fire breaks out at Shamiyah
    secondary school; arson is
    suspected.

Appendix C
(Continued)

1987

---

17. September 10, 1987
    Bomb explodes in front of the
    Kuwaiti-French bank in Paris;
    material damage.

18. October 15, 1987
    Iranian Silkworm is
    launched into a U.S.-owned
    Liberian-registered *Sangari*
    tanker at Mana Al-Ahmadi.

19. October 16, 1987
    Iranian Silkworm is launched
    into a Kuwaiti offshore oil
    island; 5 are injured.

20. October 22, 1987
    Iranian Silkworm is launched
    into a Kuwaiti offshore oil
    island.

21. October 24, 1987
    Explosion in a Pan American
    travel agency in Kuwait; material
    damage.

22. November 3, 1987
    Car bomb explodes in Kuwait
    near the Interior Ministry
    building; material damage
    to some cars.

23. November 6, 1987
    Bomb threat at the Andalus
    Theatre, Kuwait.

24. December 7, 1987
    Iran launches a Silkworm
    against Kuwaiti southern coast;
    no casualties.

**Appendix C
(Continued)**

1988

---

1. February 14, 1988
   Palestinian student
   demonstrators clash with
   police. "Several dozen"
   people are injured and
   arrested.

2. March 30, 1988
   Three Iranian speedboats
   attack Kuwait's Bubiyan Island
   military post. Two soldiers
   are injured.

3. April 5-20, 1988
   Kuwaiti airliner *Al-Jabriya*
   is hijacked en route from
   Bangkok to Kuwait and
   diverted to Mashad, Iran,
   Cyprus, and Algeria. Two
   Kuwaitis are killed.
   Hijackers believed to be
   extreme Lebanese Shiites.

4. April 9, 1988
   Bomb explodes in the Interior
   Ministry garage in Kuwait; no
   injuries.

5. April 20, 1988
   Iran launches a Scud-B
   missile against a Kuwaiti oil
   facility in Wafra, operated by
   the U.S. firm Getty Oil Company.
   No damage or injuries.

6. April 26, 1988
   Bomb blast at Saudi airlines
   office in Kuwait injures one
   security guard after Saudi Arabia
   severs diplomatic relations with
   Iran.

7. May 7, 1988
   Bomb explodes in Kuwait city's
   downtown Avis Rent-A-Car
   office; no injuries, material
   damage.

8. May 18, 1988
   Car explodes near Kuwait
   Airways Office, killing 2 Kuwaiti
   Shiites who planted the
   explosion.

9. July 8, 1988
   Iran captures 3 Kuwaiti fishing
   boats.

**Appendix C
(Continued)**

Up to June 1989

1. March 15, 1989
   33 persons, among them
   18 Kuwaitis, indicted on
   charges of plotting to
   overthrow the government.

2. March 28, 1989
   Airport receives false
   bomb threat on a Kuwaiti-
   leased aircraft.

3. May 9, 1989
   Iran confiscates a coast
   guard gunboat and 8 men
   on board, 2 non-
   Kuwaitis, are released;
   the remaining 6 crew
   members are released
   June 17, 1989.

Sources: Adapted from various Kuwaiti, regional, and international newspapers. See *Al-Qabas* (June 11, 1987), p. 5, (March 12, 1986), p. 3, (November 21, 1985), p. 1, (June 24, 1984), p. 1, (May 17, 1984), p. 2, (May 11, 1982), p. 2, (May 10, 1982), p. 7, (March 19, 1982), p. 20, (January 5, 1982), p. 1, (December 27, 1981), p. 3, (November 23, 1980), p. 5; *Al-Rai-Al-Aam* (February 2, 1984), p. 1, (May 18, 1982), p. 1, (August 31, 1981), p. 1, (July 13, 1977), p. 2, (May 27, 1985), p. 2; *Al-Itihad* (Abu Dhabi) (September 4, 1981), p. 1; *Al-Seyassah* (August 26, 1981), p. 1; *Al-Anba* (February 13, 1981), p. 1, (June 5, 1982), p. 2, (June 21, 1980), p. 2; *Al-Safir* (Beirut) (September 12, 1984), p. 3; *Al-Watan* (November 11, 1984), p. 3, (September 17, 1982), p. 2, (June 13, 1980), p. 2, (November 18, 1980), p. 2, (March 29, 1981), p. 1, (December 20, 1987), p. 5, (August 17, 1981), p. 5, (September 6, 1981), p. 1, (July 2, 1986), p. 2, (March 16, 1989), pp. 1, 21; *The Middle East Journal* (Summer 1988), p. 469, (Autumn 1980), p. 479, (Spring 1986), p. 321, (Autumn 1978), p. 463, (Winter 1974), p. 34; *The Middle East Economic Digest* (November 5, 1982), p. 39; *The Times* (London) (June 1, 1987), p. 5; *Arab News* (May 26, 1989), p. 3; *Asharq Al-Awsat* (May 21, 1989), p. 1; *Al-Majalla* (May 17, 1989), p. 25; and *New York Times* (March 9, 1989), p. 13.

Bibliography

Books

A. Arabic

Al-Adsani, Khalid Sulayman. *Nisf Aam Lil-Huk-um Al-Niyabi Fil Al-Kuwayt.* Beirut: Al-Qashaf Press, 1947.

Al-Akad, Salah. *Al-Tiyarat Al-Siyasiah Fil Al-Khalij Al-Araby.* Cairo: Anglo-Egyptian Printing, 1983.

Al-Majid, Majid. *Majlis Al-Taawun Al-Khaliji: Azmat Al-Siyasat Wal-Shariyat.* London: Ta-Ha Publishers, 1986.

Al-Nafisi, Abdullah. *Majlis Al-Taawun Al-Khaliji: Al-Itar Al-Siyasi Wal-Istrateji.* London: Ta-Ha Publishers, 1982.

Al-Naqeeb, Khaldoun H. *Al-Mujtama Wa Al-Dawlat Fil Al-Khalij Wa Al-Jazirah Al-Arabiya.* Beirut: Center for Arab Unity Studies, 1987.

Al-Rushaid, Abd Al-Aziz. *Tarikh Al-Kuwayt.* Beirut: Dar Maktabat Al-Hayat, 1971.

Al-Sarawi, Abd Al-Aziz Abdullah. *Dirasat Fil Al-Shouon Al-Ijtimaiah Wal Al-Omaliah.* Kuwait: Government Printing Press, 1965.

Al-Taliat Fi Marakat Al-Dimikra-tiah. Kuwait: Kadhima, 1984.

Dukas, Martha. *Azmat Al-Kuwayt: Al-Ilakat Al-Kuwaytiah Al-Irakiah, 1961–1963.* Beirut: Dar Al-Nahar, 1973.

Husayn, Abd Al-Aziz. *Al-Mujtama Al-Araby Bil Kuwayt.* Cairo: Institute for Higher Arab Studies, 1960.

Joudah, Ahmad Hasan. *Al-Massaleh Al-Britania Fil Kuwayt Hata 1939.* Basra: Centre for Arab Gulf Studies, 1979.

Khazal, Husayn Khalaf Al-Shaykh. *Tarikh Al-Kuwayt Al-Siyassi,* vol. 1. Beirut: Dar Al-Kutub, 1962.

———. *Tarikh Al-Kuwayt Al-Siyassi,* vol. 2. Beirut: Dar Al-Kutub, 1962.

———. *Tarikh Al-Kuwayt Al-Siyassi,* vol. 5. Beirut: Dar Al-Kutub, 1970.

Nuwfal, Sayed. *Al-Awdah Al-Siyassiah Li Amarat Al-Khalij Al-Araby Wa Janoub Al-Jazirah.* Cairo: Dar Al-Marifat, 1960.

Qalaji, Qadri. *Al-Khalij Al-Araby.* Beirut: Dar Al-Kitab Al-Araby, 1965.

Rushdi, Rasim. *Kuwayt Wa Kuwaytion: Dirasat Fil Mudhi Al-Kuwayt Wa Hadireha.* Beirut: Al-Rahbania Al-Lubaniah Press, 1965.

B. English

Abir, Mordechai. *Oil, Power and Politics.* London: Frank Cass, 1974.

Al-Baharna, Hussain. *The Arabian Gulf States: Their Legal and Political Status and Their International Problems,* 2nd ed. Beirut: Librairie de Liban, 1975.

———. *The Legal Status of the Arabian Gulf States: A Study of Their Treaty Relations and Their International Problems.* Manchester: Manchester University Press, 1968.

Axelgard, Frederick W. *A New Iraq? The Gulf War and Implications for U.S. Policy.* New York: Praeger for the Center for Strategic and International Studies, Washington, 1988.

_____. (Ed.) *Iraq in Transition: A Political, Economic and Strategic Perspective.* Boulder, CO: Westview Press, 1986.

Bidwell, Robin. *The Affairs of Kuwait 1896–1905, vol. 1, 1896–1901.* London: Frank Cass, 1971.

Brand, Laurie. *Palestinians in the Arab World: Institution Building and the Search for State.* New York: Columbia University Press, 1988.

Calverly, Eleanor Taylor. *My Arabian Days and Nights.* New York: Thomas Y. Crowell, 1958.

Catrina, Christian. *Arms Transfers and Dependence.* New York: Taylor and Francis, for the United Nations Institute for Disarmament Research in Geneva, 1988.

Chisholm, Archibald H. T. *The First Kuwait Oil Concession Agreement: A Record of Negotiations, 1911–1934.* London: Frank Cass, 1975.

Chubin, Shahram, and Charles Tripp. *Iran and Iraq at War.* Boulder, CO: Westview Press, 1988.

Coke, Richard. *The Arab's Place in the Sun.* London: Thornton Butterworth, 1929.

Cordesman, Anthony H. *The Gulf and the Search for Strategic Stability: Saudi Arabia, the Military Balance in the Gulf, and Trends in the Arab-Israeli Military Balance.* Boulder, CO: Westview Press, and London: Mansell Publishing, 1984.

_____. *The Gulf and the West: Strategic Relations and Military Realities.* Boulder, CO: Westview Press, 1988.

Cottrell, Alvin, ed. *The Persian Gulf States: A General Survey.* Baltimore: Johns Hopkins University Press, 1980.

Dann, Uriel. *Iraq under Qassem: A Political History, 1958–1963.* Pall Mall, NY: Praeger, 1969.

Darwiche, Fida. *The Gulf Exchange Crash: The Rise and Fall of the Souq Al-Manakh.* London: Croom Helm, 1986.

Dawisha, Adeed, ed. *Islam in Foreign Policy.* Cambridge: Cambridge University Press, for the Royal Institute of International Affairs, London, 1983.

Dickson, Harold R. P. *Kuwait and Her Neighbours.* London: George Allen and Unwin, 1956.

El-Ebraheem, Hassan Ali. *Kuwait and the Gulf: Small States and the International System.* Washington, D.C.: Georgetown University Center for Contemporary Arab Studies, 1984.

El-Mallakh, Ragaei. *Kuwait: Trade and Investment.* Boulder, CO: Westview Press, 1979.

Falnes, Oscar J. *The Future of the Small States.* Washington, DC: American Council on Public Affairs, 1942.

Farouk-Sluglett, Marion, and Peter Sluglett. *Iraq since 1958: From Revolution to Dictatorship.* London and New York: KDI, 1987.

Fox, Annette Baker. *The Power of Small States: Diplomacy in World War II.* Chicago: The University of Chicago Press, 1959.

Ghabra, Shafeeq N. *Palestinians in Kuwait: The Family and the Politics of Survival.* Boulder, CO and London: Westview Press, 1987.

Goldberg, Jacob. *The Foreign Policy of Saudi Arabia: The Formative Years, 1902–1918.* Cambridge, MA, and London: Harvard University Press, 1986.

Haddad, Hassan, and Basheer K. Nijim, eds. *The Arab World: A Handbook.* Wilmette, IL: Medina Press, 1978.

Handel, Michael. *Weak States in the International System.* London: Frank Cass, 1981.

Hassouna, Hussein A. *The League of Arab States and Regional Disputes: A Study of Middle East Conflicts.* Dobbs Ferry, NY: Oceana Publications, Inc., 1975.

Heckscher, Gunnar. *The Role of Small Nations–Today and Tomorrow.* London: University of London Athlone Press, 1966.

Heller, Mark, ed. *The Middle East Military Balance 1984.* Boulder, CO: Westview Press, for Tel Aviv University's Center for Strategic Studies, 1984.

Helms, Christine Moss. *Iraq: Eastern Flank of the Arab World.* Washington, DC: The Brookings Institution, 1984.

Hiro, Dilip. *Inside the Middle East.* NY: McGraw Hill, 1982.

Hull, Cordell. *The Memoirs of Cordell Hull, vol. 2.* NY: The Macmillan Co., 1948.

Hunter, Shireen. *OPEC and the Third World: The Politics of Aid.* Bloomington: Indiana University Press, 1984.

Hurewitz, Jacob C. *The Middle East and North Africa in World Politics: A Documentary Record, vol. 1.* New Haven and London: Yale University Press, 1975.

————. *The Middle East and North Africa in World Politics: A Documentary Record, vol. 2, British-French Supremacy, 1914–1945.* New Haven and London: Yale University Press, 1979.

Ismael, Jacqueline S. *Kuwait: Social Change in Historical Perspective.* Syracuse: Syracuse University Press, 1982.

Keegan, John. *World Armies.* NY: Facts on File, Inc., 1979.

Kelly, J. B. *Britain and the Persian Gulf, 1775–1880.* Oxford: Clarendon Press, 1968.

Khadduri, Majid. *Independent Iraq 1932–1958: A Study in Iraqi Politics,* 2nd ed. London: Oxford University Press, 1960.

————. *Republican Iraq: A Study in Iraqi Politics since the Revolution of 1958.* London: Oxford University Press, 1969.

————. *Socialist Iraq: A Study in Iraqi Politics since 1958.* Washington, DC: The Middle East Institute, 1978.

————. *The Gulf War: The Origins and Implications of the Iraq-Iran Conflict.* NY: Oxford University Press, 1988.

Khalil, Mohammad. *The Arab States and the Arab League: A Documentary Record, vol. 2, International Affairs.* Beirut: Khayats, 1962.

Khouja, M. W. and P. G. Sadler, *The Economy of Kuwait: Development and Role in International Finance* London: Macmillan, 1979.

Kimball, Lorenzo K. *The Changing Pattern of Political Power in Iraq: 1958 to 1971.* NY: Robert Speller and Sons, 1972.

Kramer, Martin, ed. *Shiism, Resistance, and Revolution.* Boulder, CO: Westview Press, 1987.

Layne, Linda L., ed. *Elections in the Middle East: Implications of Recent Trends.* Boulder, CO and London: Westview Press, 1987.

Legum, Colin, ed. *The Middle East Contemporary Survey, vol. 1, 1976–1977.* NY and London: Holmes and Meier, 1978.

Litwak, Robert. *Security in the Persian Gulf II: Source of Interstate Conflict.* Allenheld, PA: Osmun for International Institute for Strategic Studies, 1981.

Long, David E. *The Persian Gulf: An Introduction to Its People, Politics, and Economics.* Boulder, CO: Westview Press, 1976.

Looney, Robert. *Third-World Military Expenditure and Arms Production.* NY: St. Martin's Press, 1988.

Lorimer, J. C. *Gazetter of the Persian Gulf, Oman, and Central Asia, vol. 1, Pt. 1.* Calcutta: Superintendent Government Printing, 1915.

Malik, Hafeez, ed. *International Security in Southwest Asia.* NY: Praeger, 1984.

Marr, Phebe. *The Modern History of Iraq.* Boulder, CO: Westview Press, 1985.

Martin, Lenore G. *The Unstable Gulf: Threats from Within*. Lexington, MA: Lexington Books, 1984.

Mattione, Richard P. *OPEC's Investments and the International Financial System*. Washington, DC: The Brookings Institution, 1985.

The Middle East and North Africa, 1989, 35th ed. London: Europa Publications, 1988.

The Middle East and North Africa, 1988, 34th ed. London: Europa Publications, 1987.

The Middle East and North Africa, 1974–1975, 21st ed. London: Europa Publications, 1974.

The Middle East and North Africa, 1972–1973, 19th ed. London: Europa Publications, 1972.

The Middle East and North Africa, 1965–1965, 11th ed. London: Europa Publications, 1964.

The Middle East Review 1988, 14th ed. London: World of Information, 1987.

Mostyn, Trevor, and Albert Hourani, eds. *The Cambridge Encyclopedia of the Middle East and North Africa*. Cambridge: Cambridge University Press, 1988.

Mottale, Morris Mehrdad. *The Arms Buildup in the Persian Gulf*. Lentham, MD: University Press of America, 1986.

Muttam, John. *Arms and Insecurity in the Persian Gulf*. New Delhi: Radiant Publishers, 1984.

Nakhleh, Emile A. *The Gulf Cooperation Council: Policies, Problems and Prospects*. NY: Praeger, 1986.

Nonneman, Gerd. *Iraq, the Gulf States and the War: A Changing Relationship 1980–1986 and Beyond*. London and Atlantic Highlands: Ithaca Press, 1986.

Noyes, James H. *The Clouded Lens: Persian Gulf Security and U.S. Policy*. Stanford: Hoover Institution Press, 1979.

O'Ballance, Edgar. *The Gulf War*. London: Brassey's, 1988.

Olson, William J., ed. *U.S. Strategic Interests in the Gulf Region*. Boulder, CO: Westview Press, 1987.

Penrose, Edith, and E. F. Penrose. *Iraq: International Relations and National Development*. London: Ernest Benn, and Boulder, CO: Westview Press, 1978.

Peretz, Don. *The Middle East Today*, 3rd ed. NY: Holt, Rinehart and Winston, 1978.

Peterson, John E. *Defending Arabia*. New York: St. Martin's Press, 1986.

Pinkerton, John, ed. *A General Collection of the Best and Most Interesting Voyages and Travels in All Parts of the World*, vol. 10. London: Longman, Hurst, Rees, and Brown, Paternoster-Row, and Cadell and Davies, in the Strand, 1811.

Pipes, Daniel. *The Long Shadow: Culture and Politics in the Middle East*. New Brunswick and Oxford: Transaction, 1989.

Pridham, B. R., ed. *The Arab Gulf and the Arab World*. London: Croom Helm, 1988.

_____. *The Arab Gulf and the West*. New York: St. Martin's Press, 1985.

Quandt, William B. *Saudi Arabia in the 1980s: Foreign Policy, Security, and Oil*. Washington, DC: The Brookings Institution, 1981.

Ramazani, Rouhollah K. *Iran's Foreign Policy 1941–1973: A Study of Foreign Policy in Modernizing Nations*. Charlottesville: University Press of Virginia, 1975.

_____. *Revolutionary Iran: Challenge and Response in the Middle East*. Baltimore and London: The Johns Hopkins University Press, 1986.

_____. *The Foreign Policy of Iran: A Developing Nation in World Affairs, 1500–1941*. Charlottesville: University Press of Virginia, 1966.

_____. *The Gulf Cooperation Council: Record and Analysis*. Charlottesville: University Press of Virginia, 1988.

Rapaport, Jacques, Ernest Muteba, and Joseph J. Therattil. *Small States and Territories: Status and Problems*. NY: Arno Press, for the United Nations Institute for Training and Research (UNITAR), 1971.

Rush, Alan. *Al-Sabah: History and Genealogy of Kuwait's Ruling Family 1752–1987.* London and Atlantic Highlands: Ithaca Press, 1987.

Safran, Nadav. *Saudi Arabia: The Ceaseless Quest for Security.* Cambridge, MA, and London: The Belknap Press of Harvard University, 1985.

Sandwick, John A., ed. *The Gulf Cooperation Council: Moderation and Stability in an Interdependent World.* Boulder, CO: Westview Press; and Washington, DC: American-Arab Affairs Council, 1987.

Sanger, Richard H. *The Arabian Peninsula.* Ithaca, NY: Cornell University Press, 1954.

Sinclair, H. Richard III, and J. E. Peterson, eds. *Crosscurrents in the Gulf: Arab, Regional and Global Interests.* London: Routledge for the Middle East Institute, Washington, 1988.

Sivard, Ruth Leger. *World Military and Social Expenditures 1987–1988,* 12th ed. Washington, DC: World Priorities, 1987.

Stone, Russell A., ed. *OPEC and the Middle East: The Impact of Oil on Societal Development.* NY: Praeger, 1977.

Taheri, Amir. *Holy Terror: Inside the World of Islamic Terrorism.* Bethesda, MD: Adler & Adler, 1987.

Taylor, Michael J. H. *Encyclopedia of the World's Air Forces.* NY: Facts on File, 1988.

Tolchin, Martin, and Susan Tolchin. *Buying into America: How Foreign Money Is Changing the Face of Our Nation.* NY: Times Books, 1988.

Trevelyan, Humphrey. *The Middle East in Revolution.* Boston: Gambit, 1970.

Tripp, Charles, ed. *Regional Security in the Middle East.* New York: St. Martin's Press for the International Institute for Strategic Studies, 1984.

Twitchell, K. S. *Saudi Arabia,* 3rd ed. Princeton: Princeton University Press, 1958.

Vital, David. *The Survival of Small States: Studies in Small Power/Great Power Conflict.* London: Oxford University Press, 1971.

Wells, Samuel, F., Jr., and Mark Bruzonsky, eds. *Security in the Middle East: Regional Change and Great Power Strategies.* Boulder, CO, and London: Westview Press, 1987.

Winstone, H.C.D., and Zahra Freeth. *Kuwait: Prospect and Reality.* London: George Allen and Unwin, 1972.

Zahlan, Rosemarie Said. *The Making of the Modern Gulf States: Kuwait, Bahrain, Qatar, the United Arab Emirates and Oman.* London: Unwin Hyman, 1989.

Zirig, Lawrence. *The Middle East Political Dictionary.* Santa Barbara, CA & Oxford: ABC-CLIO Information Services, 1984.

Articles

A. Arabic

Al-Khussusi, Badr Al-Din. "Al-Nishat Al-Russy Fil Al-Khalij Al-Araby, 1987–1907." *Journal of Gulf and Arabian Peninsula Studies* (April 1979).

Al-Qinaei, Najat A. "Hadher Tijarat Al-Isleha Fil Al-Kuwayt Wa Al-Khalij Al-Araby." *Al-Biyan* (September 1983).

Bisharah, Abdullah Y. "Dawr Al-Umam Al-Mutahida Fil Istiqlal Al-Bahrayn." *Journal of the Gulf and Arabian Peninsula Studies* (July 1976).

Bissisou, Fouad. "Majlis Al-Taawun Wa Al-Stratejiah Al-Arabya." *Al-Mustaqabal Al-Araby* (1981).

B. English

Abd Al-Karim, Ibrahim. "Diplomacy of Accommodation: Changes in the Middle East." *The Fletcher Forum of World Affairs* (Winter 1989).

Ahmed, Mohamed Sid. "Egypt: The Islamic Issue." *Foreign Policy* (Winter 1987/88).

Ajami, Fouad. "Iran: The Impossible Revolution." *The Foreign Affairs* (Winter 1988/89).

Al-Sabah, Saud Nasir. "Developments in the Arabian Gulf: A View from Kuwait." *American-Arab Affairs* (Fall 1988).

Al-Saidi, Essa, and Richard U. Moench. "Oil, Prices, State Policies and Politics in Kuwait." *Arab Studies Quarterly* (Spring 1988).

Al-Tahan, Assad. "The Gulf Cooperation Council's Airpower Buildup and the Failure of U.S. FX Policy." *Strategic Studies* (Islamabad) (Fall 1987).

Amuzegar, Johangir. "Oil Wealth: A Very Mixed Blessing." *The Foreign Affairs* (Spring 1982).

Arjomand, Said Amir. "History, Structure, and Revolution in the Shiite Tradition in Contemporary Iran." *International Political Science Review* (April 1989).

Atkeson, Edward B. "The Persian Gulf: Still a Vital US Interest?" *Armed Forces Journal International* (April 1987).

Ayubi, Nazih N. M. "The Politics of Militant Islamic Movements in the Middle East." *Journal of International Affairs* (Fall/Winter 1982/83).

Batatu, Hanna. "Iraq's Underground Shiia Movements: Characteristics, Causes, and Prospects." *The Middle East Journal* (Autumn 1981).

Bill, James A. "Islam, Politics and Shiism in the Gulf." *Middle East Insight* (January/February 1984).

_____. "Populist Islam and U.S. Foreign Policy." *SAIS Review* (Winter-Spring 1989).

_____. "Resurgent Islam in the Persian Gulf." *The Foreign Affairs* (Fall 1984).

_____. "The Arab World and the Challenge of Iran." *Journal of Arab Affairs* (October 1982).

Bowen-Jones, H. "The Gulf Today: An Overview of a Region in Recession." *The Arab Gulf Journal* (October 1986).

Brewers, William D. "Yesterday and Tomorrow in the Persian Gulf." *The Middle East Journal* (Spring 1969).

Chubin, Shahram. "The Last Phase of the Iran-Iraq War: From Stalemate to Ceasefire." *Third World Quarterly* (April 1989).

Cooley, John K. "Iran, the Palestinians, and the Gulf." *The Foreign Affairs* (Summer 1979).

Cottam, Richard. "Inside Revolutionary Iran." *The Middle East Journal* (Spring 1989).

Dawisha, Adeed. "Iran's Mullahs and the Arab Masses." *The Washington Quarterly* (Summer 1983).

El-Mallakh, Ragaei, and Mihseen Kadhim. "Arab Institutionalized Development Aid: An Evolution." *The Middle East Journal* (Autumn 1976).

Entessar, Nader. "Superpowers and Persian Gulf Security: The Iranian Perspective." *Third World Quarterly* (October 1988).

Farley, Jonathan. "The Gulf War and the Littoral States." *The World Today* (July 1984).

Fuller, Graham E. "War and Revolution in Iran." *Current History* (February 1989).

Guazzone, Laura. "Gulf Cooperation Council: The Security Policies." *Survival* (March/April 1988).

Golan, Galia. "Gorbachev's Middle East Strategy." *The Foreign Affairs* (Fall 1987).

Hunter, Shireen. "Arab-Iranian Relations and Stability in the Persian Gulf." *The Washington Quarterly* (Summer 1984).

Karsh, Efraim. "Lessons of the Iran-Iraq War." *Orbis* (Spring 1989).

Katz, Mark N. "Soviet Policy in the Gulf States." *Current History* (January 1985).

Keddie, Nikki R. "Iranian Imbroglios: Who's Irrational?" *World Policy Journal* (Winter 1987/88).

Kemp, Geoffrey. "Middle East Opportunities." *The Foreign Affairs* (1988/89).

Keohane, Robert O. "Lilliputians' Dilemmas: Small States in International Politics." *International Organization* (Spring 1969).

Levy, Walter J. "The Years that the Locust Hath Eaten: Oil Policy and OPEC Development Prospects." *The Foreign Policy* (Winter 1978/79).

Lockhart, Laurence. "Outline of the History of Kuwait." *Journal of the Royal Central Asian Society* (1947).

Maddy-Weitzman, Bruce. "Islam and Arabism: The Iran-Iraq War." *The Washington Quarterly* (Autumn 1982).

Malone, Joseph J. "America and the Arabian Peninsula: The First Two Hundred Years." *The Middle East Journal* (Summer 1976).

Mezerik, Avraham G. "The Kuwait-Iraq Dispute, 1961." *International Review Service* (1961).

Moubarak, Walid E. "The Kuwait Fund in the Context of Arab and Third World Politics." *The Middle East Journal* (Autumn 1987).

Mullins, Thomas D. "The Security of Oil Supplies." *Survival* (November/December 1986).

Mylroie, Laurie A. "After the Guns Fell Silent: Iraq in the Middle East." *The Middle East Journal* (Winter 1989).

Navias, Martin S. "Ballistic Missile Proliferation in the Middle East." *Survival* (May/June 1989).

Otaqui, Shakib. "Kuwait." *The Middle East Review* (1986).

Owen, Roger. "The Arab States under Stress: The Impact of Falling Oil Prices." *World Policy Journal* (Fall 1986).

Parson, Anthony. "The Gulf States in the Eighties." *The Arab Gulf Journal* (April 1986).

Peterson, J. E. "The GCC States after the Iran-Iraq War." *American-Arab Affairs* (Fall 1988).

Precht, Henry. "Ayatollah Realpolitik." *Foreign Policy* (Spring 1988).

Raj, Christopher S. "The Iraq-Iran War and Arab Response." *IDSA Journal* (New Delhi) (January-March 1984).

Ramazani, Rouhollah K. "Iran's Foreign Policy: Contending Orientations." *The Middle East Journal* (Spring 1989).

———. "Iran's Islamic Revolution and the Persian Gulf." *Current History* (January 1985).

———. "Iran's Search for Regional Cooperation." *The Middle East Journal* (Spring 1976).

———. "The Iran-Iraq War and the Persian Gulf Crisis." *Current History* (January 1988).

Rashid, Ahmed. "Pakistan, Afghanistan, and the Gulf." *MERIP Reports* (September-October 1987).

Ross, Dennis. "Soviet Views toward the Gulf War." *Orbis* (Fall 1984).

Rubin, Barry. "Drowning in the Gulf." *Foreign Policy* (Winter 1987/88).

Rustow, Dankwart A. "Realignments in the Middle East." *The Foreign Affairs* (1985).

Segal, David. "The Iran-Iraq War: A Military Analysis." *The Foreign Affairs* (Summer 1988).

Shehab, Fakhri. "Kuwait: A Super-Affluent Society." *The Foreign Affairs* (April 1964).

Sick, Gary. "Iran's Quest for Superpower Status." *The Foreign Affairs* (Spring 1987).
_____ . "Trial by Error: Reflections on the Iran-Iraq War." *The Middle East Journal* (Spring 1989).
Sivan, Emmanuel. "Sunni Radicalism in the Middle East and the Iranian Revolution." *International Journal of Middle East Studies* (February 1989).
Smith, Roland C. "Coalition Air Defense in the Persian Gulf." *Airpower Journal* (Fall 1987).
Southwell, C.A.P. "Kuwait." *Journal of the Royal Society of Arts* (December 11, 1953).
Stork, Joe, and Martha Wenger. "US Ready to Intervene in Gulf War." *MERIP Reports* (July-September 1984).
"Tribes with Flags." *The Economist* (February 6, 1988).
Tuma, Elias H. "The Rich and the Poor in the Middle East." *The Middle East Journal* (Autumn 1980).
Twinam, Joseph W. "America and the Gulf Arabs." *American-Arab Affairs* (Fall 1988).
Viorst, Milton. "Out of the Desert: Kuwait." *The New Yorker* (May 16, 1988).
Von Dornoch, Alex (pseudonym). "Iran's Violent Diplomacy." *Survival* (May/June 1988).
Williams, Maurice J. "The Aid Programs of the OPEC Countries." *The Foreign Affairs* (January 1976).
Wright, Robin. "The Islamic Resurgence: A New Phase?" *Current History* (January 1988).
Yuryev, V. "Kuwait Facing the Future." *International Affairs* (Moscow) (March 1984).

Government Documents

A. Arabic

Al-Kuwait Al-Youm. January 3, 1988 and June 28, 1989.
Kuwait Fund for Arab Economic Development. *Nashat Al-Sandouq Fil Al-Duwal Al-Nameyat Hata April 30, 1988.* Kuwait: The Fund, International Cooperation Department, May 1988.
Ministry of Foreign Affairs. *Al-Diplomasion Fil Al-Diwan Al-Aam Wa Bathat Al-Kuwayt Al-Mutamida Fil Al-Kharij.* Kuwait: April 1989.

B. Farsi

Moslem Students of Khomeini's Line. *Dikhalathai Amerika der Kishwarhay Islamy: Kuwait II.* Teheran: University of Teheran and Islamic Guidance Ministry, N.D. Documents captured during the Iranian students' occupation of the American embassy in Teheran in November 1979.

C. English

British Government. India Office and Library Records (IOR, London). File R/15/5/226, August 8, 1935, no. D.O.C. 250. File R/15/5/225, no. c/104, March 13, 1939. File 15/5/228, no. 149/39/49, July 18, 1949, May 16, 1949, and March 26, 1949. File 15/5/126, no. 155, February 14, 1930. File 15/5/317, no. 258, March 27, 1948.
_____ . Public Record Office (PRO, Kew). File 3/18/88, F.O. 371/126905, November 14, 1957, no. EA 1022/2, and December 3, 1957, no. EA 1022/2. File 3/18/88,

F.O. 371/126899, January 9, 1957, no. EA 1018/1, January 25, 1957, no. EA. 1018/5, and May 2, 1957, no. EA. 1018/9.

Iraqi Government. Ministry of Foreign Affairs. *The Facts about Kuwait, II.* Baghdad: Ministry of Foreign Affairs, August 1961.

Kuwaiti Government. Central Bank of Kuwait. *The Kuwaiti Economy in Ten Years: Economic Report for the Period 1969–1979.* Kuwait: Dar Al-Seyassah, 1980.

––––––. *Quarterly Statistical Bulletin, October–December 1987.* Kuwait: CBK, 1988.

Kuwaiti Government. General Board for the South and Arabian Gulf. *Services Extended by the State of Kuwait to the South and Arabian Gulf.* Kuwait: The Ministry of Foreign Affairs, July 1987.

Kuwaiti Government. *The Kuwaiti-Iraqi Crisis.* Kuwait: Government Printing Press, 1961.

Kuwaiti Government. Ministry of Foreign Affairs. *Diplomatic and Consular Corps in Kuwait.* Kuwait: January 1989.

Kuwaiti Government. Ministry of Guidance and Information. *Kuwait Today: A Welfare State.* Nairobi: Quality Productions, N.D.

Kuwaiti Government. Ministry of Information. *Kuwait: Facts and Figures 1988.* Kuwait: Ministry of Information, 1988.

Kuwaiti Government. Permanent Mission of Kuwait to the UN. *Statement by His Highness Sheikh Jaber Al-Ahmad Al-Sabah.* 43rd Session, UN General Assembly. New York, September 28, 1988.

––––––. *Speech of the Kuwaiti Foreign Minister to the 40th Session of the General Assembly.* New York, September 26, 1985.

––––––. *Kuwaiti Foreign Minister's Statement to the United Nations, General Assembly 36th Session.* New York, September 29, 1981.

Kuwaiti Government. Ministry of Planning. *Annual Statistical Abstract 1988.* Kuwait: Central Statistical Office, 1988.

––––––. *Annual Statistical Abstract 1987.* Kuwait: Central Statistical Office, 1987.

––––––. *Annual Statistical Abstract 1986.* Kuwait: Al-Mughawi Press, 1986.

––––––. *Annual Statistical Abstract 1982.* Kuwait: Central Statistical Office, 1982.

––––––. *Annual Statistical Abstract 1977.* Kuwait: Central Statistical Office, 1977.

––––––. *Annual Statistical Abstract 1976.* Kuwait: Central Statistical Office, 1976.

––––––. *Statistical Yearbook of Kuwait 1974.* Kuwait: Central Statistical Office, 1974.

––––––. *Annual Statistical Abstract 1973.* Kuwait: Central Statistical Office, 1973.

Kuwaiti Government. The Planning Board. *Statistical Abstract 1970.* Kuwait: Central Statistical Office, 1970.

––––––. *Statistical Abstract 1968.* Kuwait: Central Statistical Office, 1968.

––––––. *Statistical Abstract 1966.* Kuwait: Central Statistical Office, 1966.

––––––. *Statistical Abstract 1965.* Kuwait: Government Printing Press, 1965.

––––––. *Statistical Abstract 1964.* Kuwait: Central Statistical Office, 1964.

United Nations. *General Assembly Plenary Meetings.* 29th Session, 2249th meeting. New York, September 30, 1974.

––––––. *Official Records General Assembly.* 18th Session, 122nd meeting. New York, September 17-October 14, 1963.

––––––. *Security Council Official Records, 39th Year 1984.* New York: UN, 1985.

––––––. New York, May 1984.

––––––. 1034th meeting. New York, May 7, 1963.

––––––. 16th Year, Supplement for July, August, and September 1961.

––––––. 958th meeting. New York, July 5, 1961.

U.S. Government. Arms Control and Disarmament Agency. *World Military Expenditures and Arms Transfers 1988.* Washington, DC: ACDA, June 1989.

_____. *World Military Expenditures and Arms Transfers 1987.* Washington, DC: ACDA, March 1988.

_____. *World Military Expenditures and Arms Transfers 1986.* Washington, DC: ACDA, April 1987.

_____. *World Military Expenditures and Arms Transfers 1985.* Washington, DC: ACDA, August 1985.

_____. *World Military Expenditures and Arms Transfers 1972–1982.* Washington, DC: ACDA, April 1984.

_____. *World Military Expenditures and Arms Trade 1963–1973.* Washington, DC: ACDA 1974.

_____. *World Military Expenditures and Arms Trade 1970–1979.* Washington, DC: ACDA, March 1982.

_____. *World Military Expenditures and Arms Transfers 1967–1976.* Washington, DC: ACDA, July 1978.

U.S. Government. Central Intelligence Agency. *The World Factbook 1988.* CIA: Directorate of Intelligence, 1988.

U.S. Congress. Congressional Research Service. *Disruption of Oil Supply from the Persian Gulf: Near-Term U.S. Vulnerability (Winter 1987/88),* November 1, 1987.

_____. *The Persian Gulf Crisis: U.S. Military Operations,* October 7, 1987.

_____. *The Persian Gulf and the U.S. Naval Presence: Issues for Congress,* August 3, 1987.

U.S. Congress. House of Representatives. *Proposed Arms Sales to Kuwait.* Hearings before the Subcommittee on Arms Control, International Security and Science, and on Europe and the Middle East. July 1988. 100th Congress, 2nd Sess. Washington, DC: USGPO, 1988.

_____. *Mine Warfare.* Hearings before the Subcommittee on Seapower and Strategic and Critical Materials. September 9, 1987. 100th Cong., 1st Sess. Washington, DC: USGPO, 1988.

_____. *National Security Policy Implications of United States Operations in the Persian Gulf.* Report of the Defense Policy Panel and Investigations Subcommittee. July 1987. 100th Cong., 1st Sess. Washington, DC: USGPO, 1987.

_____. *Kuwaiti Tankers.* Hearings before the Committee on Merchant Marine and Fisheries. June and August 1987. 100th Cong., 1st Sess. Washington, DC: USGPO, 1987.

_____. *The Persian Gulf Controversy.* Democratic Study Group, Special Report no. 100-9. June 9, 1987.

_____. *Overview of the Situations in the Persian Gulf.* Hearings and Markup before the Committee on Foreign Affairs. May and June 1987. 100th Cong., 1st Sess. Washington, DC: USGPO, 1987.

_____. *Islamic Fundamentalism and Islamic Radicalism.* Hearings before the Subcommittee on Europe and the Middle East. June 24, July 15, and September 30, 1985. 99th Cong., 1st Sess. Washington, DC: USGPO, 1985.

_____. *Federal Response to OPEC Country Investments in the United States, Part 2—Investments in Sensitive Sectors of the U.S. Economy: Kuwait Petroleum Corp. Takeover of Santa Fe International Corp.* Hearings, Subcommittee on Government Operations. October 20, 22, November 24, and December 9, 1981. 97th Cong., 1st Sess. Washington, DC: USGPO, 1982.

_____. *Proposed Sales to Kuwait of Air-to-Air Missiles.* Hearings before subcommittee on International Political and Military Affairs, October 24, 1975. 94th Cong., 1st Sess. Washington, DC: USGPO, 1976.

U.S. Congress. Senate. *U.S. Presence in the Persian Gulf: Cost and Policy Implications.* Report to the Committee on Appropriations. 1988. Washington, DC: USGPO, January 1988.

————. *War in the Persian Gulf: The U.S. Takes Sides.* Staff report to the Committee on Foreign Relations. October 1987.

————. *U.S. Military Forces to Protect "Re-Flagged" Kuwaiti Oil Tankers.* Hearings before the Committee on Armed Services. June 5, 11, and 16, 1987. 100th Cong., 1st Sess. Washington, DC: USGPO, 1987.

U.S. Foreign Area Studies. *Persian Gulf States: Country Studies.* Edited by Richard F. Nyrop. Washington, DC: USGPO, 1985.

————. *Area Handbook for the Persian Gulf States.* Edited by Richard F. Nyrop. Washington, DC: USGPO, 1977.

U.S. Department of Commerce. *Business America*, April 10, 1989, and February 12, 1987.

————. *Foreign Economic Trends and Their Implications for the United States, "Kuwait: Key Economic Indicators."* Prepared by the American embassy in Kuwait. Washington, DC: USGPO, January 1989.

————. *International Direct Investment: Global Trends and U.S. Role, 1988 Edition.* Washington, DC: USGPO, 1988.

————. *Survey of Current Business.* May 1989.

U.S. Department of Defense. *Terrorist Group Profiles.* Washington, DC: USGPO, 1988.

————. *A Report to the Congress on Security Arrangements in the Persian Gulf.* Prepared by Casper W. Weinberger. June 15, 1987.

U.S. Department of State. *Country Report on Human Rights Practices for 1988.* Report submitted to the Senate Committee on Foreign Relations and House Committee on Foreign Affairs. February 1989. 101st Cong., 1st Sess. Washington, DC: USGPO, 1989.

————. *Bulletin*, September and October 1988.

————. *Background Notes: Kuwait.* Washington, DC: Bureau of Public Affairs, March 1988.

————. *U.S. Policy in the Persian Gulf.* Special Report no. 166. July 1987.

————. *U.S. Policy in the Persian Gulf and Kuwaiti Reflagging.* Current Policy, no. 9. June 1987.

The World Bank. *The World Bank Annual Report 1987.* Washington, DC: The World Bank, 1987.

Annual Reports, Lectures, Conferences, Occasional Papers, Reports, etc.

A. Arabic

Al-Hassan, Bilal. *Filistineyeen Fil Al-Kuwayt: Dirasat Ehsaeyeeh.* Beirut: Palestine Liberation Organization Research Center, February 1974.

Al-Nafisi, Abdullah. "Mantiqat Al-Khalij Bin Al-Bued Al-Araby Wal-Islamy." Unpublished paper, Kuwait, 1988.

Al-Rashed, Rashed. "Al-Tawasout Fil Siyassat Al-Kuwayt Al-Kharijiya." Lecture given at a training course, Department of Political Science, University of Kuwait, April 1, 1984.

Al-Shaheen, Sulaiman Majid. "Al-Tafawoudh Fil Siyassat Al-Kuwayt Al-Kharijiya." Lecture given at a training course, Department of Political Science, University of Kuwait, April 15, 1986.

Arab Organization for Human Rights. *Huqooq Al-Insan Fil Al-Alam Al-Araby.* Cairo: International Press, 1988.

Kuwait News Agency. *Khamsa-eishreen Sanna Min Al-Kuwayt Al-Haditha.* Kuwait: KUNA, February 1986.

———. *Ikhtitaf Al-Jabriyah.* Kuwait: KUNA, July 1988.

———. *Majlis Al-Taawun Al-Khaliji.* Kuwait: KUNA, January 1983.

———. File No. 8. Kuwait: KUNA, April 1984.

B. *English*

Al-Sabah, Saud N. *A Kuwaiti View of Middle Eastern and International Affairs.* Lectures of Kuwaiti Ambassador in the United States. Washington, DC: 1983.

Amnesty International. *Amnesty International Report.* London: Amnesty International Publications, 1988.

Bisharah, Abdullah. "The Gulf Cooperation Council: Its Nature and Outlook." Address by the National Council on US-Arab Relations, September 23, 1986.

CBS. *60 Minutes* (February 14, 1988).

Cottrell, Alvin J., and Frank Bray. *Military Forces in the Persian Gulf.* The Washington Papers, no. 6. Washington, DC: The Center for Strategic and International Studies, 1978.

Defense Information Center. *Staff Report.* Washington, DC: DIC, 1988.

The Economic Intelligence Unit. *Iran and Iraq: The Next Five Years.* London: Economist Publications, 1987.

Foreign Policy Association. *Great Decisions 1989.* New York: Foreign Policy Association, 1989.

Gulf International Bank. *Gulf Economic and Financial Report: Gulf Economic Indicators,* vol. 3, no. 1. Bahrain: Gulf International Bank, December 1988.

———. *Gulf Economic Outlook 1989,* vol. 4, no. 1. Bahrain: Gulf International Bank, January 1989.

International Committee for the Defense of Human Rights in the Gulf and Arabian Peninsula (I.C.H.R.G. & A.P.). Report No. 9/89/22K. London and Nashville, TN: I.C.H.R.G. & A.P., April 1989.

The International Institute for Strategic Studies. *The Military Balance, 1988–1989.* London: IISS, 1988.

———. *The Military Balance, 1987–1988.* London: IISS, 1987.

———. *The Military Balance, 1986–1987.* London: IISS, 1986.

International Monetary Fund. "Kuwait: Economy Adjusts to Sharp Drop in Oil Revenue." *IMF Survey* (March 23, 1987).

Kelly, Anne M. *The Soviet Naval Presence during the Iraq-Kuwait Border Dispute: March-April 1973.* Professional Paper no. 122. Washington, DC: Center for Naval Analyses, June 1974.

King, Ralph. *The Iran-Iraq War: The Political Implications.* Adelphi Paper no. 219. London: IISS, Spring 1987.

The Middle East Research Institute. *Kuwait.* Dover, NH: Croom Helm for the University of Pennsylvania, MERI Report, 1985.

The Middle East: U.S. Policy, Israel, Oil and the Arabs, 2nd ed. Washington, DC: Congressional Quarterly (October 1975).

Milton, D. I. *Geology of the Arabian Peninsula: Kuwait.* Geological Survey Professional Paper no. 560-F. Washington, DC: USGPO, 1967.

Murphy, Richard W. *Protecting U.S. Interests in the Gulf.* Remarks by Assistant Secretary of State, on May 20, 1988. Washington, DC: National Council on US-Arab Relations, 1988.

The National Bank of Kuwait. *Kuwait and Gulf Cooperation Council: Economic and Financial Bulletin.* Kuwait: NBK, 1987.

_____ . *Kuwait: Interim Economic and Financial Report, Winter 1988.* Kuwait: NBK, 1988.

The National Press Club. A speech by Kuwait's Crown Prince and Prime Minister, Saad Al-Abdullah. Washington, D.C., July 13, 1988.

Peterson, J. E. *The Arab Gulf States: Steps toward Political Participation.* The Washington Papers, no. 131. New York: Praeger, with The Center for Strategic and International Studies, Washington, 1988.

Richman, Sheldon L. *Where Angels Fear to Tread: The United States and the Persian Gulf Conflict.* Washington, DC: CATO Institute, Policy Analysis no. 90, September 9, 1987.

Roberts, John. *The Gulf, Integration, and OPEC: Overseas Downstream Activities.* Occasional Paper no. 4. Boulder, CO: International Research Center for Energy and Economic Development, 1988.

Sherbiny, Naim A. *Arab Financial Institutions and Developing Countries.* Staff Working Paper no. 794. Washington, DC: The World Bank, 1986.

Stockholm International Peace Research Institutew. *SIPRI Yearbook 1988: World Armaments and Disarmament.* London: Oxford University Press, 1988.

_____ . *SIPRI Yearbook 1987: World Armaments and Disarmament.* London: Oxford University Press, 1987.

_____ . *World Armaments and Disarmament: SIPRI Yearbook 1980.* London: Taylor and Francis, 1980.

_____ . *World Armaments and Disarmament: SIPRI Yearbook 1977.* Cambridge, MA and London: MIT Press, 1977.

_____ . *World Armaments and Disarmament: SIPRI Yearbook 1975.* Cambridge, MA and London: MIT Press, 1975.

Taecker, Kevin R. *U.S.-GCC Relations: Economic and Financial Issues.* Washington, DC: National Council on U.S.-Arab Relations, 1987.

United Services Institute for Defense Studies, London, ed. *Rusi and Brassey's Defense Yearbook 1984.* Oxford: Brassey's Defense Publishers, 1984.

Urquhart, Brian, and Gary Sick, eds. *The United Nations and the Iran-Iraq War.* New York: Ford Foundation Conference Report, August 1987.

Voice of America. "Symposium on Gulf Security and the Iran-Iraq War." Washington, DC: May 6, 1988.

Webb, James H., Jr. "National Strategy, the Navy, and the Persian Gulf." Lecture by the Secretary of the Navy to the Los Angeles World Affairs Council on October 9, 1987. *World Affairs Journal* (Fall 1987).

Weinberger, Caspar W. *Security Arrangements in the Gulf.* Washington, DC: National Council on US-Arab Relations, 1988.

Zonis, Marvin, and Daniel Brumberg. *Khomeini, the Islamic Republic of Iran, and the Arab World.* Harvard Middle East paper, Modern Series, no. 5. Cambridge, MA: Harvard University, 1987.

Magazines, Newspapers, and Periodicals

A. Arabic (Published in Kuwait Unless Stated Otherwise)

Al-Ahram (Cairo)
Al-Anba
Al-Arabi

Al-Hadaf
Al-Itihad (Abu Dhabi)
Al-Majalla (London)
Al-Majallis
Al-Mjtama
Al-Nahar (Beirut)
Al-Qabas
Al-Rai (Jordan)
Al-Rai al-Aam
Al-Rissalat
Al-Riyadh (Riyadh)
Al-Taliat
Al-Watan
Al-Watan Al-Araby (Paris)
Al-Yaqza
Asharq Al-Awsat (London)
Majalat Al-Ashouh al-Araby (Beirut)
Sout Al-Khalij
Sout Al-Shaab (Jordan)

B. Farsi

Shaheed (Teheran)

C. English (Published in the United States Unless Stated Otherwise)

Arab News (Riyadh)
Arab Report and Record (London)
Aramco World Magazine (Houston)
Armed Forces Journal International
Aviation Week and Space Technology
The Baghdad Observer (Baghdad)
The Banker (London)
The Boston Globe
The British Broadcasting Corporation (BBC). Summary of World Broadcasts, Part 4, The Middle East and Africa (SWB).
Business Week
The Christian Science Monitor
Coventry Evening Telegraph (U.K.)
The Economist (London)
Euromoney (London)
Facts on File
The Financial Times (London)
Flight International (Surrey, U.K.)
Foreign Broadcast Information Service (FBIS), Daily Report: Near East and South Africa
Institutional Investor
Intelligence Digest (U.K.)
International Defense Review (Geneva)
International Management (London)
Jane's Defense Weekly (London)
Kayhan International (Teheran)

Keesing's Contemporary Archives
Keesing's Record of World Events
The Kuwaiti Digest (Kuwait Oil Company)
Kuwait Times (Kuwait)
Los Angeles Times
The Middle East (London)
The Middle East and African Economist
The Middle East Economic Digest (London)
The Middle East Economic Survey (Cyprus)
The Middle East International
Middle East Monitor
The Middle East News Agency Bulletin (Cairo)
The Middle East Report (MERIP)
Newsweek
The New York Times
Oil and Gas Journal
Platt's Oilgram News
The Reporter: The Magazine of Facts and Ideas
The South (London)
The Spectator (London)
The Sunday Times London)
Time
The Times (London)
U.S. News and World Report
The Wall Street Journal
The Washington Post
Western Mail (Cardiff, U.K.)
World Oil

Interviews

A. Kuwait

Al-Ali, Ali Jaber. Managing Director, Marketing, Kuwait Petroleum Corporation. April 11, 1988.

Al-Ateeqi, Abdul-Rahman. Advisor to the Amir, former minister of finance. March 31, 1988.

Al-Bader, Abdul-Fattah. Chairman and Managing Director, Kuwait Oil Tanker Co. April 12, 1988.

Al-Dawoud, Faisal Ali. Under-Secretary, Ministry of Defense. March 30, 1988.

Al-Ghanim, Abdullah Yusuf. Former minister of electricity and water. April 5, 1988.

Al-Nafisi, Abdullah. Political scientist. Former member of the National Assembly. March 29, 1988.

Al-Osaimi, Saud Mohammad. Minister of State for Foreign Affairs. April 4, 1988.

Al-Sabah, Jaber Al-Ali. Former deputy prime minister and minister of information. April 9, 1988.

Al-Shaheen, Sulaiman Majid. Undersecretary, Ministry of Foreign Affairs. April 5 and 6, 1988.

El-Ebraheem, Hassan. Political scientist. Former minister of education. April 11, 1988.

Howell, W. Nathaniel. United States Ambassador to Kuwait. April 11, 1988.

Hussain, Abdul-Aziz. Advisor to the Amir. Former minister of state for cabinet affairs. March 29, 1988.

Sheldon, C. Miles. Vice President, Santa Fe International Corporation, and Chairman and President, Chesapeake Shipping, Inc. April 9, 1988.

B. *New York*

Abolhassan, Mohammad A. Kuwait's Ambassador and Permanent Representative to the United Nations. March 15, 1988.

C. *Washington, D.C.*

Al-Sabah, Saud Nasir. Kuwait's Ambassador to the United States. November 10, 1987.

Quinton, Anthony. Former American ambassador to Kuwait. November 12, 1987.

Index